D1011158

STEPFAMILIES
Who Benefits? Who Does Not?

STEPFAMILIES
Who Benefits? Who Does Not?

Edited by
Alan Booth
Judy Dunn
Pennsylvania State University

IEA LAWRENCE ERLBAUM ASSOCIATES, PUBLISHERS
1994 Hillsdale, New Jersey   Hove, UK

Lawrence Erlbaum Associates, Inc., Publishers
365 Broadway
Hillsdale, New Jersey 07642

Cover design by Mairav Salomon-Dekel

Library of Congress Cataloging-in-Publication Data

Stepfamilies : who benefits? who does not? / edited by Alan
Booth, Judy Dunn.
    p. cm.
    Contains papers from the National Symposium on
Stepfamilies held Oct. 14–15, 1993 at the Pennsylvania State
University.
    Includes bibliographical references and index.
    ISBN 0-8058-1544-9 (acid-free paper)
    1. Stepfamilies--United States--Congresses. I. Booth, Alan,
1935– . II. Dunn, Judy, 1939– . III. National Symposium
on Stepfamilies (1993 : Pennsylvania State University)
HQ759.92.S76   1994
306.874--dc20   94-13294
                                                      CIP

Books published by Lawrence Erlbaum Associates are printed on
acid-free paper, and their bindings are chosen for strength and durability.

Printed in the United States of America
10 9 8 7 6 5 4 3 2 1

Contents

PART II
HOW DO STEPFAMILIES FUNCTION AS CHILDREARING ORGANIZATIONS?

PART III
HOW DO STEPFAMILIES FUNCTION AS SOURCES OF SUPPORT?

PART IV
BUILDING RESEARCH AND POLICY AGENDAS—WHAT IS NEEDED?

Preface

Stepfamilies are one of the fastest growing family types in industrial nations. Nearly one third of all Americans is now a stepparent, stepchild, stepsibling, or some other member of a stepfamily. Compared to other family groups, the stepfamily has been neglected both with respect to research and to policy. With this in mind, the National Symposium on Stepfamilies was held October 14–15, 1993 at the Pennsylvania State University to bring together some of the best minds in the country to focus on four questions related to stepfamilies.

- Marriages that create stepfamilies—Why do they occur? Fail? Succeed?
- How do stepfamilies function as childrearing organizations?
- How do stepfamilies function as sources of support?
- Building research and policy agendas—What is needed?

The stepfamily symposium is the first of a series of national symposia to be held annually to deal with a wide range of family issues. Planning for the series and the first symposium occurred at several levels. Dennis Hogan, director of the Pennsylvania State University Population Research Institute, was enthusiastic about the idea. Not only did he raise funds for the symposium, but he aided with initial planning. Judy Dunn, director of the Center for the Study of Child and Adolescent Development, raised funds for the symposium and agreed to be a co-organizer of this and future symposia. A national advisory committee was formed that reviewed alternative topics and helped us select the topic for the first event. Faculty and students at the Population research Institute and the Center for the Study of Child and Adolescent Development also helped us select stepfamilies as the first topic.

The symposium was a 2-day event entailing four sessions, one focusing on each question. Each session had a lead speaker who presented a paper on the question.

Each paper had three discussants, each of whom was responsible for commenting on the lead speaker's paper as well as bringing to bear his or her own work on the question. The lead papers, discussant papers, and overview chapters by the organizers of the symposium constitute the contents of this volume.

Speakers and discussants were selected for the high quality of their prior work related to the topic and for their divergent points of view on each questions. Our goal was to provide the reader with current information on the topic and to provoke new ways of thinking about stepfamilies.

ACKNOWLEDGMENTS

There are many people to thank for assisting with the development and organization of the symposium. We are indebted to the Population Research Institute, Center for the Study of Child and Adolescent Development, Department of Sociology, and the Intercollege Research Programs that provided funds for the symposium. We are indebted to Beatrix Hamburg, Ron Haskins, Robert Michael, Brent Miller, David Reiss, Sandra Scarr, Graham Spanier, and Linda Waite who, as members of the advisory committee, spent time reviewing and commenting on symposium proposals. We appreciate the advice and encouragement throughout the process of planning and conducting the symposium of faculty and graduate students in the Pennsylvania State University Departments of Sociology and Human Development and Family Studies. The contributions of Joy Barger, Cassie Johnstonbaugh, Ramona King, and Sherry Yocum in assisting with the administration of the symposium were invaluable. Special thanks to Professors Bonnie Barber, Nan Crouter, Nancy Landale, and Dan Lichter for their excellent work in presiding over the four sessions and for contributing greatly to the flow of ideas during each session.

Alan Booth
Judy Dunn

MARRIAGES THAT CREATE STEPFAMILIES—WHY DO THEY OCCUR? FAIL? SUCCEED?

1 The Evolution of Marriage and the Problem of Stepfamilies: A Biosocial Perspective

David Popenoe
Rutgers University

One of the fastest growing family types in every advanced industrial nation has been the stepfamily. A stepfamily occurs when a two-biological-parent family is not formed or breaks up and the custodial parent mates with a new partner, or when both biological parents die and the custody of a child is assumed by a new family. Using a simple definition, a *stepfamily* is a family in which at least one member of the adult couple is a stepparent (Beer, 1989, p. 7). To better understand the nature of stepfamilies, the reasons for their increase in number, and the problems they pose, this introductory chapter examines the biological and social (biosocial) bases of human families, how marriage and family life have evolved in human history, and recent family change.

In 1990, 11.3% of U.S. children under age 18 lived with two parents married to each other, one of whom was their stepparent, while 21.6% lived with their mother only, 3.1% lived with their father only, 57.7% lived with both their biological parents, and the remaining 6.3% lived with neither parent or were "unknown or unaccounted for" (U.S. Bureau of the Census, 1992).[1] Demographer Paul C. Glick (1989) estimated that about one third of all children today

---

[1]The percentage of stepchildren would, of course, be higher if children over age 18 were added, and if stepchildren living with unmarried parents were included. Data on the latter are unavailable. Children of unmarried stepparents are typically classified as living in mother-only families, and a substantial number of stepchildren are probably so classified. In Great Britain, 9% of children under 16 lived in 1985 with a natural mother and a stepfather, 7% in legally married and 2% in nonmarital cohabiting unions (Kiernan, 1992). It is also important to note that a higher percentage of children than indicated "live in a stepfamily"; they are the biological children of the parents, stepsiblings but not stepchildren. An estimated one third of all children living in stepfamilies fall into this category (Glick, 1989).

3

may be expected to become stepchildren before they reach age 18. Looking at the picture more broadly, he suggested that one out of every three Americans is now a stepparent, a stepchild, a stepsibling, or some other member of a stepfamily and "more than half of Americans today have been, are now, or will eventually be in one or more step situations during their lives" (Larson, 1992, p. 36).

Stepfamilies have been present throughout world history, owing mainly to the high death rate of parenting adults. In the early 17th century in colonial Virginia, for example, only an estimated 31% of White children reached age 18 with both parents still alive.[2] Yet, although historical data are scarce, stepfamilies were probably never so common as they are today. In most stable agrarian societies, widespread opposition to remarriage was prevalent, especially for women with children (Macfarlane, 1986.) When stepfamilies did occur, they typically involved close relatives of the deceased parents. Even in premodern England, where remarriage appears to have been tolerated and even encouraged, data from 19 English villages during the period 1599–1811 indicate that only 4.3% of all children lived in stepfamilies at any given time (Laslett, 1977). It is important to add that in many premodern societies, children were raised as much by relatives and by the larger community as by the nuclear family, and the structure of the nuclear family was probably of considerably less importance for childrearing than is the case today.

Although historical data on stepparenting in the United States are lacking, relatively good data exist on changes over time in the percentage of children living in other than intact, two-parent families for all reasons, including divorce, desertion, and nonmarital births. During the late 19th and early 20th centuries, an estimated one third of children spent some part of their childhood living in other than intact families (Hernandez, 1993). By the middle of the 20th century the situation had improved substantially, due largely to steeply diminishing death rates and relatively low marital dissolution rates. The chances that a child born in the late 1940s and early 1950s would not be living at age 17 with both biological parents were, by one estimate, only about 20% (Bumpass & Sweet, 1989). This was probably an all-time historical high point in the prevalence of the intact two-biological-parent family.

Since 1960, however, the chances of spending part or all of one's childhood outside an intact family have grown dramatically. According to various estimates, the chances that a child born around 1980 will not be living at age 17 with both biological parents have increased to over 50% (Hernandez, 1993). Thus, we have rapidly gone from an intact-family apogee to what is probably an historical nadir. In 1960, an estimated 83% of all children were living with their two

---

[2]This figure improved to almost 50% by the early 18th century (Rutman & Rutman, 1984). By the turn of the 20th century, the parental death rate had declined dramatically, but was still high; about 75% of 15-year-olds had two living parents (Uhlenberg, 1983), as did 72% of 18-year-olds (Hernandez, 1993). By 1940, most of the modern decline in parental death rate had occurred; about 88% of children born at that time still had two living parents when they finished childhood.

married, biological parents; by 1990, this figure was 58%.[3] During this three-decade period, the percentage of stepchildren under age 18 living with a stepparent has climbed from 6.7% to 11.3%.[4] More than 9 out of 10 stepchildren live with their biological mother and a stepfather.

Accounting for this recent increase in family fragmentation are two main factors: voluntary marital dissolution and nonmarital births. The chances today that a first marriage will end in divorce or separation stand at over 50%, following a gradual increase in the divorce rate over the past 150 years. About three out of five divorcing couples have at least one child (Bumpass, 1990). The growth of nonmarital births is more recent and more dramatic; nonmarital births as a percent of all births increased from 5.3% in 1960 to 28% today. In contrast, the death of parents has become an insignificant factor in family fragmentation. Well over 90% of children reach age 18 with both parents still alive.

THE PROBLEM OF STEPFAMILIES

Many, and perhaps most stepfamilies today lead contented home lives and produce happy and successful children. But a growing body of evidence suggests that the increase of stepfamilies has created serious problems for child welfare (Ihinger-Tallman, 1988). Virtually all of the children of nonmarital births and marital dissolution end up in one of two family types: single-parent families (usually mother-headed), or stepfamilies. Contrary to the view of some social scientists in recent years, who believed that the effects of family fragmentation on children were both modest and ephemeral, there is now substantial evidence to indicate that the child outcomes of these alternative family forms are significantly inferior to those of families consisting of two biological parents. Compared to those in intact families, children in single-parent and stepfamilies are significantly more likely to have emotional and behavioral problems, to receive the professional help of psychologists, to have health problems, to perform poorly in school and drop out, and to leave home early (Bray, Berger, Boethel, Maymi, & Touch, 1992; Dawson, 1991; Hetherington & Jodl, this volume; Zill, 1988; Zill & Schoenborn, 1990). Moreover, some of these negative effects have been shown to persist into adult life.

Social scientists used to believe that, for positive child outcomes, stepfamilies were preferable to single-parent families. Today, we are not so sure. Stepfamilies typically have an economic advantage, but some recent studies indicate that the children of stepfamilies have as many behavioral and emotional problems as the children of single-parent families, and possibly more (e.g., Kiernan, 1992).

---

[3]Estimated from U.S. Bureau of the Census (1992) and Hernandez (1993). Estimates for 1960 from personal communication with Hernandez (September, 1993).

[4]Estimated from U.S. Bureau of the Census (1992) and Hernandez (1993). Estimates for 1960 from personal communication with Hernandez (September, 1993).

Stepfamilies apparently have been regarded as problematic at all times and in all societies, perceived as a family form that is sometimes necessary, but to be avoided if possible. The stepmother in Western societies, for instance, has long been a focus of scorn in nursery rhymes and folk tales (Collins, 1991). In folk literature from around the world, stepparents commonly appear in a highly unfavorable light. Today, stepfamilies may have become even more problematic than in the past because they are created mostly by divorce and nonmarital births rather than by the death of a parent. Many studies have verified that children whose birth families have been disrupted by divorce show more emotional and behavioral problems than those whose families have been disrupted by the death of a parent (e.g., Kiernan, 1992; Timms, 1991; Zill, 1988). For stepchildren, the continuing existence of a biological parent can create additional problems due to the complexity of relationships and the possibility for increased interpersonal conflict.

Certain problems are more prevalent in stepfamilies than in other family forms. A common finding is that stepparents provide less warmth and communicate less well with their children than do biological parents (Thomson, McLanahan, & Curtin, 1992). A number of studies have found that a child is far more likely to be abused by a stepfather than by the biological father (Daly & Wilson, 1985; Gordon, 1989; Russell, 1983, 1984; Wilson, Daly, & Weghorst, 1980). One Canadian investigation found that "preschoolers in Hamilton [Ontario] living with one natural and one stepparent in 1983 were 40 times as likely to become child abuse statistics as like-aged children living with two natural parents" (Wilson & Daly, 1987, p. 228). On the basis of this and other studies, these investigators concluded that "stepparenthood per se remains the single most powerful risk factor for child abuse that has yet been identified" (Daly & Wilson, 1988, pp. 87–88). Compared to children in intact and single-parent households, they suggest, "stepchildren are not merely 'disadvantaged,' but imperiled" (Wilson & Daly, 1987, p. 230).

As in single-parent families, a major problem of the stepfamily phenomenon is the net loss of fathering in children's lives. Some 80% of divorced fathers remarry, and a large portion of these fathers transfer their parenting to stepchildren; this has been described as a "transient father" syndrome or a system of "child swapping" (Furstenberg, 1988). Many studies have shown that stepfathering acts to diminish contact between original fathers and their biological children (Furstenberg & Nord, 1985; Furstenberg, Nord, Peterson, & Zill, 1983; Mott, 1990; Seltzer & Bianchi, 1988; White, this volume).[5] In their turn, stepfathers take a considerably less active role in parenting than do custodial biological

---

[5]Mott (1990), using 1979–1986 data from the National Longitudinal Survey of Labor Market Experience of Youth, determined that about 60% of youth who did not have a resident biological father "had access to a male figure either in or out of the home who may potentially be considered a father or father substitute." He was unable to determine, however, how many of these men actually filled the various role obligations of a father.

fathers, according to many studies, and frequently become disengaged from their stepchildren following the establishment of a stepfamily (Bray, 1988; Hetherington, 1987; White, this volume). "Even after two years," it is reported, "disengagement by the stepparent is the most common parenting style" (Hetherington, Stanley-Hagan, & Anderson, 1989, p. 308).

Another problematic aspect of stepfamilies is their high breakup rate, higher than that of two-biological-parent families. According to the most recent census data, more than 62% of remarriages among women under age 40 will end in divorce, and the more that children are involved, the higher the redivorce rate. Thus, not only is the quality of family life in stepfamilies typically inferior to that of biological-parent families, but the children of stepfamilies face a greater chance of family breakup than they did in their original families (White & Booth, 1985). By one estimate, about 15% of all children born in recent decades will go through at least two family disruptions before coming of age (Furstenberg, 1990).

In summary, according to the available evidence, stepfamilies tend to have less cohesive, more problematic, and more stressful family relationships than intact families, and probably also than single-parent families. Put more strongly by a recent article in *Psychology Today*, stepfamilies "are such a minefield of divided loyalties, emotional traps, and management conflicts that they are the most fragile form of family in America" ("Shuttle Diplomacy," 1993).

BIOSOCIAL BASES OF FAMILY LIFE

In order to better understand the special problems that stepfamilies pose, it is necessary to delve into the fundamental biosocial nature of human family life. Even though family life today is heavily shaped by a massive layer of culture, the predispositions of our biological make-up are ever present. It is almost certainly the case that families are more than just arbitrary social constructs that can be redesigned at will; they are partly rooted in biology, especially because they intimately concern what is most basic to life—the reproduction of the species.[6]

Human beings have evolved as biological organisms through the process of natural selection generated by differential reproduction. The Darwinian explanation of evolution is accepted by virtually all biologists; there are no competing theories that have any evidential support (Barkow, 1989; Goldsmith, 1991; Hinde, 1987). From a Darwinian perspective, all living things are motivated by a

---

[6]It is necessary, especially for a social science audience, for me to insert some caveats. (a) Biology does not necessarily determine behavior; it merely predisposes people to act in certain ways rather than others, or to feel more comfortable acting one way rather than another. (b) Our biological nature is not necessarily immutable; it is subject to much personal and cultural control. (c) What is biologically inherent in human nature is not necessarily "good" or "right." Good and right are cultural concepts, designed to guide human behavior in ways that benefit society as a whole.

"drive" to survive and reproduce, and the nature of human beings today is partly the result of the expression of this drive throughout the millions of years of our species' development. The distinctive qualities of the human species were heavily shaped in what is referred to as the environment of evolutionary adaptedness (EEA), which consisted of small tribal groupings of hunter-gatherers in a wood and grasslands (Savanna) ecology, and was organized around relatively tight-knit nuclear families designed for food procurement and the procreation and socialization of the young.[7] Those human beings best adapted to this environment were more likely to survive, reproduce, and produce successful offspring (Leakey & Lewin, 1992).

One of the most distinctive traits of the human species is our family system— a nuclear family grouping in which the biological father is not only identified, but is also normally involved in the upbringing of his children. The human family was probably the first of our social institutions, and was a major factor in enabling us to become the dominant species on earth. Within the rest of the animal kingdom, the fatherless mother–child family unit largely prevails. There are few animal species in which the male plays much of a role in childrearing beyond that of sperm donor.[8] But owing to the pronounced and lengthy dependence of human offspring on adults (partly the result of having such large and complex brains), human mothers required significant help from others in order to survive, and the biological father was the most highly motivated to provide that help. Anthropologists Jane and Chet Lancaster (1987) put the matter as follows:

> In the course of evolution, the keystone in the foundation of the human family was the capturing of male energy into the nurturance of young, most specifically for the collaborative feeding of weaned juveniles. The human family is a complex organizational structure for the garnering of energy to be transformed into the production of the next generation, and its most essential feature is the collaboration of the male and female parent in the division of labor. (p. 192)

In the words of biosociologist Pierre L. van den Berghe (1988), "the human family is, very simply, the solution our hominid ancestor evolved over three to five million years to raise our brainy, slow-maturing . . . highly dependent, and, therefore, very costly (in terms of parental investment) babies" (p. 43).

From the perspective of evolutionary biology, the organization of the human

---

[7]There is evidence that, still to this day, "we enjoy being in savannah vegetation, prefer to avoid both closed forests and open plains, will pay more for land giving us the impression of being on a savannah, mold recreational environments to be more like savannahs, and develop varieties of ornamental plants that converge on the shapes typical of tropical savannahs" (Orians, 1980, cited in Symons, 1985, p. 137).

[8]In only about 3% of all mammal species do males form a long-term relationship with a female. Monogamy is most common among birds; 90% of bird species are monogamous. High rates of avian monogamy are found because nestling birds are so helpless, and avian mothers (who don't lactate) are commonly no better suited to parenting tasks than fathers (Mock & Fujioka, 1990).

nuclear family is based on two inherited biological predispositions that confer reproductive success, one that operates between parent and child, and the other between parent and parent. The first is a predisposition to advance the interests of genetic relatives before those of unrelated individuals, so-called inclusive fitness, kin selection, or nepotism (Hamilton, 1964). With respect to children, this means that men and women have likely evolved to invest more in children who are related to them than in those who are not (Smith, 1988). The world over, such biological favoritism tends to be the rule.

The second biological predisposition is for males and females to have some emotional affinity for each other beyond the sexual act, and to establish pair bonds (Hamilton, 1984; Lovejoy, 1981). We tend to fall in love with one person at a time. Although we think of love attachments as being highly social in character, they also have a strong biological component (Hinde, 1987). There exists an "affective attachment" between men and women that causes us to be infatuated with each other, to feel a sense of well-being when we are together with a loved one, and to feel jealous when others attempt to intrude into our relationship. Around the world today, almost all adults pair-bond with someone of the opposite sex for at least a portion of their lives, and monogamous relationships are the rule (even in the 85% of known societies that permit or prefer polygyny). All known human societies have recognized the existence of the pair bond, and have given it formal sanction through the institution of marriage (van den Berghe, 1990). In summary, as Dobash, Dobash, Wilson, and Daly (1992) wrote:

> It is a cross-culturally and historically ubiquitous aspect of human affairs that women and men form individualized unions, recognized by themselves and by others as conferring certain obligations and entitlements, such that the partners' productive and reproductive careers become intertwined. (p. 84)

Yet, the human family is not an especially stable institution. It exists in a delicate balance between the centripetal bonding forces and centrifugal forces that operate in the opposite direction—to pull family members apart. One fundamental reason for family instability is that, at heart, human beings are probably more self-interested than truly altruistic, even toward our own relatives and intimates. We act, first and foremost, in the interest of self-survival. But another reason is that the male–female bond, especially when compared to the mother–infant bond, is notoriously fragile. Although marriage is universal, divorce has also been a central feature of human social life. It has recently been suggested that, in the EEA, the practice of monogamy may have meant that a man only stayed with a women until their child was out of infancy, a period of about 4 years (Fisher, 1992).

Possibly the most disintegrating force acting on the human pair bond is the male sexual drive. Can anyone really believe that the male sex drive was designed to ensure lifelong sexual fidelity to one mate? As anthropologist Donald Symons (1985) summarized, "human sexuality, especially male sexuality, is by its very nature ill-designed to promote marriage, and gender differences in sexuality do not seem to be complementary" (p. 151). Universally, men are the more sexually driven and promiscuous, while women are more relationship-oriented. Sex researcher Alfred Kinsey once said, "Among all peoples, everywhere in the world, it is understood that the male is more likely than the female to desire sexual relations with a variety of partners" (Daly & Wilson, 1983, p. 281).

Sexual and Reproductive Strategies

To understand the male difference, and why human pair bonds are in many ways so fragile, we must consider the radically dissimilar sexual and reproductive strategies of males and females (Trivers, 1972). Biologically, the primary reproductive function for males is to inseminate, and for females is to harbor the growing fetus. Because male sperm are numerous and female eggs are relatively rare (both being the prime genetic carriers), a distinctive sexual or reproductive strategy is most adaptive for each sex. Males, much more than females, have the capacity to achieve vast increases in reproductive success by acquiring multiple mates. One man with 100 mates could have hundreds of children, but one women with 100 mates could not have many more children than she could have with just one mate. Males, therefore, have more incentive to spread their numerous sperm more widely among many females, and females have a strong incentive to bind males to themselves for the long-term care of their more limited number of potential offspring.

The woman's best reproductive strategy is to ensure that she maximizes the survivability of the one baby she is able to produce every few years through gaining the provision and protection of the father (or, today, the government!). The man's best strategy, however, may be twofold. He wants his baby to survive, yes, and for that reason he may provide help to his child's mother. But, at the same time, it is relatively costless to him (if he can get away with it) to inseminate other women, and thereby help to further insure that his genes are passed on. Using the popular terms suggested by evolutionary scientists Patricia Draper and Henry Harpending (1982), male reproductive strategy can range from the promiscuous and low paternal-investment "cad" approach, in which sperm is widely distributed with the hope that more offspring will survive to reproduce, to the "dad" approach, in which a high paternal investment is made in a limited number of offspring.

Why aren't all men promiscuous cads? Because, in addition to the pull of the biological pair-bonding and parenting predispositions discussed previously, virtually all human societies have established strong cultural sanctions that seek to limit male promiscuity and protect the sanctity of the family. Some anthropologists have suggested that the chief function of the culturally elaborated kinship structures that human beings have devised, and which provide the social basis of premodern societies, is to "protect the mother–infant bond from the relative fragility and volatility of the male–female bond" (Tiger & Fox, 1971, p. 71). The famous anthropologist Bronislaw Malinowski, in *Sex, Culture and Myth* (1930), pointed out the way in which kinship structures perform this function (cited in Moynihan, 1986):

> In all human societies the father is regarded by tradition as indispensable. The woman has to be married before she is allowed legitimately to conceive . . . An unmarried mother is under a ban, a fatherless child is a bastard. This is by no means only a European or Christian prejudice; it is the attitude found amongst most barbarous and savage peoples as well . . . The most important moral and legal rule concerning the physiological side of kinship is that no child should be brought into the world without a man—and one man at that—assuming the role of sociological father, that is, guardian and protector, the male link between the child and the rest of the community. (pp. 169–170)

Paternal Certainty

If a man is to stay with one woman rather than pursue many different women, according to sociobiologists, the "paternal certainty" of his offspring is extremely important. A woman can be certain about her own offspring, but a man cannot be. Because the biological goal is to pass on one's genes, it would be genetic folly for a man to spend his life with one woman unknowingly raising someone else's child in place of his own. For this reason, some evolutionists believe that monogamy arose first, and that high paternal investments evolved only after monogamy had produced a decrease in uncertainty concerning the paternity of offspring (Peck & Feldman, 1988).

The likely impact of the paternal certainty issue can be seen throughout the world today. Studies have shown that family systems in which paternity tends not to be as acknowledged or is downplayed relative to maternity, and systems in which paternal investments are minimal, are those in which confidence of paternity is low (Flinn, 1992, p. 80). In other words, a male tends to invest in his mate's children only when his paternal confidence is high. As anthropologists Steven Gaulin and Alice Schlegel (1980) put it, "cultural patterns leading to heavy male investment in wife's children are common only where mating patterns make it likely that such investment benefits bearers of the male's genes" (p. 308).

Paternal certainty may be an important, and is certainly a relatively unexamined, evolutionary insight to bear in mind when analyzing social conditions in modern societies. The evidence suggests that paternal certainty is diminishing in our time, with these same predicted consequences of unacknowledged paternity, the downplaying of fatherhood, and decreasing paternal investment.

CULTURAL CONTEXTS

The predominance of the primordial hunter-gatherer lifestyle began to decline some 10,000 years ago with the rise of horticultural societies and a more settled way of life. With the warming of the earth and the end of the Ice Age, plant food resources increased and big game hunting declined in importance. Rudimentary technologies of agriculture and the domestication of animals were put into widespread use. Since then (an extremely short period of time in the history of the species), human social life has changed dramatically, with enormous increases in population densities and in the scale and technological sophistication of societies (Lenski, Lenski, & Nolan, 1991). Over time, the emergence of plow agriculture and food surpluses led to the rise of agrarian societies. With the development of class hierarchies and, eventually, the state, cooperation and trust among kinfolk as the main bases of social order gave way to power and domination by the few, leading to the endless tribal conflicts, wars, and the many other violent forms of struggle for the control of resources that have characterized recorded human history.[9]

During the most recent stages of the development of the human species, rapidly paced cultural evolution has overtaken slow-moving biological evolution as the main force of social change (Hallpike, 1986; Scott, 1989). One result is that family structures around the world today are widely variable, determined more by cultural differences than by biological predispositions. Cultural differences, in turn, are strongly related to levels of economic and social development, and to ecological circumstance.

Associated with the rise of horticultural and agrarian societies was a fundamental shift in people's attitudes toward reproduction (Lancaster & Lancaster, 1987). When people perceive that the resources necessary to sustain life and reproductive success are abundant and generally available to all, as was presumably the case among our hunter-gatherer ancestors, the reproductive strategy is to have as many children as possible and share and share alike. Reproduction is limited only by the need of parents to sustain themselves, which in hunter-gatherer societies may have caused women to bear children only about once every 4 years. This strategy still prevails today in remote parts of the world.

But with increased density of population and wealth, people came to perceive that resources were limited, that major differentials existed between who survived and who did not, and that survival was very much dependent on who controlled the most resources. It was no longer sufficient merely to rear as many offspring as possible and hope that they would survive to reproduce. Reproductive strategies became individually tailored to maximize the use and control of resources. It was necessary to try to guarantee children access to resources in the

---

[9]For an intriguing perspective that the rise of complex, culturally based societies represents a "social cage" that has produced tensions with our primate biological legacy, see Maryanski and Turner (1993).

form of education or inheritance, for example, so that they would have an advantage over other parents' children.

Marriage and Divorce in Premodern Societies

The new perception of resource scarcity in complex societies generated a dramatic transformation in family life and kinship relations, including concern for the "legitimacy" of children, the rise of inheritance laws, and the careful control of female sexuality. The nuclear family gave way to the complex, extended family; the conjugal unit became imbedded in an elaborate kinship network. The father role of authority figure and head of household grew in importance, whereas the status of women deteriorated. Sociologist Martin King Whyte (1978) found, in a comparative analysis of data on 93 preindustrial societies drawn from the Human Relations Area Files, that "in the more complex cultures, women tend to have less domestic authority, less independent solidarity with other women, more unequal sex restrictions . . . and fewer property rights" (p. 172).

Through the institutionalization of cultural norms and sanctions, complex societies have become heavily devoted to socially controlling male and female sexual strategies. The most important social institution serving this purpose is marriage. Marriage can be defined simply as "a relationship within which a group socially approves and encourages sexual intercourse and the birth of children" (Frayser, 1985, p. 248). As this definition suggests, marriage as an institution is best thought of in terms of group norms rather than individual pursuits. The norms of marriage include some degree of mutual obligation between husband and wife, the right of sexual access (usually, but not inevitably exclusive), and persistence in time. Throughout most of recorded history, until recently, most marriages were arranged (although the principals typically had a say in the matter); they were less alliances of two individuals than of two kin networks, typically involving an exchange of money or goods.

Various theories have been put forth to explain the fundamental purposes of marriage. But certainly one purpose is, as noted previously, to hold men to the pair bond, thereby helping to ensure high quality offspring and, at the same time, helping to control the open conflict that would result if men were allowed unlimited ability to pursue the "cad" strategy with other men's wives. As demographer Kingsley Davis (1985) stated:

> The genius of the family system is that, through it, the society normally holds the biological parents responsible for each other and for their offspring. By identifying children with their parents, and by penalizing people who do not have stable reproductive relationships, the social system powerfully motivates individuals to settle into a sexual union and take care of the ensuing offspring. (pp. 7–8)

Margaret Mead is purported to have said, with male biology strongly in mind, that there is no society in the world where men will stay married for very long unless culturally required to do so. Although biology may pull men in one direction, culture has sought to pull them in another. The cultural pull can be seen in the marriage ceremony. Reinforced by ritual and public acknowledgment, the ceremony stresses the long-term commitment of the male, the durability of the marital relationship, and the importance of the union for children. A major intent of the ceremony is to solidify a strong social bond in addition to the sexual tie.

Marriages around the world are not necessarily monogamous, however. In about 85% of the world's premodern societies, marital polygyny (one man, several women) is condoned, and in many of these societies it is actually preferred and practiced to the extent possible. Yet, even in these societies, the great majority of men (and all women) live monogamously. Why do some premodern societies prefer or permit (simultaneous) polygyny, while others do not? There is no definitive answer to this question, although many researchers have investigated it (Betzig, 1986; Lee & Whitbeck, 1990). Polygyny may have been quite limited in the EEA, as it is among hunter-gatherer societies today. Due to the generation of great wealth and economic inequalities, polygyny probably increased with the rise of agriculture. Wealth is essential for securing mates in all polygynous societies; the well-to-do men are most likely to have polygynous marriages.

Divorce is almost as universal as marriage. Societies differ greatly in the degree to which divorce actually occurs, but there are few societies in which it is totally absent or absolutely forbidden. Low divorce societies tend to be those in which women have little relative autonomy, especially in the economic sphere. The growing economic autonomy of women is a principal factor accounting for increased divorce in modern societies over the past 150 years (Goode, 1993; Phillips, 1988). The leading causes for divorce around the world, however, are drawn directly from the realm of evolutionary biology—adultery (especially women's) and infertility (Betzig, 1989).

Marriage and Divorce in Urban-Industrial Societies

Just a couple of hundred years ago, after people had been living for many millennia in agrarian societies, a relatively few societies shifted to an urban and industrial way of life. This is the way of life to which most societies in the world today appear to be headed (Goode, 1970). Urban-industrial societies, of course, have created their own, new problems. But they have dramatically reduced poverty and, through the associated rise of liberal democracy, eased those conditions in complex agrarian societies that generated gross inequalities of income and status. Women, for example, are in the process of regaining the relatively equal status they presumably had in early hunter-gatherer societies.

In urban-industrial societies, reproductive concerns about the quantity of children have largely given way to concerns about quality. Children in these societies require massive parental investments if they are to succeed, and childrearing has become extraordinarily expensive in terms of time and money. The low birth rates and small average family sizes found in these societies, therefore, may be considered an adaptive reproductive strategy.

Simultaneous polygyny is not permitted in any society that, to date, has achieved urban-industrial status. Among the many reasons for mandating monogamy is that it is fairer to both women and men, equality being one of the supreme values of the modern period. In the United States today, we take for granted that monogamy is the natural and preferred form of marriage although, increasingly, the high marital breakup rate suggests that "serial monogamy" or "successive polygamy" is the actual institutional form of our time.

In the preindustrial West, at least in northwest Europe, a relatively nuclear family structure existed for many centuries prior to the Industrial Revolution, unlike the situation in most of the rest of the world where complex, extended families predominated. The modern nuclear family that accompanied the emergence of urban-industrialism and cultural modernity in the West was distinctly different from its preindustrial predecessor, however. The rise of this new family form, in the words of historian Lawrence Stone (1977), was "one of the most significant transformations that has ever taken place, not only in the most intimate aspects of human life, but also in the nature of social organization" (p. 687). In structure, the modern family was smaller, even more nuclear in the sense of being split off from relatives, and more stable because there were fewer early deaths of husbands and wives (Kertzer, 1991). But it was in the tone or quality of family life that the modern family was truly unique. The new family form was emotionally intense, privatized, and child-oriented; in authority structure, it was relatively egalitarian; and it placed a high value on individualism in the sense of individual rights and autonomy.

Today, the modern nuclear family—what we now call the "traditional nuclear family"—is denigrated by some scholars in the belief that it dreadfully oppresses women. Yet, the nuclear family that predominated in the United States from the early 1800s through the 1950s probably represented, for most married women, a significant life improvement. As historian Carl N. Degler (1980) noted: "the marriage which initiated the modern family was based upon affection and mutual respect between the partners, both at the time of family formation and in the course of its life. The woman in the marriage enjoyed an increasing degree of influence or autonomy within the family" (pp. 8–9). Lawrence Stone (1977) suggested that this was "the first family type in history which was both long-lasting and intimate" (p. 679).

The big winners from the emergence of the modern nuclear family, however, were not women, but children. In preindustrial Europe, parental care of children does not seem to have been particularly prominent, and such practices as infanticide, wet nursing, child fosterage, and the widespread use of lower status surrogate caretakers were common (Draper & Harpending, 1987). According to evidence assembled by demographer Sheila Ryan Johansson (1987), "malparenting in the form of extreme parental neglect (or even abuse) must have been widespread" (p. 68). Draper and Harpending (1987) suggested that one of the greatest achievements of the modern nuclear family was the return to the high-investment nurturing of children by their biological parents, the kind of parenting characteristic of our hunter-gatherer ancestors. As appraised by Degler (1980):

> The attention, energy and resources of parents in the emerging modern family were increasingly centered upon the rearing of their offspring. Children were now perceived as being different from adults and deserving not only of material care but of solicitude and love as well. Childhood was deemed a valuable period in the life of every person and to be sharply distinguished in character and purpose from adulthood. Parenthood thus became a major personal responsibility, perhaps even a burden. (pp. 8–9)

Family stability during this era, together with parental investments in children, may have been greater than at any other time in history. Cultural sanctions concerning marriage were powerfully enforced, and thanks to ever lowering death rates and low divorce rates, both parents were typically able to see their children through to adulthood. This remarkably high family stability helps to explain why the family situation in the United States today appears so troubled, particularly in the minds of the older generation.

RECENT FAMILY AND CULTURAL CHANGE
IN AMERICA

In the past half century, the U.S. family has been on a social roller coaster. The ups and downs have been quite astonishing. Following World War II, the United States entered a two-decade period of extraordinary economic growth and material progress. Commonly referred to as simply "the 50s," it was the most sustained period of prosperity in U.S. history. Together with most other industrially developed societies of the world, this nation saw improvements in the levels of health, material consumption, and economic security that had scant historical precedent. For most Americans, the improvements included striking increases in longevity, buying power, personal net worth, and government-sponsored economic security.

The 1950s was also an era of remarkable familism and family togetherness, with the family as an institution undergoing unprecedented growth and stability within the middle and working classes. The marriage rate reached an all-time high, the birth rate returned to the high levels of earlier in the century, generating the baby boom, and the divorce rate leveled off. Home, motherhood, and child-centeredness reigned high in the lexicon of cultural values. A higher proportion of children were growing up in stable, two-parent families than ever before in U.S. history (Cherlin & Furstenberg, 1988, p. 294; Modell, Furstenberg, & Strong, 1978).

Beginning in the 1960s, however, a series of unanticipated social and cultural developments took place that shook the foundations of the modern nuclear family. As the authors of a recent history of the U.S. family (Mintz & Kellogg, 1988) said, "what Americans have witnessed since 1960 are fundamental challenges to the forms, ideals, and role expectations that have defined the family for the last century and a half" (p. 204). Men abandoned their families at an unprecedented rate, leaving behind broken homes and single-parent, female-headed households. Women relinquished their traditional mother/housewife roles in unexpectedly large numbers and entered the labor force. The percentage of births taking place outside of marriage skyrocketed. Highly permissive sexual behavior became acceptable, accompanied by the widespread dissemination of pornography.

Not only did the modern nuclear family become fragmented, but participation in family life went into a precipitous decline (Popenoe, 1993). A calculation by demographers indicates that while the proportion of one's adult life spent living with spouse and children was 62% in 1960, the highest in our history, in just 25 years this figure dropped to 43%, the lowest in our history (Watkins, Menken, & Bongaarts, 1987).

Underlying these family-related trends was an extraordinary shift in cultural values and self-definition. An abrupt acceleration occurred in the long-run cultural shift, associated with the rise of modernity, from communitarian or collectivist values to the values of individualism. Trust in, and a sense of obligation toward, the larger society and its institutions rapidly eroded; the traditional moral authority of social institutions such as schools, churches, and governments withered. What emerged, instead, was a new importance given by large segments of the population to the personal goal and even moral commandment of expressive individualism or "self-fulfillment" (Bellah, Madsen, Sullivan, Swidler, & Tipton, 1985). In public opinion polls, Daniel Yankelovich (1994) found that people today place a lower value on what we owe others as a matter of moral obligation, on self-sacrifice, on social conformity, and on restraint in matters of physical pleasure and sexuality, and we place a higher value on self-expression, individualism, self-realization, and personal choice.

The institution of marriage was particularly hard hit. "At no time in history, with the possible exception of Imperial Rome," Kingsley Davis (1985) said, "has the institution of marriage been more problematic than it is today" (p. 21). Davis may only have been thinking of Western history, but his point is probably still valid. Many marriages, those involving close companionship and intimacy between well-matched people, may provide more personal satisfaction than marriages ever have before. But marriage has also been deinstitutionalized on a scale that is unprecedented. The distinguished French sociologist Louis Roussel (1989) suggested, in fact, that a double deinstitutionalization has occurred: Individuals are more hesitant to enter or commit themselves to institutional marriage roles, and societies have weakened their normative sanctions over such roles.

The marriage rate has steadily declined over the past few decades, from 76.7 marriages per 1,000 unmarried women in 1970, to 54.2 in 1990. The divorce rate, although it has leveled off, remains at an historically high level. Marriage has become a voluntary relationship which individuals can make and break at will. As one indicator of this shift, the legal regulation of marriage and divorce has become increasingly lax (Glendon, 1989; Jacob, 1988; Sugarman & Kay, 1990). In summary, fewer people ever marry, those who marry do so at a later age, a smaller proportion of life is spent in wedlock, and marriages are of a shorter duration (Espanshade, 1985).

The underlying causes for the decline of marriage and the high divorce rate are numerous and not fully understood (Goode, 1993; Phillips, 1988). Widely recognized causal factors include material affluence (it weakens the family's traditional economic bond), higher psychological expectations for marriage, secularization, and rapidly changing gender roles. Much of the evidence, however, points to the fact that the recent changes in marriage and divorce are fundamentally rooted in the cultural shift from a collectivist to an individualist ethos, and are related to the decline of social institutions in general.

Divorce feeds upon itself, and today we have what can be called a "divorce climate." The more divorce there is, the more "normal" it becomes, with fewer negative sanctions to oppose it, and the more potential remarriage partners become available. One of the significant attitudinal changes of recent years is the rising acceptance of divorce, especially when children are involved. Divorces involving children used to be in the category of "unthinkable." Today, children are only a minor inhibitor of divorce, slightly more so when the children are male than female (Heaton, 1990; Morgan, Lye, & Condran, 1988; Waite & Lillard, 1991). As one measure of the acceptance of divorce involving children, the proportion of persons answering "no" to the question, "should a couple stay together for the sake the children?" jumped from 51% to 82% between 1962 and 1985 (Thornton, 1989). In other words, less than one fifth of the population today believes that the presence of children should deter parents from breaking up.

The high voluntary dissolution of marriages might not be a serious problem if only adults were involved although, even then, it certainly generates considerable instability and anxiety. The problem is that young children, if they are to grow up successfully, still need strong attachments to parents. The evidence strongly suggests that parental bonds with children have suffered in recent years, and that the tremendous parenting advantages of the modern nuclear family are on the wane. As Samuel Preston (1984), former president of the Population Association of America, suggested, "Since 1960 the conjugal family has begun to divest itself of care for children in much the same way that it did earlier for the elderly" (p. 443). Quantitative measures of such divestiture are the absenteeism rate of fathers, the decline in the amount of time that parents spend with their children, and the growing portion of a child's life that is spent alone, with peers, in day care, in school, and watching television (Hewlett, 1991; Louv, 1990).

THE SOCIAL RESPONSE TO STEPFAMILIES

The decline of marriage and the increase of divorce are, of course, the major contributors to the recent growth of stepfamilies. Because childrearing is such a time- and energy-consuming activity, it has always been a difficult activity for a lone parent to successfully accomplish. On this ground alone, in addition to the parent's desire to have a new partner for his or her own sake, it seems entirely reasonable for the custodial parent of minor children following a death or divorce, and for the woman who has a nonmarital birth, to seek to replace the missing biological parent. Yet, as is now evident, this action generates serious problems of its own.

One approach to addressing these problems is to provide more collective assistance to stepfamilies. It is surely the case, especially in view of the diminution of kinship and neighborhood groupings, that stepfamilies need our collective help and understanding more than ever. But we should not confuse short-run actions aimed at helping stepfamilies with long-run solutions. If the argument presented in this chapter is correct, and the family is fundamentally rooted in biology and at least partly activated by the "genetically selfish" activities of human beings, childrearing by nonrelatives is inherently problematic. It is not that unrelated individuals are unable to do the job of parenting, it is just that they are not as likely to do the job well. Stepfamily problems, in short, may be so intractable that the best strategy for dealing with them is to do everything possible to minimize their occurrence.

Unfortunately, many members of the therapeutic and helping professions, together with a large group of social science allies, now take the view that the trend toward stepfamilies cannot be reversed. In a recent book on stepfamilies, for example, sociologist William R. Beer (1989) began, "For better or worse, the stepfamily is the family of the future" (p. 1). Just as the nuclear family was adapted to the industrial society, he suggested:

> the stepfamily is a family form well matched to post-industrial society. This kind of society is typified by an emphasis on personal freedom and emotional fulfillment, sexual experimentation and egalitarianism, a reduced importance of kinship and consequent salience of nonfamily agencies that care for and educate the young, nurture the elderly, and carry on almost all economic activity. (p. 7)

A close companion to this belief in stepfamily inevitability and optimum fit with a changing society is the view that we should now direct most of our attention toward understanding the familial processes of stepfamilies, and seek to develop social policies and interventions that will assist children's adjustment to them. In turn, the problems of stepfamilies are seen to be ones of "incomplete institutionalization" and "role ambiguity" (Cherlin, 1978; Giles-Sims, 1984; Giles-Sims & Crosbie-Burnett, 1989). Once stepfamilies become more common and accepted, it is argued, and once our society comes to define the roles of stepparenthood more clearly, the problems of stepfamilies will diminish.

This may be a largely incorrect understanding of the situation. The reason why unrelated stepparents find their parenting roles more stressful and less satisfying than biological parents is probably due much less to social stigma and to the uncertainty of their obligations, as to the fact that they gain fewer intrinsic emotional rewards from carrying out those obligations. The parental relationship is unique in human affairs. In most social relationships, the reciprocity of benefits is carefully monitored and an imbalance is regarded as exploitative. But in the parental relationship, as evolutionary psychologists Martin Daly and Margo Wilson (1988) pointed out, "the flow of benefits is prolongedly, cumulatively, and ungrudgingly unbalanced" (p. 83). They continued: "Organisms have evolved to expend their very lives enhancing the fitness prospects of their descendants. . . .Parental investment is a precious resource, and selection must favor those parental psyches that do not squander it on nonrelatives" (p. 83). On the inherent emotional difficulties of parenting by nonrelatives, Daly and Wilson (1988) cited one study (Duberman, 1975) that found "only 53% of stepfathers and 25% of stepmothers could claim to have 'parental feeling' toward their stepchildren, and still fewer to 'love' them" (p. 84).

If, as the findings of evolutionary biology strongly suggest, there is a biological basis to parenting, we must question the view, widespread in the social sciences, that parenthood is merely a social role anyone can play if only they learn the part. Again, Daly and Wilson (1987) were forceful on this point:

> The prevalent conception of parenthood itself as a "role" (with stepparenthood being another role, partially overlapping that of natural parenthood) is profoundly misleading in its implication of arbitrary substitutability. A role is something that any competent actor who has studied the part can step into, but parental love cannot be established at will. Parents care profoundly—often selflessly—about their children, a fact with immense behavioral consequences about which the shallow metaphor of "parental roles" is mute. (p. 117)

This is not to deny, of course, that strong feelings of parental love can be activated in substitute parents, including many and perhaps most stepparents and most adoptive parents. As Daly and Wilson (1988) noted, the psychology of parental love "can, after all, be activated with surprising intensity toward a nonhuman pet" (p. 84). One could even say, as Lynn White (this volume) does, that in view of biological predispositions, "stepfamilies are amazingly successful." The only point is that, given their very special nature, parental feelings and parental love are inherently more difficult to develop among persons unrelated to a given child.

The difficulties of parenting by unrelated individuals can also be found in adoption situations, where a growing body of evidence suggests that adopted children fare somewhat worse than do children from intact families (Brodzinsky, Radice, Huffman, & Merkler, 1987; Deutsch, 1992; Lindholm & Touliatos, 1980). Bear in mind that parents of adopted children have noteworthy parenting advantages over stepparents in that they tend to have fewer conflicting relationships with biological parents and, having freely and deliberately decided to adopt, they may be more strongly motivated to the task of childrearing. Unlike most stepparents, their entry into the parenting relationship is not incidental to the establishment of the adult pair bond. Also, because in most adoption situations neither parent is related to the child, from a sociobiological perspective there is "no exploitation of one partner's efforts for the other's fitness benefit" (Daly & Wilson, 1988, p. 84).

The biosocial perspective presented in this essay leads to the conclusion that we as a society should be doing much more to halt the growth of stepfamilies. It is important to give great respect to those stepfamilies that are doing their job well, and to provide both assistance and compassion for those that are experiencing difficulties. But such efforts should not overshadow the paramount importance of public policies designed to promote and preserve two-biological-parent families, and of endeavors to reverse the cultural drift toward radical individualism and the decline of marriage.

Only very limited suggestions can be provided within the confines of this essay as to what such public policies and cultural endeavors might entail. An overriding goal of public policy should be to increase the proportion of children who grow up with their two married parents and decrease the proportion of children who do not. We should seek to promote family formation through marriage and discourage nonmarital pregnancies, to foster stable and enduring marriages, and to decrease the prevalence of divorce (National Commission on America's Urban Families, 1993). Appropriate measures include (a) the widespread promotion of premarital counseling and marital enrichment programs, (b) the reform of state laws on marriage and divorce so that the social importance of marriage is explicitly stated and meaningful waiting periods for divorce are adopted or extended in cases involving minor children, (c) promulgation of the view at all levels of society that nonmarital pregnancies are wrong and that fatherhood is a lifelong commitment, (d) redesign of the current welfare system so that marriage and the family are empowered rather than denigrated, (e) and revision of the federal tax code to provide more favorable treatment for married couples.

The power of public policy, however, pales in comparison with the general drift of our culture. Fortunately, there are some hopeful signs that a cultural

turnaround is possible (Popenoe, 1994). As previously noted, a rapidly acceler-
ated cultural trend from collectivist values that favor social bonds to individualist
values that favor personal choice, has been a prominent social fact of recent
decades. But cultural change can be dialectical and cyclical as well as linear. Not
all cultural values can simultaneously be maximized, and one generation comes
to value, because they have less of it, what their parent's generation rejected. The
1950s was an era of strong social bonds. Taking these bonds largely for granted,
the baby boom children of the 1950s shifted during the late 1960s and 1970s in
the direction of what had been relatively lacking in their lives—personal
choice/self-fulfillment.

In the 1990s (30 years and one generation later), a cultural mini-shift back to
social bonds may be underway. There appears to be a new realization that, as
much as each individual desires personal choice, we also need—and society
surely needs—strong social bonds. In the family sphere, some have called this
cultural shift "the new familism" (Popenoe, 1992). With the very important
exception that an enduring sense of family obligation and the desire to put
children first are held as paramount values, the new familism does not represent a
call to return to the modern (traditional) nuclear family. In place of the male
domination and full-time housewife of the earlier family form, the new nuclear
family ideal is a 50/50 division of power and decision making between husband
and wife, and a firm understanding that both women and men will share a
common (though not necessarily identical) commitment to the work force over
the course of their lives.

The new familism shift is led by the maturing baby boomers, now at the
family stage of the life cycle and family-oriented as never before. Spurred both
by concerns for their own offspring and by growing evidence that recent family
changes have hurt children, the huge cohort of middle-aged, childrearing baby
boomers have already clearly shifted the media in a more profamily direction. As
the baby boomers age and become even more aware of the importance of social
bonds, the effect of this huge cohort on our cultural values could be enormous.

Another group potentially involved in the cultural shift is the "babyboom
echo" children of the divorce revolution, now coming into adulthood with a
troubled childhood to look back on and a new resolve to avoid the path their
parents took. Their situation is ambivalent, however. They tend to favor marital
permanence more than their own parents did, for example, perhaps because they
do not take the family as much for granted as their parents did (Moore & Stief,
1989). But will their insecure childhoods prove damaging to their family hopes,
as suggested by the evidence that children of divorce have a higher rate of divorce
in their own marriages? We can only hope that this empirical finding will not
stand the test of time.

Another source of cultural change is the economy. If affluence breeds radical
individualism, then moderate economic decline may generate more family solidarity through promoting a "hunkering-down" attitude in which people look to

their social ties for support, and married couples have fewer opportunities to break up. However, the unemployment and poverty an economic downturn inevitably fosters is no one's prescription for a happy marriage. Finally, there is the social institution typically overlooked by social scientists—religion. If the accumulated sociological evidence is correct, religion has long played an important role in promoting marriage and family solidarity. There are some signs of a religious reawakening in the United States. Whether a new religiosity in fact develops, and what it may mean for marriage, remains to be seen. But one thing seems clear. Marriage, an institution with a profound social purpose, cannot long prevail in a culture based solely on personal expression and individual interest.

REFERENCES

Barkow, J. H. (1989). *Darwin sex and status: Biological approaches to mind and culture*. Toronto: University of Toronto Press.

Beer, W. R. (1989). *Strangers in the house: The world of stepsiblings and half-siblings*. New Brunswick, NJ: Transaction Publishers.

Bellah, R. N., Madsen, R., Sullivan, W. M., Swidler, A., & Tipton, S. M. (1985). *Habits of the heart: Individualism and commitment in american life*. Berkeley: University of California.

Betzig, L. (1986). *Despotism and differential reproduction: A Darwinian view of history*. New York: Aldine de Gruyter.

Betzig, L. (1989). Causes of conjugal dissolution: A cross-cultural study. *Current Anthropology, 30*, 654–676.

Bray, J. H. (1988). Children's development during early remarriage. In E. M. Hetherington & J. D. Arasteh (Eds.), *Impact of divorce, single parenting, and stepparenting on children* (pp. 279–298). Hillsdale, NJ: Lawrence Erlbaum Associates.

Bray, J. H., Berger, S. H., Boethel, C. L., Maymi, J. R., & Touch, G. (1992, August). *Longitudinal changes in stepfamilies: Impact on children's adjustment*. Paper presented at the annual meeting of the American Psychological Association, Washington, DC.

Brodzinsky, D. M., Radice, C., Huffman, L., & Merkler, K. (1987). Prevalence of clinically significant symptomatology in a nonclinical sample of adopted and nonadopted children. *Journal of Clinical Child Psychology, 16*(4), 350–356.

Bumpass, L. L. (1990). What's happening to the family: Interactions between demographic and institutional change. *Demography, 27*(4), 483–498.

Bumpass, L. L., & Sweet, J. A. (1989). Children's experience in single-parent families: Implications of cohabitation and marital transitions. *Family Planning Perspectives, 6*, 256–260.

Cherlin, A. (1978). Remarriage as an incomplete institution. *American Journal of Sociology, 84*, 634–650.

Cherlin, A., & Furstenberg, F. F., Jr. (1988). The changing european family: Lessons for the American reader. *Journal of Family Issues, 9*(3), 291–297.

Collins, S. (1991). British stepfamily relationships, 1500–1800. *Journal of Family History, 16*(4), 331–344.

Daly, M., & Wilson, M. (1983). *Sex, evolution, and behavior* (2nd ed.). Belmont, CA: Wadsworth.

Daly, M., & Wilson, M. (1985). Child abuse and other risks of not living with both parents. *Ethology and Sociobiology, 6*, 197–210.

Daly, M., & Wilson, M. (1987). The Darwinian psychology of discriminative parental solicitude. *Nebraska Symposium on Motivation*.

Daly, M., & Wilson, M. (1988). *Homicide.* New York: Aldine de Gruyter.

Davis, K. (1985). The meaning and significance of marriage in contemporary society. In K. Davis (Ed.), *Contemporary marriage* (pp. 1–21). New York: Russell Sage Foundation.

Dawson, D. A. (1991). Family structure and children's health and well-being: Data from the 1988 National Health Interview Survey on Child Health. *Journal of Marriage and the Family, 53*(3), 573–584.

Degler, C. N. (1980). *At odds: Women and the family in America from the Revolution to the present.* New York: Oxford University Press.

Deutsch, C. K. (1992). The overrepresentation of adoptees in children with the attention deficit disorder. *Behavioral Genetics, 12*(2), 231–238.

Dobash, R. P., Dobash, R. E., Wilson, M., & Daly, M. (1992). The myth of sexual symmetry in marital violence. *Social Problems, 39*(1), 71–87.

Draper, P., & Harpending, H. (1982). Father absence and reproductive strategy: An evolutionary perspective. *Journal of Anthropological Research, 38*(3), 255–273.

Draper, P., & Harpending, H. (1987). Parent investment and the child's environment. In J. B. Lancaster, J. Altmann, A. S. Rossi, & L. R. Sherrod (Eds.), *Parenting across the life span: Biosocial dimensions* (pp. 207–235). New York: Aldine de Gruyter.

Duberman, L. (1975). *The reconstituted family: A study of remarried couples and their children.* Chicago, IL: Nelson-Hall.

Espenshade, T. J. (1985). The recent decline of american marriage. In K. Davis (Ed.), *Contemporary marriage* (pp. 53–90). New York: Russell Sage Foundation.

Fisher, H. (1992). *Anatomy of love: The natural history of monogamy, adultery, and divorce.* New York: Norton.

Flinn, M. V. (1992). Paternal care in a Caribbean village. In B. S. Hewlett (Ed.), *Father-child relations: Cultural and biosocial contexts* (pp. 57–84). New York: Aldine de Gruyter.

Frayser, S. (1985). *Varieties of sexual experience: An anthropological perspective on human sexuality.* New Haven, CT: HRAF Press.

Furstenberg, F. F., Jr. (1988). Child care after divorce and remarriage. In E. M. Hetherington & J. D. Arasteh (Eds), *Impact of divorce, single parenting, and stepparenting on children* (pp. 245–261). Hillsdale, NJ: Lawrence Erlbaum Associates.

Furstenberg, F. F, Jr. (1990). Divorce and the American family. *Annual Review of Sociology, 16,* 379–403.

Furstenberg, F. F., Jr., & Nord, C. W. (1985). Parenting apart: Patterns of childbearing after marital disruption. *Journal of Marriage and the Family, 47*(4), 893–905.

Furstenberg, F. F., Jr., Nord, C. W., Peterson, J. L., & Zill, N. (1983). The life course of children of divorce: Marital disruption and parental contact. *American Sociological Review, 48*(2), 656–658.

Gaulin, S. J. C., & Schlegel, A. (1980). Paternal confidence and paternal investment: A cross-cultural test of a sociobiological hypothesis. *Ethology and Sociobiology, 1,* 301–309.

Giles-Sims, J. (1984). The stepparent role: Expectations, behavior and sanctions. *Journal of Family Issues, 5,* 116–130.

Giles-Sims, J., & Crosbie-Burnett, M. (1989). Stepfamily research: Implications for policy, clinical interventions, and further research. *Family Relations, 38*(1), 19–23.

Glendon, M. A. (1989). *The transformation of family law.* Chicago: University of Chicago Press.

Glick, P. C. (1989). Remarried families, stepfamilies, and stepchildren: A brief demographic profile. *Family Relations, 38*(1), 24–27.

Goldsmith, T. H. (1991). *The biological roots of human nature.* New York: Oxford University Press.

Goode, W. J. (1970). *World revolution and family patterns.* New York: The Free Press.

Goode, W. J. (1993). *World changes in divorce patterns.* New Haven, CT: Yale University Press.

Gordon, M. (1989). The family environment of sexual abuse: A comparison of natal and stepfather abuse. *Child Abuse and Neglect, 13,* 121–130.

Hallpike, C. R. (1986). *The principles of social evolution*. Oxford: Clarendon.

Hamilton, W. D. (1964). The genetic evolution of social behavior: I, II. *Journal of Theoretical Biology, 7*, 7–52.

Hamilton, III, W. J. (1984). Significance of paternal investment by primates to the evolution of adult male-female associations. In D. M. Taub (Ed.), *Primate paternalism* (pp. 309–335). New York: Van Nostrand.

Heaton, T. B. (1990). Marital stability throughout the child-rearing years. *Demography, 27*(1), 55–63.

Hetherington, E. M. (1987). Family relations six years after divorce. In K. Pasley & M. Ihinger-Tollman (Eds.), *Remarriage and stepparenting today: Current research and theory* (pp. 185–205). New York: Guilford.

Hetherington, E. M., Stanley-Hagan, M., & Anderson, E. R. (1989). Marital transitions: A child's perspective. *American Psychologist, 44*(2), 303–312.

Hernandez, D. J. (1993). *America's children*. New York: Russell Sage Foundation.

Hewlett, S. A. (1991). *When the bough breaks: The cost of neglecting our children*. New York: Basic Books.

Hinde, R. A. (1987). *Individuals, relationships and culture: Links between ethology and the social sciences*. New York: Cambridge University Press.

Ihinger-Tallman, M. (1988). Research on stepfamilies. *Annual Review of Sociology, 14*, 25–48.

Jacob, H. (1988). *Silent revolution: The transformation of divorce law in the United States*. Chicago: University of Chicago Press.

Johansson, S. R. (1987). Neglect, abuse, and avoidable death: Parental investment and the mortality of infants and children in the European tradition. In R. J. Gelles & J. B. Lancaster (Eds.), *Child abuse and neglect: Biosocial dimensions* (pp. 57–93). New York: Aldine de Gruyter.

Kertzer, D. I. (1991). Household history and sociological theory. *Annual Review of Sociology, 17*, 155–179.

Kiernan, K. E. (1992). The impact of family disruption in childhood on transitions made in young adult life. *Population Studies, 46*, 213–234.

Lancaster, J. B., & Lancaster, C. S. (1987). The watershed: Change in parental-investment and family formation strategies in the course of human evolution. In J. B. Lancaster, J. Altmann, A. S. Rossi, & L. R. Sherrod (Eds.), *Parenting across the life span: Biosocial dimensions* (pp. 187–205). New York: Aldine de Gruyter.

Larson, J. (1992, January). Understanding stepfamilies. *American Demographics*, 36–40.

Laslett, P. (1977). *Family life and illicit love in earlier generations*. New York: Cambridge University Press.

Leakey, R., & Lewin, R. (1992). *Origins reconsidered*. New York: Doubleday.

Lee, G. R., & Whitbeck, L. B. (1990). Economic systems and rates of polygyny. *Journal of Comparative Family Studies, 21*(1), 13–24.

Lenski, G., Lenski, J., & Nolan, P. (1991). *Human societies* (6th ed.). New York: McGraw-Hill.

Lindholm, B. W. & Touliatos, J. (1980). The psychological adjustment of adopted and nonadopted children. *Psychological Reports, 46*(1), 307–310.

Louv, R. (1990). *Childhood's future*. Boston, MA: Houghton Mifflin.

Lovejoy, C. O. (1981). The origin of man. *Science, 211*(4480), 341–350.

Macfarlane, A. (1986). *Marriage and Love in England 1300–1840*. New York: Basil Blackwell.

Maryanski, A., & Turner, J. H. (1993). *The social cage: Human nature and the evolution of society*. Stanford, CA: Stanford University Press.

Mintz, S., & Kellogg, S. (1988). *Domestic revolutions: A social history of American family life*. New York: The Free Press.

Mock, D. W., & Fujioka, M. (1990). Monogamy and long-term pair bonding in vertebrates. *Trends in Ecology and Evolution, 5*(2), 39–43.

Modell, J., Furstenberg, F. F., Jr. & Strong, D. (1978). The timing of marriage in the transition to adulthood: Continuity and change, 1860–1975. *American Journal of Sociology*, *84*, S120–S150.

Moore, K. A., & Stief, T. M. (1989). *Changes in marriage and fertility behavior: Behavior versus attitudes of young adults*. Washington, DC: Child Trends.

Morgan, S. P., Lye, D., & Condran, G. (1988). Sons, daughters, and the risk of marital disruption. *American Journal of Sociology*, *94*(1), 110–129.

Mott, F. L. (1990). When is a father really gone? Paternal-child contact in father absent homes. *Demography*, *27*(4), 499–517.

Moynihan, D. P. (1986). *Family and nation*. San Diego, CA: Harcourt Brace.

National Commission on America's Urban Families. (1993). *Families first*. Washington, DC: U.S. Government Printing Office.

Orians, G. H. (1980). Habitat selection: General theory and applications to human behavior. In J. S. Lockard (Ed.), *The evolution of human social behavior*. New York: Elsevier.

Peck, J. R., & Feldman, M. W. (1988). Kin selection and the evolution of monogamy. *Science*, *240*, 1672–1674.

Phillips, R. (1988). *Putting asunder: A history of divorce in Western society*. Cambridge: Cambridge University Press.

Popenoe, D. (1992). Fostering the new familism: A goal for America. *The Responsive Community*, *2*(4), 31–39.

Popenoe, D. (1993). American family decline, 1960–1990: A review and appraisal. *Journal of Marriage and the Family*, *55*(3), 527–542.

Popenoe, D. (1994). The family condition of America: Cultural change and public policy. In H. Aaron, T. Mann, & T. Taylor (Eds.), *Values and public policy* (pp. 81–112). Washington, DC: Brookings Institute.

Preston, S. (1984). Children and the elderly: Divergent paths for America's dependents. *Demography*, *21*, 435–457.

Roussel, L. (1989). *La famille incertaine*. Paris: Editions Odile Jacob.

Russell, D. E. H. (1983). The incidence and prevalence of intrafamilial and extrafamilial sexual abuse of female children. *Child Abuse and Neglect*, *7*, 133–146.

Russell, D. E. H. (1984). The prevalence and seriousness of incestuous abuse: Stepfathers vs. biological fathers. *Child Abuse and Neglect*, *8*, 15–22.

Rutman, D. B., & Rutman, A. H. (1984). *A place in time: Middlesex County, Virginia, 1650–1750*. New York: Norton.

Scott, J. P. (1989). *The evolution of social systems*. New York: Gordon & Breach.

Seltzer, J. A., & Bianchi, S. M. (1988). Children's contact with absent parents. *Journal of Marriage and the Family*, *50*, 663–677.

Shuttle diplomacy. (1993, July/August). *Psychology Today*, p. 15.

Smith, M. S. (1988). Research in developmental sociobiology: Parenting and family behavior. In K. B. MacDonald (Ed.), *Sociobiological perspectives on human development* (pp. 271–292). New York: Springer-Verlag.

Stone, L. (1977). *The family, sex and marriage in England 1500–1800*. New York: Harper & Row.

Sugarman, S. D., & Kay, H. H. (Eds.). (1990). *Divorce reform at the crossroads*. New Haven, CT: Yale University Press.

Symons, D. (1985). Darwinism and contemporary marriage. In K. Davis (Ed.), *Contemporary marriage* (pp. 133–155). New York: Russell Sage Foundation.

Thomson, E., McLanahan, S. S., & Curtin, R. B. (1992). Family structure, gender, and parental socialization. *Journal of Marriage and the Family*, *54*(2), 368–378.

Thornton, A. (1989). Changing attitudes toward family issues in the United States. *Journal of Marriage and the Family*, *51*(4), 873–893.

Tiger, L., & Fox, R. (1971). *The imperial animal*. New York: Holt, Rinehart & Winston.

Timms, D. W. G. (1991). *Family structure in childhood and mental health in adolescence* (Project Metropolitan Research Report No. 32). Stockholm, Sweden: University of Stockholm.

Trivers, R. L. (1972). Parental investment and sexual selection. In B. Campbell (Ed.), *Sexual selection and the descent of man* (pp. 136–179). Chicago: Aldine-Atherton.

Uhlenberg, P. (1983). Death and the family. In M. Gordon (Ed.), *The American family in historical perspective* (pp. 169–178). New York: St. Martin's Press.

U.S. Bureau of the Census. (1992). *Marriage, divorce, and remarriage in the 1990s* (Current Population Reports, pp. 23–180). Washington, DC: U.S. Government Printing Office.

van den Berghe, P. L. (1988). The family and the biological base of human sociality. In E. E. Filsinger (Ed.), *Biosocial perspectives on the family* (pp. 39–60). Newbury Park, CA: Sage.

van den Berghe, P. L. (1990). *Human family systems: An evolutionary view.* Prospect Heights, OH: Waveland Press.

Waite, L., & Lillard, L. A. (1991). Children and marital disruption. *American Journal of Sociology, 96*(4), 930–953.

Watkins, S. C., Menken, J. A., & Bongaarts, J. (1987). Demographic foundations of family change. *American Sociological Review, 52*(3), 346–358.

White, L. K., & Booth, A. (1985). The quality and stability of remarriages: The role of stepchildren. *American Sociological Review, 50*(5), 689–698.

Whyte, M. K. (1978). *The status of women in preindustrial societies.* Princeton, NJ: Princeton University Press.

Wilson, M. I., Daly, M., & Weghorst, S. J. (1980). Household composition and the risk of child abuse and neglect. *Biosocial Science, 12*, 333–340.

Wilson, M. I., & Daly, M. (1987). Risk of maltreatment of children living with stepparents. In R. J. Gelles & J. B. Lancaster (Eds.), *Child abuse and neglect: Biosocial dimensions* (pp. 215–232). New York: Aldine de Gruyter.

Yankelovich, D. (1994). How changes in the economy are reshaping American values. In H. J. Aaron, T. Mann, & T. Taylor (Eds.), *Values and public policy* (pp. 16–53). Washington, DC: Brookings Institute.

Zill, N. (1988). Behavior, achievement, and health problems among children in stepfamilies: Findings from a national survey of child health. In E. M. Hetherington & J. D. Arasteh (Eds.), *Impact of divorce, single parenting, and stepparenting on children* (pp. 325–368). Hillsdale, NJ: Lawrence Erlbaum Associates.

Zill, N., & Schoenborn, C. A. (1990, November). *Developmental, learning, and emotional problems: Health of our nation's children, United States, 1988 advance data* (Report No. 120). Washington, DC: National Center for Health Statistics.

2 Stepfamilies in the United States: Challenging Biased Assumptions

Marilyn Coleman
University of Missouri

Popenoe (chap. 1, this volume) concluded that stepfamilies are a problem in U.S. society. He even suggests "that we as a society should be doing much more to halt the growth of stepfamilies." How did he come to this conclusion? What is his evidence?

It appears to me that Popenoe took a position on the issue (his position being that stepfamilies are a social problem) and then selectively sifted through the literature to find material to support that stand. As I read the Popenoe chapter, a wonderful quote by Ashley Brilliant, came to mind, "If I hadn't believed it, I wouldn't have seen it." Popenoe saw what he believed in the literature, ignoring or overlooking evidence that did not fit his preconceived beliefs. As a result, I believe that his chapter contains *statements lacking adequate empirical support, selective use of research to support his theoretical position,* and that it is *relatively simplistic, ignoring the diversity and complexity of stepfamilies.* In general, the chapter is a disappointment.

STATEMENTS LACKING EMPIRICAL SUPPORT

Some statements in Popenoe's chapter appear to be solely based on his opinion—at least, no empirical support is provided. In fact, empirical data would often refute his opinions. For example, Popenoe states that "stepfamilies were probably never so common as they are today" (chap. 1, this volume). This is simply not true. An 1878 social survey of the Black households of Rowanty Township in Dinwiddie County, Virginia, provides data that "prove that serial marriage and the stepfamily, initially observable in slavery, became characteristic features of the postemancipation black family" (Manfra & Dykstra, 1985, p. 20). Thirty-two percent of all households in Rowanty Township contained stepfamilies, more than in the United States today.

Another unsupported claim is Popenoe's statement that social scientists *used* to think that stepfamilies were preferable to single-parent families, but now believe that stepchildren have as many behavioral and emotional problems as children in single-parent families, if not more. Because investigation of stepfamilies by social scientists is a relatively recent phenomenon (Coleman & Ganong, 1990), I am not sure which social scientists Popenoe believes used to think that stepchildren had fewer problems than children in single-parent families. It is doubtful that more than a few social scientists ever seriously considered that the remarriage of a child's parent would reduce behavioral and emotional problems. Remarriage is not an antidote for problems that may have stemmed from disturbances in the first marriage, problems created by an adversarial divorce process, or problems associated with the economic poverty of life in a single-parent household. It is not clear whether or not Popenoe's solution is for divorced parents to remain single, but that appears to be where his logic would lead.

Popenoe stresses early in the chapter that "not only is the quality of family life in stepfamilies typically inferior to that of biological-parent families, but the children of stepfamilies face a greater chance of family breakup than they did in their original families." He provides no evidence to support his judgment regarding the quality of stepfamily life, and it should be noted that there is only a marginal difference in divorce rates for first-marriage families and remarried families. Castro Martin and Bumpass (1989) found that two variables associated with lower socioeconomic status—lower educational achievement and being married the first time as teenagers—accounted for the difference in rates of divorce in remarriages compared to first marriages. A more accurate statement would have been that children of *certain* stepfamilies face a greater chance of family breakup.

SELECTIVE USE OF RESEARCH TO SUPPORT A THEORETICAL POSITION

Popenoe bases many of his claims for the need to halt the growth of stepfamilies on sociobiological theory, a theory that has been highly criticized as ignoring human free will and justifying existing injustices (Green, 1989; Sharpe, 1991). Popenoe's argument is that the family is "fundamentally rooted in biology and at least partly activated by the 'genetically selfish' activities of human beings," which results in childrearing by nonrelatives being inherently problematic. I believe that unwarranted stigma and harm often arises from this application of sociobiological theory to stepfamilies. In his chapter, Popenoe applies the theory to negative outcomes in adopted children, as well.

The particular application of sociobiology to stepparenting that creates the most stigma is in the area of child abuse. Popenoe cites numerous studies that conclude that children are far more likely to be abused by a stepparent than by a biological parent, without mentioning any of the serious problems with this body of research (Ganong & Coleman, in press) or noting that only a very small percentage of stepparents ever abuse their stepchildren. According to R. Gelles (personal communication, October 1993), it is difficult, at best, to draw valid conclusions from the empirical work on child abuse in stepfamilies. The veracity of the data is always questionable, with the most reliable data being officially reported abuse that resulted in a fatality.

In contrast to research reported by Popenoe, Malkin and Lamb (in press) found that biological parents were *more* likely than nonbiological parents to severely abuse and to kill their children, rather than to cause them major physical injuries. Although their findings suggest that children living with caretakers other than two biological parents are at greater risk for child abuse, they are not preferentially victimized by the stepparents. In other words, stepchildren may be at greater risk for abuse than are children in first-marriage families, but the risk does not necessarily come from the stepparent.

Gelles and Harrop (1991), using data from the Second National Family Violence Survey, found that the rate of overall violence was significantly *lower for stepchildren than for all other children.* Considerably better information is needed before sociobiology is applied as the explanatory factor for child abuse in stepfamilies and, perhaps, before it is applied to stepfamilies at all.

One of Popenoe's assertions is that a major stepfamily problem is a net loss of fathering because fathers transfer their parenting from their biological children to their stepchildren when they remarry, a system referred to as *child swapping* by Furstenberg (1988). This statement contradicts sociobiological theory, which predicts that parents would be inclined to invest more resources in maximizing their own reproductive success (i.e., their biological children) than in their stepchildren. The theory, as defined by Popenoe, would not predict child swapping.

Another incidence of selective use of research is Popenoe's conclusion which followed his reading Ihinger-Tallman's (1988) review of stepfamily research. Popenoe states that "a growing body of evidence suggests that the increase of stepfamilies has created serious problems for child welfare" (chap. 1, this volume). Although Ihinger-Tallman certainly noted that considerable research suggests less positive outcomes for stepchildren compared with children in first-marriage families, she also urged caution in drawing conclusions, and remarked that, "although the patterns that emerge from the most recent research depict children in stepfamilies as having a more difficult experience developmentally and interpersonally than do children in first families, these patterns apply to a *minority* of children . . . it is probably too soon to draw firm conclusions about the effects on children of living in a stepfamily" (p. 35).

Hetherington and colleagues, who reviewed approximately the same body of research as Ihinger-Tallman, concluded that "Divorce and remarriage are often associated with experiences that place children at increased risk for developing social, psychological, behavioral, and academic problems. Yet divorce and remarriage also can remove children from stressful or acrimonious family relationships and provide additional resources for children" (Hetherington, Stanley-Hagan, & Anderson, 1989, p. 310). These authors also suggested that researchers have begun to move away from the view of stepfamilies as atypical or pathogenic and, instead, are focusing upon the diversity of children's responses to remarriage and to factors that disrupt or facilitate children's adjustment to stepfamily living. Popenoe's treatment of the literature, however, is at odds with these trends.

Neither Ihinger-Tallman or Hetherington and colleagues appeared to share Popenoe's alarm about the effects of remarriage on children's welfare, and these two major reviews of the stepfamily literature hardly support his assertion that "contrary to the view of some social scientists in recent years, who believed that the effects on children of family fragmentation were both modest and ephemeral, there is now substantial evidence to indicate that the child outcomes . . . are significantly inferior to those in families consisting of two biological parents" (chap. 1, this volume). I believe he overstated the evidence. Although several studies have found statistically significant differences between children in first-married families and stepchildren, the differences between the two groups are generally too small to have much practical meaning. The effect size or magnitude of the differences are, in fact, modest.

DISREGARD OF STEPFAMILY COMPLEXITY AND DIVERSITY

Nowhere in the chapter does Popenoe give recognition to the tremendous diversity and complexity of stepfamilies. For example, he makes no mention of potential differences between stepfather, stepmother, and blended stepfamily households; he ignores variations such as the child's age at remarriage, years in the stepfamily, number of siblings and stepsiblings, and contact with the nonresidential parent. By viewing stepfamilies as one monolithic group, he has limited himself to a superficial and simplistic interpretation of stepfamily functioning. His one reference to diversity, that stepfamilies are more problematic today because they are now created by divorce rather than death, is not only simplistic, it is unsettling. He relies on three studies to support his assertion, only one of which is based on a U.S. population (Zill, 1988). Zill found that, children living in stepmother households following divorce rather than bereavement had more emotional and behavioral problems, but this was not true of children living in stepfather households. Considering that the vast majority of stepchildren live in stepfather households, Popenoe's assertion should have been qualified. Keep in mind that fathers have typically been awarded physical custody only when the mother abandoned the children or was unfit in some way (e.g., substance abuse, mental problems). The circumstances that commonly led to the father being awarded custody are likely to have contributed a great deal to the children's problems. This interpretation of Zill's finding is much less unsettling than the unconvincing, alternative one, that children are better off if their parents die than if they divorce and remarry.

Much of the research cited by Popenoe was conducted by demographers or other social scientists using secondary data sets. Although secondary data sets provide valuable information, they do have limitations: They often fail to account for the complexity of stepfamilies; they typically rely on self-report questionnaires, often of unknown validity and reliability and collected from only one family member; they seldom have evolved from theory; and they are nearly always limited in the measurement of the variables of interest.

DISAPPOINTING ASPECTS OF THE CHAPTER

Popenoe's solutions to the problems of stepfamilies do not address family problems related to substance abuse, inadequate education, unemployment and underemployment, poverty, inadequate child care and health care, and the accelerating level of violence in our culture. His solution appears to include limiting remarriage unless the biological parent had died. He equates a moderate economic decline with family solidarity, and suggests that current signs of a religious reawakening in the United States (Glenn, 1987; & Thornton, 1989, refute any such signs) will promote family solidarity. His suggestion of a return to the families of the 1950s with egalitarian values of the nineties seems unrealistic at best.

Popenoe makes almost no mention of the excellent research on stepfamilies that has taken place in recent years (e.g., the body of work by Ahrons, Hetherington and Clingempeel, Kurdek and Fine, to name a few). These researchers are among those conducting longitudinal studies, using multilevel–multivariable–multimeasure designs, paying greater attention to theory, trying to account for the complexity of stepfamily structures, and gathering information about previously understudied topics such as stepmother–stepchild relationships. The work of these scholars has made it clear that a complete understanding of the effects of remarriage on children cannot be obtained from only one method of gathering information.

There are other disappointing aspects to the Popenoe chapter. For example, Popenoe seems to equate low divorce rates with "stability" and "remarkable familism and family togetherness." This equation is tenuous at best. Popenoe's seeming nostalgia for the "stable" family life of the 1950s is not uncommon among family scholars. Such nostalgia was critiqued extensively by Skolnick

(1991) in *Embattled Paradise* and Coontz (1992), in *The Way We Never Were*, among others. Family science has been characterized by Osmond (1987) as being extremely conservative and having a "narrow focus on the interior of families in the American middle class" (p. 103). In my opinion, Popenoe's chapter, had that narrow focus.

The most disappointing aspect of Popenoe's chapter is that he does not directly speak to the topic of this volume. By painting stepfamilies with such a broad and negative brush, he provides us with no insight regarding which children benefit from remarriage and which do not. If he had engaged in a more objective search for the truth about stepfamilies, or more specifically, for the effects of remarriage on children, he would probably have concluded that "it depends . . ." The research question would then become, "It depends on what?" *Who benefits? Who does not?*

REFERENCES

Castro Martin, T., & Bumpass, L. (1989). Recent trends in marital disruption. *Demography, 26,* 37–51.

Coleman, M., & Ganong, L. (1990). Remarriage and stepfamily research in the 80s: New interest in an old family form. *Journal of Marriage and the Family, 52,* 925–940.

Coontz, S. (1992). *The way we never were: American families and the nostalgia trap.* New York: HarperCollins.

Furstenberg, F. F. (1988). Child care after divorce and remarriage. In E. M. Hetherington & J. Arasteh (Eds.), *Impact of divorce, single parenting, and stepparenting on children.* Hillsdale, NJ: Lawrence Erlbaum Associates.

Ganong, L., & Coleman, M. (1994). *Remarried family relationships.* Newbury Park, CA: Sage.

Gelles, R., & Harrop, J. (1991). The risk of abusive violence among children with nongenetic caretakers. *Family Relations, 40,* 78–83.

Glenn, N. (1987). Social trends in the United States: Evidence from sample surveys. *Public Opinion Quarterly, 51,* S109–S126.

Green, M. (1989). *Theories of human development: A comparative approach.* Englewood Cliffs, NJ: Prentice-Hall.

Hetherington, E. M., Stanley-Hagan, M., & Anderson, E. R. (1989). Marital transitions: A child's perspective. *American Psychologist, 44*(2), 303–312.

Ihinger-Tallman, M. (1988). Research on stepfamilies. *Annual Review of Sociology, 14,* 25–48.

Malkin, C., & Lamb, M. (in press). Child maltreatment: A test of sociobiological theory. *Journal of Comparative Family Studies.*

Manfra, J., & Dykstra, R. (1985). Serial marriage and the origins of the Black stepfamily: The Rowanty evidence. *The Journal of American History, 72*(1), 18–44.

Osmond, M. (1987). Radical-critical theories. In M.B. Sussman & S. Steinmetz (Eds.), *Handbook of marriage and the family.* New York: Plenum.

Skolnick, A. (1991). *Embattled paradise.* New York: Basic Books.

Sharpe, L. (1991, June). Science and religion: From warfare over sociobiology to a working alliance. *Current Contents,* pp. 6–13.

Thornton, A. (1989). Changing attitudes toward family issues in the United States. *Journal of Marriage and the Family, 51*(4), 873–893.

Zill, N. (1988). Behavior, achievement, and health problems among children in stepfamilies: Findings from a national survey of child health. In E. M. Hetherington & J. Arasteh (Eds.), *Impact of divorce, single parenting, and stepparenting on children* (pp. 325–368). Hillsdale, NJ: Lawrence Erlbaum Associates.

3 Remarriages and Stepfamilies Are Not Inherently Problematic

Lawrence A. Kurdek
Wright State University

My strongest reactions to Popenoe's chapter were disappointment and irritation. I was disappointed because the chapter didn't comprehensively address two major components of its title: Why do stepfamilies succeed and why do stepfamilies fail? In view of the limited data relevant to this question, I had expected a critical review of the factors that determine both relationship commitment (e.g., Kurdek, 1993a) and relationship stability (e.g., Kurdek, 1993b) in remarriages involving children. No such review was presented.

Instead, Popenoe uses a biosocial perspective to make sweeping claims about the nature of family life that result in the conclusion that society should do more to halt the growth of stepfamilies. My position is that these claims are based on an uncritical review of evidence that is open to alternative and even opposing interpretations and conclusions. I address five of these claims in turn.

CHILDREN OF STEPFAMILIES HAVE AS MANY BEHAVIORAL AND EMOTIONAL PROBLEMS AS THE CHILDREN OF SINGLE-PARENT FAMILIES, AND POSSIBLY MORE

My response to this claim has four parts: (a) comparisons between family structures should include mention of the size of any obtained differences between these family structures, (b) comparisons among divorce-related family structures need to take into account the number of parental divorces experienced, (c) the key family structure comparison involves stepfamilies and single divorced-parent families, and (d) comparisons involving stepfamilies need to consider the structural heterogeneity of stepfamilies. I expand on each of these parts.

In their influential meta-analysis of parental divorce and children's well-being, Amato and Keith (1991) presented information on the nature of differences between children in intact families and children in stepfamilies. True to the pattern Popenoe describes, relative to children in intact families, those in stepfamilies had more conduct problems, lower psychological adjustment, and lower self-esteem. However, across all outcomes, children in stepfamilies placed only 0.17 of a standard deviation below those in intact families. Although reliable, the differences between the two groups are fairly weak and point to considerable overlap in the distributions of scores for children in the stepfamily and intact family groups.

Based on evidence from the life events, attachment, and family process literatures (Brody, Neubaum, & Forehand, 1988; Capaldi & Patterson, 1991), there is reason to expect that the children and adolescents most at risk for behavioral and emotional problems are not those in stepfamilies, but those who have experienced multiple parental divorces and, consequently, multiple parenting transitions. Although evidence on this point is limited (Capaldi & Patterson, 1991; Kurdek & Fine, 1993; Kurdek, Fine, & Sinclair, in press-a, in press-b), it is consistent.

Studies that have examined the effects of parenting transitions on child and adolescent outcomes have typically compared four groups. These are children living continuously with both biological parents, children who have experienced one parental divorce and live with a single mother, children who have experienced one parental divorce and have made the additional transition to living with a mother and stepfather, and children who have experienced more than one parental divorce. Because of their relatively small numbers, children living with single divorced fathers and children living in stepmother families are usually excluded (see Kurdek & Fine, 1993).

Across a range of outcome variables and sources of information, it is the multiple divorce group—not the stepfamily group—that differs most strongly and negatively from the two-parent group. In fact, few differences emerge between children living continuously with both biological parents and either children living with a singly divorced mother or children living in a stepfather family. These findings lead to the plausible conclusion that what negatively affects children's well-being is not so much the kind of family structure in which they happen to reside, but the history of the quality and consistency of the parenting they receive.

From a parenting transitions perspective, one wonders about the logic of comparing stepfamilies to continuous two-biological-parent families. If the issue is that making the transition to a stepfamily imposes stresses above and beyond those experienced as a result of the transition to a divorced, single-parent family (Capaldi & Patterson, 1991), then the comparison of interest is that between children in divorced, single-parent families and children who have entered into stepfamilies after parental divorce. It is of note that Amato and Keith's (1991) meta-analysis (which did not take into account the number of divorces experienced) indicated that the effect size associated with differences between children from divorced, single-parent families and those from stepfamilies across a range of outcomes was not significant.

Despite the emphasis Popenoe places on family structure, he fails to recognize that stepfamilies themselves are quite structurally diverse. To his credit, he does note that stepfamilies may result from parental death, parental abandonment, or parental divorce. However, he does not mention that there may be important differences between stepfather families and stepmother families (Brand, Clingempeel, & Bowen-Woodard, 1988; Fine & Kurdek, 1992; Kurdek & Fine, 1993), or that the remarriage history of each spouse may affect the stability of the remarriage (Booth & Edwards, 1992; Kurdek, 1993b). Nor does he state that a joint consideration of the husbands' and wives' parent and custody status relevant to previous marriages leads to at least nine types of stepfamilies, and highlights the distinction between residential and nonresidential stepfamilies (Clingempeel, Brand, & Segal, 1987), or that a substantial number of children—as many as 300,000 children for women in second marriages alone—are born into stepfamilies (Wineberg, 1992). Given such diversity within stepfamily structures, the general and unqualified claim that stepfamilies are no better than single-parent families is unfounded.

STEPFAMILIES ARE MORE UNSTABLE THAN INTACT FAMILIES

Popenoe claims that one problematic aspect of stepfamilies is their high breakup rate. However, a close reading of the limited data on this topic reveals that the findings on this issue are actually inconsistent. Most of the evidence concerns the stability of second marriages. Some of these studies (Furstenberg & Spanier, 1984; Martin & Bumpass, 1989) report no difference in the marital stability of second marriers with and without children. Others report slightly higher instability rates for second marriers with children compared to those without children (Becker, Landes, & Michael, 1977; McCarthy, 1978; see also Booth & Edwards, 1992). Still others report that for second-marriers, a slightly increased instability rate occurs only for dissolutions occurring within the first 5 years of remarriage and that the birth of children to a mother in a second marriage increases the stability of that remarriage (Wineberg, 1992).

In short, because stepfamilies are a diverse group, it is misleading to characterize their stability as if they represented a homogeneous group. The current evidence gives every reason to expect that stability rates of remarriages vary by divorce history and parent history of each spouse (White & Booth, 1985); length of remarriage; age, gender, and pattern of residence for stepchildren; and whether mutual children are born to spouses in the stepfamily (Ganong & Coleman, 1988; Wineberg, 1992).

A BIOSOCIAL PERSPECTIVE LEADS TO THE CONCLUSION THAT STEPFAMILIES ARE INTRACTABLY PROBLEMATIC

Popenoe claims that in order to understand the special problems posed by stepfamilies, one must consider the biosocial nature of human family life. Based on an evolutionary biology perspective, Popenoe states that the organization of the human nuclear family is based on two inherited biological predispositions that confer reproductive success. The first predisposition operates between parents and children and entails advancing the interests of genetic relatives over those of unrelated individuals. The second predisposition operates between parents and concerns affective attachments between males and females. These seem like reasonable propositions.

Popenoe further notes that family instability can be linked to the fact that human beings are more interested in themselves than in their own relatives, results from men being more sexually driven and promiscuous than women, and that because human pair bonds are fragile, men and women follow different reproductive strategies: Men inseminate as many women as possible, whereas women withhold reproductive access until they can be certain that the male will commit his resources to his offspring.

I see two major problems with using these points to support the argument that childrearing by nonrelatives is inherently problematic. First, Popenoe ignores evidence that although the roles consistent with each gender's reproductive strategy do a reasonable job of accounting for differences between men and women in sexual attraction and mate selection (e.g., Buss & Schmitt, 1993; Kenrick, Groth, Trost, & Sadalla, 1993), these same roles actually contribute to relationship problems and relationship instability. In what he termed the *fundamental paradox*, Ickes (1993) noted a tension between what genes predispose us to do in finding a mate and what current culture prescribes us to do in living happily with that mate. That is, although our evolutionary past may account for partner attraction, our cultural present accounts for how nonexploitative, equal partner relationships are established and maintained.

Second, Popenoe does not use the term *paternal investment* very clearly, but I assume he means that biological fathers in stable marriages are directly—and not just genetically—involved in childrearing. However, most of the normative descriptive data on this topic indicate that although fathers believe they should be directly involved in their children's lives, most are not (Thompson & Walker, 1989). In fact, the general paternal investment of residential biological fathers is so widely known to be low that there is a growing body of research attempting to identify the circumstances under which fathers actually are actively involved with their children (e.g., Harris & Morgan, 1991; Phares, 1992).

Addressing these data on paternal investment from a systems perspective, it would seem that fathers have an indirect effect on their children by directly affecting their wives' parenting competence (Belsky, 1984; Demo, 1992). Thus, the bystander role played by some stepfathers may be functionally similar to the indirect parenting role played by some biological fathers. In summary, the key issue for most stepfamilies (i.e., stepfather families) may not be paternal investment, but whether maternal investment and maternal competence are negatively affected by mothers making the transition from a divorced parent to a remarried parent.

FAMILY LIFE IN THE 1950S WAS BETTER THAN CONTEMPORARY FAMILY LIFE

I agree with Popenoe that it is important to place family life within a larger sociocultural context. Further, no one could disagree that divorce rates began to accelerate in the 1960s. However, I strongly disagree with Popenoe's claim that the 1950s were an era of remarkable familism and family togetherness. Certainly, marital stability rates were high at this time in history. Nonetheless, there is ample evidence that stable marriages are not necessarily happy or healthy marriages (Gordon & O'Keefe, 1984; Heaton & Albrecht, 1991; Straus & Sweet, 1992). In addition, prospective longitudinal studies that have assessed the same group of children when they lived with both parents as well as when they lived with a divorced single parent (e.g., Cherlin et al., 1991; Shaw, Emery, & Tuer, 1993) indicate that the relatively adverse functioning of children who have experienced parental divorce is predicted by conditions in the intact family that existed well before the divorce. Children's divorce-related problems, then, may really be problems attributed to pathogenic processes within the intact family.

What irritates me most about the claim of familism in the 1950s is that it seems to value marital stability for stability's sake. Home, motherhood, and children did rank high among U.S. cultural values, yet current data on middle-aged persons who were children during this era strongly suggest that what transpired in many of these families belied these values. That is, the culture of the family was at odds with the conduct of the family (LaRossa & Rietzes, 1993). How can Popenoe extol the somewhat superficial endorsement of familism during this era in light of evidence that many children in these highly stable families were exposed to an interconnecting web of family conflict, domestic violence, harsh and inconsistent discipline, alcoholism, and, in some instances, abuse and neglect (Domenico & Windle, 1993; Nash, Hulsey, Sexton, Harralson, & Lambert, 1993)? Two biological parents were physically present in many of these families, but at what cost? Further, the current inability of many parents to supervise and to express warmth to their children may, in part, be a backlash to the kind of parenting they experienced as children. To the extent that parents model childrearing styles, many modern parents seem to have adopted an "anti-style." In summary, it is unlikely that family life in the 1950s was better than contemporary family life.

THE FAMILY IS BEING DEINSTITUTIONALIZED

Popenoe rightly notes that marriage as a social institution has evolved in form and function to adapt to new economic, social, cultural, and even psychological settings. But for some reason, Popenoe does not seem to think that the current nature of the institution of marriage reflects this continuous process of economic, social, cultural, and psychological change. One of the most peculiar aspects to Popenoe's chapter is that although he endorses a grand model of change (the biosocial, evolutionary perspective), he urges us as members of society to put an end to a family form that could be viewed as the result of the very economic, social, cultural, and psychological changes that preceded it.

This unfounded and unrealistic exhortation ignores certain contextual conditions that are not likely to change. Like it or not, women are no longer economically dependent on their husbands. Like it or not, women no longer need to define themselves in terms of their social roles as wives and mothers. Like it or not, women benefit from participating in roles other than or in addition to that of mother. Like it or not, men and women are going to renege on vows of lifetime commitments to one person because life with that one person sometimes reaches intolerable limits that could not be foreseen at the time of marriage. Finally, like it or not, as a result of these economic, social, cultural, and psychological dimensions of contemporary life, many children will experience the stresses associated with parenting transitions. In sum, rather than being de-institutionalized, it seems to me that marriage is being re-institutionalized to adapt to a new set of economic, social, cultural, and psychological conditions (Scott, 1993).

Although Popenoe and I disagree about the institutional status of marriage, we happily agree that social policies can and should be designed to facilitate marital happiness and, as a result, the development of children in these marriages. On my own list, these policies include (a) educating adolescents and young adults about expected changes in the course of marriage, (b) providing adolescents and young adults with the skills to handle relationship conflict in constructive ways, (c) facilitating the physical, emotional, and financial investment of biological fathers in their children, (d) elevating the status and pay scales of women in general and childcare professionals in particular, (e) ensuring the availability of high quality day care and after-school care, and (f) making readily available the services of health-care professionals trained to optimize family life, however idiosyncratically that might be defined.

REFERENCES

Amato, P. R., & Keith, B. (1991). Parental divorce and the well-being of children: A meta-analysis. *Psychological Bulletin, 110*, 26–46.

Becker, G. S., Landes, E. M., & Michael, R. T. (1977). An economic analysis of marital instability. *Journal of Political Economy, 85*, 1141–1187.

Belsky, J. (1984). The determinants of parenting: A process model. *Child Development, 55*, 83–96.

Booth, A., & Edwards, J. N. (1992). Starting over: Why remarriages are more unstable. *Journal of Family Issues, 13*, 179–194.

Brand, E., Clingempeel, W. G., & Bowen-Woodard, K. (1988). Family relationships and children's psychological adjustment in stepmother and stepfather families. In E. M. Hetherington & J. D. Arasteh (Eds.), *Impact of divorce, single parenting, and stepparenting* (pp. 299–324). Hillsdale, NJ: Lawrence Erlbaum Associates.

Brody, G. H., Neubaum, E., & Forehand, R. (1988). Serial marriage: A heuristic analysis of an emerging family form. *Psychological Bulletin, 103*, 211–222.

Buss, D. M., & Schmitt, D. P. (1993). Sexual strategies theory: An evolutionary perspective on human mating. *Psychological Review, 100*, 204–232.

Capaldi, D. M., & Patterson, G. R. (1991). Relation of parental transitions to boys' adjustment problems: I. A linear hypothesis. II. Mothers at risk for transitions and unskilled parenting. *Developmental Psychology, 27*, 489–504.

Cherlin, A. J., Furstenberg, F. F., Jr., Chase-Lansdale, P. L., Kiernan, K. E., Robins, P. K., Morrison, D. R., & Teitler, J. O. (1991). Longitudinal studies of effects of divorce on children in Great Britain and the United States. *Science, 252*, 1386–1389.

Clingempeel, W. G., Brand, E., & Segal, S. (1987). A multilevel-multivariable-developmental perspective for future research on stepfamilies. In K. Pasley & M. Ihinger-Tallman (Eds.), *Remarriage and stepparenting: Current research and theory* (pp. 65–93). New York: Guilford.

Demo, D. H. (1992). Parent–child relations: Assessing recent changes. *Journal of Marriage and the Family, 54*, 104–117.

Domenico, D., & Windle, M. (1993). Intrapersonal and interpersonal functioning among middle-aged female adult children of alcoholics. *Journal of Consulting and Clinical Psychology, 61*, 659–666.

Fine, M. A., & Kurdek, L. A. (1992). The adjustment of adolescents in stepfather and stepmother families. *Journal of Marriage and the Family, 54*, 725–736.

Furstenberg, F. F., & Spanier, G. B. (1984). The risk of dissolution in remarriage: An examination of Cherlin's hypothesis of incomplete institutionalization. *Family Relations, 33*, 433–444.

Ganong, L. H., & Coleman, M. (1988). Do mutual children cement bonds in stepfamilies? *Journal of Marriage and the Family, 50*, 687–698.

Gordon, L., & O'Keefe, P. (1984). Incest as a form of family violence: Evidence from historical case records. *Journal of Marriage and the Family, 46*, 27–34.

Harris, K. M., & Morgan, S. P. (1991). Fathers' involvement in parenting sons and daughters. *Journal of Marriage and the Family, 53*, 531–544.

Heaton, T. B., & Albrecht, S. L. (1991). Stable unhappy marriages. *Journal of Marriage and the Family, 53*, 747–758.

Ickes, W. (1993). Traditional gender roles: Do they make, and then break, our relationships? *Journal of Social Issues, 49*, 71–85.

Kenrick, D. T., Groth, G. E., Trost, M. R., & Sadalla, E. K. (1993). Integrating evolutionary and social exchange perspectives on relationships: Effects of gender, self-appraisal, and involvement level on mate selection criteria. *Journal of Personality and Social Psychology, 64*, 951–969.

Kurdek, L. A. (1993a). *Determinants of relationship commitment: evidence from gay, lesbian, dating heterosexual, and married heterosexual couples.* Manuscript submitted for publication.

Kurdek, L. A. (1993b). Predicting marital dissolution from demographic, individual-differences, interdependence, and spouse discrepancy variables: A 5-year prospective longitudinal study of newlywed couples. *Journal of Personality and Social Psychology, 64*, 221–242.

Kurdek, L. A., & Fine, M. A. (1993). The relation between family structure and young adolescents' appraisals of family climate and parenting behavior. *Journal of Family Issues, 14*, 279–290.

Kurdek, L. A., Fine, M. A., & Sinclair, R. J. (in press-a). The relation between parenting transitions and adjustment in young adolescents: A multi-sample investigation. *Journal of Early Adolescence.*

Kurdek, L. A., Fine, M. A., & Sinclair, R. J. (in press-b). School competence in sixth graders: Parenting transitions, family climate, and peer norm effects. *Child Development.*

LaRossa, R., & Rietzes, D. C. (1993). Continuity and change in middle class fatherhood, 1925–1939: The culture–conduct connection. *Journal of Marriage and the Family, 55*, 455–468.

Martin, T. C., & Bumpass, L. L. (1989). Recent trends in marital disruption. *Demography, 26*, 37–51.

McCarthy, J. (1978). A comparison of the probability of the probability of first and second marriages. *Demography, 15*, 345–360.

Nash, M. R., Hulsey, T. L., Sexton, M. C., Harralson, T. L., & Lambert, W. (1993). Long-term sequelae of childhood sexual abuse: Perceived family environment, psychopathology, and dissociation. *Journal of Consulting and Clinical Psychology, 61*, 276–283.

Phares, V. (1992). Where's Poppa? The relative lack of attention to the role of fathers in child and adolescent psychopathology. *American Psychologist, 47*, 656–664.

Scott, M. M. (1993). Recent changes in family structure in the United States: A developmental-systems perspective. *Journal of Applied Developmental Psychology, 14*, 213–230.

Shaw, D. S., Emery, R. E., & Tuer, M. D. (1993). Parental functioning and children's adjustment in families of divorce: A prospective study. *Journal of Abnormal Child Psychology, 21*, 119–134.

Straus, M. A., & Sweet, S. (1992). Verbal aggression in couples: Incidence rates and relationships to personal characteristics. *Journal of Marriage and the Family, 54*, 346–357.

Thompson, L., & Walker, A. J. (1989). Women and men in marriage, work, and parenthood. *Journal of Marriage and the Family, 51*, 845–872.

White, L. K., & Booth, A. (1985). The quality and stability of remarriages: The role of stepchildren. *American Sociological Review, 50*, 689–698.

Wineberg, H. (1992). Childbearing and dissolution of the second marriage. *Journal of Marriage and the Family, 54*, 879–887.

4

Biology, Evolutionary Theory, and Family Social Science

Norval D. Glenn
University of Texas

In his provocative chapter, Popenoe presents a biosocial perspective, which he clearly thinks is likely to be correct. According to this view, stepparenting is inherently problematic because adults have an inborn tendency to invest greater resources in children with whom they share genes than in other children. And Popenoe points out that the biosocial perspective leads to the conclusion that "we as a society should be doing much more to halt the growth of stepfamilies" (chap. 1, this volume).

Even though Popenoe is not dogmatically committed to the perspective he describes, his serious consideration of it is bound to elicit strong and emotional criticism from some quarters. Many family social scientists are highly resistant to any biosocial perspective (a point to which I return later), and those who believe that all or most recent family changes in the United States and other modern societies are desirable, or at least inevitable, tend to be offended by any suggestion that there should be attempts to reverse the changes. Such persons think that dwelling on pathology, or possible pathology, in single-parent families or stepfamilies only tends to stigmatize and make life more difficult for persons in such families; that social policy should be designed to help nontraditional families and to accommodate society to their needs, rather than to inhibit their formation.

Unfortunately, this well-intentioned concern about stigmatizing persons in nontraditional families may contribute to human misery rather than lessen it. Any stigma attached to stepfamilies has declined appreciably in recent years, and it is unlikely that stigma now ranks high among the causes of stress and discomfort of persons in those families, or that the content of scholarly publications has much effect on the amount of stigma. On the other hand, to the extent that concern about stigma restricts the free exchange and consideration of ideas, it hampers the accumulation of sound and empirically verified knowledge and thus the development of effective social policies. Therefore, the perspective described by Popenoe deserves serious and unbiased consideration rather than out-of-hand rejection by those who find it offensive for ideological reasons. Of course, uncritical acceptance should also be avoided.

My goal here, which I may only partially attain, is to evaluate Popenoe's chapter objectively.

THE UTILITY OF BIOSOCIAL PERSPECTIVES IN EXPLAINING CONTEMPORARY BEHAVIOR AND SOCIAL ARRANGEMENTS

As Popenoe points out, evolutionary theory maintains that all living things are motivated "in some deep sense" to survive and reproduce, and there is no current major theoretical challenge to that proposition. Moreover, hardly anyone who accepts any version of evolutionary theory would challenge the view that, in the environment of evolutionary adaptiveness (EEA), those genetically determined behavioral dispositions that contributed to "inclusive fitness" (IF) came to predominate. It is obvious, for instance, that if mutation should produce a gene that inclined men to prefer to mate with postmenopausal women, that gene would not become prevalent and might not survive. It is likely, although perhaps not quite so obvious, that certain mating dispositions of human males and females (such as the former's tendency to prefer multiple and relatively young sex partners), evolved in the EEA because they contributed to IF.

What is debatable is the extent to which behavior and social arrangements in contemporary societies reflect IF-enhancing proclivities that evolved in the EEA. As Popenoe points out, in the modern world, cultural evolution has replaced biological evolution as the main force driving social change. Although biology continues to place limits on the nature of the culture that can predominate in viable human societies, culture can, to some extent, offset the effects of genetic predispositions and shape the specific behaviors that result from those inclinations. Since the "demographic transition," when voluntary fertility limitation became widespread, many persons in modern societies obviously have not acted in such a way as to maximize their IF. For instance, a married couple who choose to have only two children even though they have the resources to provide for the material needs of more are not maximizing their genetic contribution to future generations. Furthermore, behavioral predispositions that increased IF in the EEA may not have the same effect in modern societies. To illustrate, a man's preference to mate with a female in the early part of her reproductive life should have contributed to the man's IF in earlier times, but will not necessarily do so today if most women limit their childbearing to two or three children.[1]

Most evolutionary biologists admit that evolved characteristics that once contributed to IF may not do so in modern societies, and most point out that there probably is no widespread tendency among humans to be consciously concerned about maximizing their IF. Some biologists leave open the possibility that conscious intent may be a proximal cause of much behavior that contributes to IF, but generally, evolutionary theory only assumes that people tend to act as though they are consciously concerned about the birth and survival of persons who will carry their genes.

However, many of these authors who abjure conscious intent as an explanatory variable write in a teleological language that makes it appear that they do believe people consciously strive for IF. An example is the term, *reproductive strategy*, which Popenoe and virtually all evolutionary theorists use. When this term is applied to such forms of life as insects or reptiles, it clearly does not refer to a conscious plan, but a human strategy ordinarily involves conscious planning to attain a consciously held goal. Furthermore, when evolutionary biologists describe how they think humans change their behavior in order to maximize their IF under new circumstances, they seem to believe in a kind of motivation that works very much like conscious intent. An example of this is when Popenoe posits that increased density of population and wealth may have brought about a change in reproductive strategies.

A more defensible kind of evolutionary theory, in my opinion, is one that posits only the kind of evolved behavioral tendencies that do not change rapidly with changed circumstances or perceptions of circumstances, but only at the glacial pace at which evolution presumably occurred in the EEA. Popenoe writes (chap. 1, this volume) that the low birth rates and small family sizes found in modern societies "may be considered an adaptive reproductive strategy," but I find his argument unconvincing. It must be based on an assumed conscious intent to increase IF, or some kind of subconscious motivation that operates very much as conscious intent would operate, and there seems to me to be little evidence for such motivation in modern societies. Popenoe's argument must also be based on an assumption that increased concern with quality of offspring has generally contributed to IF, or at least has not diminished it, and I think that is unlikely. Of course, to the extent that concern with quality enhances the health of offspring and increases the probability that they will survive to reproduce themselves, it

---

[1]Although a man's preference to mate with a woman in the early stage of her reproductive life may not contribute to his IF if she has only two or three children, a similar preference of other males (namely, those who mate with the man's female descendants and collateral kin), will tend to contribute to his IF by shortening the distance between generations.

contributes to IF. However, modern concerns about the quality and success of offspring go far beyond health and survival, being concentrated on characteristics, such as social standing and psychological adjustment, that contribute little or nothing to IF. Parents are likely to *reduce* their IF when they try to enhance their offsprings' quality through formal education, because education tends to lower fertility (especially among females).[2]

The weaker version of evolutionary theory—the one that I prefer—is not necessarily very useful in explaining behavior and social arrangements in modern societies, but it is not incompatible with the thesis that adults tend to invest more heavily in children who are biologically related to them than in other children. The proximal mechanism through which such a tendency would operate is not apparent, however, and the widespread emotional and physical abandonment of children by their biological fathers in modern societies indicates that any such tendency is not a very strong and dependable predictor of male behavior. And the fact that stepfathers often invest more resources in stepchildren with whom they live than in biological children with whom they do not live indicates that the tendency posited by Popenoe's biosocial perspective either does not exist or can be overridden by other proclivities.[3] The evidence that casts doubt on Popenoe's thesis does not disprove it, and no one can honestly say they know for sure that the thesis is incorrect, but the negative evidence is strong enough to make alternative explanations for the problems of stepfamilies attractive.

· For instance, one might hypothesize that a stepparent–stepchild relationship tends to be problematic if the two persons do not bond when the stepchild is in infancy or early childhood. The huge literature on parent–child attachment largely ignores fathers, or only considers how fathers affect the mother–infant bond, but it contains suggestive evidence that a parent's willingness to invest in a child depends at least partly on early parent–child bonding.[4] If so, early bonding may have about the same effects as those attributed to gene sharing, according to Popenoe's biosocial perspective.[5] This explanation is, of course, highly speculative, but it seems to fit the data at least as well as does Popenoe's. It can account, for instance, for many fathers' unwillingness to invest in their biological children, since many fathers fail to bond with those offspring.

---

[2]Numerous studies have found fertility to be lower, and voluntary childlessness to be higher, among highly educated persons than among others (e.g., Baum & Cope, 1980; Houseknecht, 1978; Silka & Kiesler, 1977).

[3]When greater investment in stepchildren than in biological children occurs, the reason may be the tendency for men's relationships with children to be mediated by their wives (Furstenberg & Cherlin, 1991), and one could probably devise a biosocial explanation for this tendency.

[4]For a summary of much of this literature, see Peterson and Rollins (1987).

[5]The fact, cited by Popenoe, that adoptive children have greater problems, on average, than biological children is not strong evidence against this explanation, because poorer prenatal care of adoptive children could account for the difference.

IS STEPPARENTING INHERENTLY PROBLEMATIC?

What is ultimately important is not the correctness or incorrectness of either of these explanations, but rather, whether or not stepparenting is really inherently problematic. The literature on stepparenting (including several of the chapters in this volume), strongly suggests that it is. The reasons may not be much more complicated than the commonsensical, ad hoc explanations frequently given in the literature. Stepparents and stepchildren do not ordinarily choose one another; they enter into a relationship that is incidental to the attraction of two adults to one another. The probability that there will be strong mutual liking is rather low because the screening and testing for compatibility that usually precede the bonding of adults—as occurs in friendship or marriage—often has not occurred. And whatever it is that tends to bond a parent and an infant to one another has not been present either.

Therefore, even though I am not convinced that stepparenting is inherently problematic for the reason that Popenoe gives, I agree with his view that step-families are, in general, not an ideal family form, and that, everything else being equal, it would be better if we had more intact two-parent families and fewer stepfamilies. His statement that the biosocial perspective leads to the conclusion that we as a society should be doing more to halt the growth of stepfamilies is highly provocative, especially when it is taken out of context. However, the steps Popenoe thinks should be taken to retard the growth of stepfamilies are widely advocated, no doubt primarily by persons who would not agree with his biosocial perspective. It is important that he does not advocate steps to inhibit the remarriage of divorced custodial parents or the marriage of never-married single parents; if he did, his position would indeed be problematic. The evidence that children tend to fare worse in stepfamilies than in single-parent families is not strong enough to support a policy of discouraging the marriages by which stepfamilies are formed. It is not at all unusual to advocate policies to discourage nonmarital pregnancies and to foster stable and enduring marriages, and if the language were changed to "successful marriages" rather than stable and enduring ones, Popenoe's policy stance would hardly be controversial at all.

BRINGING BIOLOGY BACK IN

The importance of Popenoe's chapter does not solely depend on the correctness of the biosocial perspective it presents or the soundness of the policy implications drawn from that perspective. Because Popenoe is only one of a very few "mainstream" family social scientists to have embraced or seriously considered biological explanations for problems in modern families, his chapter may embolden others to venture into territory where they have feared to tread. If it helps to break down the unscientific barriers to consideration of biological factors that have plagued much of social science for the past few decades, it will be an important contribution.

The roots of the resistance to biosocial perspectives are in the early decades of this century, when sociology, social psychology, and cultural anthropology fought crude biological explanations of human behavior and social arrangements in order to gain a place in the academic panoply. The use of biological determinism by racists, fascists, and various reactionary social movements during the 1920s, 1930s, and 1940s reinforced distaste for biological perspectives, so that by mid-century, an extreme environmentalism prevailed in many branches of social science. Debates about the relative importance of heredity and environment were focused on ability and performance, and in his presidential address to the American Sociological Association in 1961, Robert E. L. Faris claimed that "in most of the population the levels of performance actually reached have virtually no relation to innate capacities" (p. 838). According to Faris, about the only part played by biology is to set varying but high upper limits on human capabilities, and those limits are largely irrelevant, because virtually no one comes close to reaching them. That view, which seems quaint and naive in view of current understandings about how environment and heredity interact, was by no means held by all sociologists and social psychologists, but it and similar views were quite prevalent.

This extreme environmentalism was no more defensible on intellectual or empirical grounds than the biological determinism it challenged, and it has gradually yielded to more sophisticated views that posit complex interactions of environmental and hereditary influences. Nevertheless, there is still enough resistance to biosocial explanations among social scientists to retard interdisciplinary communication and cooperation and to impede the needed integration of biological and social-environmental perspectives on human behavior and institutions. For instance, a sociologist who tenders a biological explanation for phenomena for which there are popular social and cultural explanations still risks damage to his or her reputation and virtual ostracism by some factions in the discipline.[6]

Popenoe's major thesis may or may not be correct, but let us hope that his chapter helps to launch a new era of objectivity and openness to biological explanations in family social science.

REFERENCES

Baum, R., & Cope, D. R. (1980). Some characteristics of intentionally childless wives in Britain. *Journal of Biosocial Science, 12,* 287–299.

---

[6]In contrast, most branches of psychology have been relatively open to biological explanations, and thus family social scientists trained in psychology are probably a great deal more receptive on the average to biological perspectives than are those trained in sociology.

Faris, R. E. L. (1961). Reflections on the ability dimension in human society. *American Sociological Review, 26,* 835–843.

Furstenberg, F. F., Jr., & Cherlin, A. J. (1991). *Divided families: What happens to children when parents part.* Cambridge, MA: Harvard University Press.

Houseknecht, S. K. (1978). *Achieving females and the decision to remain childless.* Paper presented at the annual meeting of the Groves Conference on Marriage and the Family, Washington, DC.

Peterson, G. W., & Rollins, B. C. (1987). Parent–child socialization. In M. B. Sussman & S. K. Steinmetz (Eds.), *Handbook of marriage and the family* (pp. 471–507). New York: Plenum.

Silka, L., & Kiesler, S. (1977). Couples who choose to remain childless. *Family Planning Perspectives, 9,* 16–25.

11

HOW DO STEPFAMILIES FUNCTION AS CHILDREARING ORGANIZATIONS?

5 Stepfamilies as Settings for Child Development

E. Mavis Hetherington
Kathleen M. Jodl
University of Virginia

Marital transitions have become increasingly common in the lives of children and families. With one half of all first marriages ending in divorce and most divorced adults eventually remarrying, a divorce or a remarriage is no longer a non-normative event, despite a leveling off in the rate of marital dissolution over the last decade. Moreover, if data on couples who separate but never legally divorce are included in figures for marital dissolution, the rate increases to 60% of all first marriages. Among African-American couples, rates of separation and divorce are even higher, with the length of separation prior to divorce often longer and the likelihood of remarriage even lower (Cherlin, 1992). By the age of 16, 40% of White children and 75% of African-American children in the United States will experience a parental separation or divorce. Most of these children will spend an average of 5 years in a single-parent household (Bumpass & Sweet, 1989), with 85% to 90% of them placed in the custody of their biological mother (Depner & Bray, 1993; Furstenberg, 1990).

Life in a single-parent family is often only temporary, given that estimates of rates of remarriage are 66% (Norton, 1991) to 75% (Cherlin, 1992) for women and 80% for men. Before the youngest child reaches the age of 18, 40% of family members currently in a first marriage will eventually become members of a stepfamily (Glick, 1989), with 86% of these stepfamilies composed of a biological mother and stepfather (U.S. Bureau of the Census, 1989). Because separation and divorce rates are at least as high in second marriages as in first marriages, many children and parents become involved in a series of family transitions. Thus, divorce and remarriage should not be viewed as single static life events, but as part of a complex chain of marital transitions and family reorganizations associated with alterations in family roles and relationships and

55

the adjustment of family members (Hetherington, 1993). The disequilibrium in the immediate aftermath of a transition is usually followed by a redefinition of relationships and restabilization of the new family system (Hetherington & Clingempeel, 1992).

Each transition presents families with changes and new adaptive challenges, and the response to these challenges will be influenced by previous family functioning and experiences. Roles and relationships in the first marriage will shape the response to divorce and life in a single-parent family, and previous family experiences will modify the adapatation of family members to a remarriage (Hetherington, 1993).

Adaptation to marital transitions should be considered at the level of individual differences and in the contexts of the entire family system and the larger social milieu of peer networks, extended families, neighborhoods, schools, and work. Furthermore, developmental factors play a central role in the adjustment of children and families to marital transitions. Family members age and confront changing normative challenges as they deal with changes associated with divorce, life in a single-parent household, and remarriage. Family members may be more sensitive to changes, stresses, and opportunities presented by marital transitions at some developmental periods than in others, and certain developmental changes may trigger latent, delayed effects of divorce and remarriage.

A systems approach to family functioning assumes that family members are part of an interdependent emotional and relational system (Bray & Berger, 1993). Each individual within the family unit is part of a dynamic, in which behavior in one subsystem impacts behavior in other subsystems (Hetherington & Clingempeel, 1992). Adaptation at one level in the family system can influence adaptation in another domain of functioning. The marital, parent–child, and sibling subsystems are linked in an intricate network of feedback loops, with alterations occurring at various levels within the system concurrently and over time, as families adapt to individual, intrafamilial and extrafamilial change (Bray & Berger, 1993). Whether these mutually influential family processes and subsystems operate in the same way, and are similar in their contributions to the development of children in nondivorced families and stepfamilies, is open to question.

CHALLENGES TO REMARRIED FAMILIES

Remarriage can be viewed as potentially beneficial to the overall functioning of children and parents in single-parent households. Remarriage usually increases the family income, and the addition of a new stepparent may also provide emotional and childrearing support that could be salutary for both custodial parents and stepchildren (Zill, Morrison, & Coiro, 1993).

Despite the apparent advantages of remarriage, research has failed to consistently demonstrate benefits in achievement, social and emotional development, or conduct disorders for children growing up in stepfamilies compared to those in single-parent households (Zill, 1988). Benefits are most likely to be found in preadolescent boys, and when the remarriage occurred at an early age (Hetherington, Cox, & Cox, 1985; Zill et al., 1993). The newly reconstituted stepfamily must cope with certain stresses and strains unique to this family form that may override any potential advantages of remarriage. As Papernow (1984) noted, a typical starting point for many stepfamilies is one that would not be viewed as auspicious from a family systems perspective: "a weak couple system, a tightly bonded parent–child alliance and potential 'interference' in family functioning from an 'outsider'" (p. 346).

Stepfamilies differ from other family forms in their patterns of functioning, organization, and relationships. Defining and developing appropriate and acceptable roles within the family unit is a major challenge confronting stepfamilies, and constructive functional relationships in stepfamilies may differ from those in nondivorced families or in divorced, single-parent households. Unlike divorce, which involves the exit of a family member, remarriage is unique in that it involves the entrance of a new and, for children, a potentially unwelcome member into a family unit with a shared family history and established roles and relationships (Hetherington, 1993). Alterations in the family constellation is often a source of stress and rivalry for the children of a disrupted marriage, and this may be especially marked if the remarriage involves not only the entrance of a stepparent, but the blending of children from both the mothers' and fathers' previous marriages into a single household (Zill et al., 1993). Thus, it is not surprising that clincians note problems in cross-generational alliances, the establishment of appropriate boundaries in stepfamilies, scapegoating, and loyalty conflicts (Visher & Visher, 1988). Researchers report stepfamilies have more conflict about childrearing and the financial support of children, less cohesion, ambiguous or disparate role expectations, more stress, and more problems in childrearing and child adjustment than families in first marriages (Anderson & White, 1986; Bray, 1988; Bray & Berger, 1993; Zill et al., 1993).

Stepfamilies' success in coping with the challenges that confront them depends in part on their initial expectations and beliefs. Clinicians suggest that when remarried families use traditional nuclear family roles and relationships as the ideal against which they measure themselves, problems are inevitable (Visher & Visher, 1988).

This chapter uses data from three longitudinal studies involving stepfamilies to examine how stepfamilies deal with five main challenges to family functioning.

The first challenge is the establishment and maintainance of a strong marital relationship. This task may be particularly difficult in the context of remarriage since a stepparent must cope with the task of simultaneously constructing a stable marital relationship and a functional parent–child relationship (Hetherington & Clingempeel, 1992).

A second challenge involves the task of the biological parent in simultaneously sustaining a close relationship with children, building a marital relationship, and resolving loyalty conflicts.

The third task involves the establishment of the stepparent–stepchild relationship. Beyond the construction of a strong marital relationship, the stepparent has the additional challenge of developing and defining an acceptable, appropriate, and constructive role as a stepparent within the reconstituted family. Due to a lack of societal norms and supports for parents, role expectations may not be clearly delineated in stepfamilies (Cherlin, 1981). The delineation of the stepparent role is not a unilateral process controlled by the stepparent, but involves negotiation among all family members, including the children, biological parent, noncustodial parent, and even grandparents. The custodial parents' expectations and restrictions on the kind and amount of acceptable involvement in parenting by their new spouse limits the stepparent's role. In addition, the behavior of the stepchild is particularly important in shaping the stepparent's role.

A fourth challenge involves the child's adaptation to his or her biological parents' new marital relationship, adjustment to the presence of a stepparent, and alterations in the relationship between the biological custodial parent and child.

A final challenge is that of maintaining or building supportive, or at least nondestructive, sibling relationships. This task may be more difficult as sibling relationships become more complex and move beyond those containing only full biological siblings to those with half siblings and unrelated siblings from both of the parents' previous marriages. This chapter focuses on how these five challenges are met and their consequences for children's adjustment in stepfamilies.

THREE LONGITUDINAL STUDIES
OF MARITAL TRANSITIONS

The studies on which this chapter are based include: (a) Study 1: The Virginia Longitudinal Study of Divorce and Remarriage (Hetherington, 1993), (b) Study 2: The Hetherington and Clingempeel Study of Divorce and Remarriage (Hetherington & Clingempeel, 1992), and (c) Study 3: The National Study of Nonshared Environment (Reiss et al., 1994). Although all of these studies used an ecological developmental family systems framework, similar constructs (and often similar measures), each contributed unique information about family functioning, individual adjustment, and adaptation to remarriage and life in a stepfamily. All studies involved both male and female children and had nondivorced families as comparison groups.

Studies 1 and 2 also had a comparison group of families headed by a divorced, nonremarried mother. Study 1 was not originally intended as a study of remarriage, but of divorced and nondivorced families. However, stepfamilies emerged over time as divorced parents remarried. Studies 1 and 2 examined stepfather families, whereas Study 3 included a variety of stepfamily forms.

Study 1 had the longest time span of any of the studies examining children and families—an 11-year period, from the time the children were 4 until they were 15. In this study, time of remarriage was not controlled through sample selection, but was assessed when the parents who had been in the married and divorced group in the initial sample opted to remarry.

Study 2 was designed to study adaptation in stepfamilies with an early adolescent child in the first 26 months following a remarriage. This might be viewed as a study of the initial crisis period following a second marriage.

Study 3, although it also involved adolescent children, included stepfamilies who had been married at least 5 years and could therefore be viewed as established, stabilized stepfamilies. Moreover, Study 3 had two siblings of varying degrees of biological relatedness who were intensively studied as target children, whereas Studies 1 and 2 had one target child who was intensively studied over time. However, a subgroup of children in Study 1 and Study 2 also had siblings who were studied much less extensively in order to examine the influence of the sibling relationship on the development of the target child.

The Virginia Longitudinal Study of Divorce

The Virginia Longitudinal Study of Divorce and Remarriage (Hetherington, 1993) was designed to examine adaptation following divorce in mother-custody families. The initial sample was composed of 144 middle-class, White families, half nondivorced, half divorced, half with a target son, and half with a target daughter 4 years of age. Children and families were studied at 2 months, 1 year, 2 years, 6 years, 8 years (truncated battery), and 11 years post-divorce. Nondivorced families were studied at equivalent time intervals. Of the original sample, 121 families remained in the study until the final follow-up, when the children were 15. At the six-year follow-up, when the children were 10, the sample was expanded to include 180 families, and in the final follow-up, the sample was expanded to 300 families evenly distributed across a remarried mother–stepfather group, a nonremarried mother-custody group, and a nondivorced group (Hetherington, 1993).

The Hetherington and Clingempeel Study of Divorce and Remarriage

This 2-year longitudinal study (Hetherington & Clingempeel, 1992) examined the effect of marital transitions on family functioning and early adolescent adjustment in 202 families. Three groups of White, middle-class families were investigated: (a) newly remarried families with a biological custodial mother and a stepfather, (b) single-parent families with a divorced custodial mother who had been divorced for the same length of time as the mothers in the stepfamilies, but who had never remarried, and (c) nondivorced families. Three waves of data

were collected at 4 months, 17 months, and 26 months following remarriage
(Hetherington & Clingempeel, 1992).

The National Study of Nonshared Environment

The primary aim of the National Study of Nonshared Environment was to examine the contribution of nonshared environment, that is experiences that differ for siblings in the same family, to the development of both competence and psychopathology during adolescence. However, this study also offered an unusual opportunity to examine the functioning and development of children in different kinds of stepfamilies (Reiss et al., 1994). A national sample comprised of 720 two-parent families with a pair of same-sex adolescent siblings no more than 4 years apart in age was obtained. It consisted of six groups of families with siblings of varying degrees of genetic relatedness. These six family types included: (a) families with dizygotic twins, (b) families with monozygotic twins, (c) stepfamilies with full siblings where both children were from the mother's previous marriage, (d) stepfamilies with half siblings where one child was from the mother's previous marriage and one was born in the remarriage, (e) blended stepfamilies with unrelated siblings (one from the mother's previous marriage and one from the father's previous marriage), and (f) nondivorced families with full siblings (intact). The stepfamilies were stabilized stepfamilies who had been remarried for an average of almost 9 years.

In this chapter, we sometimes refer to *simple* and *complex* stepfamilies. Simple stepfamilies are those in which only children from the mother's previous marriage are present in the family. Complex stepfamilies are those in which siblings in the family vary in biological relatedness to the mother and father.

It was expected that more complex relationships would be associated with more problems in the parent–child relationship and in the adjustment of children. In contrast, the quality of the sibling relationship was expected to be influenced by the biological relationship of the specific sibling pair rather than the complexity in biological relationships among all family members. (Twin findings are not discussed in this chapter.) Four years after the initial assessment, a second assessment of 404 families with both adolescents still remaining in the home was conducted. Only preliminary analyses from the first assessment are available for this chapter.

Methods and Constructs

Multimethod, Multimeasure, Multi-Informant Assessment. Multiple measures, multiple methods, and multiple informants were used to gather information on family functioning and children's adjustment in all three longitudinal studies. Each wave of data collection involved a large set of interviews, questionnaires, standardized test measures and observations of family problem-solving sessions in various dyadic, triadic, and tetradic combinations of parents, sibling, and adolescent target children. In Study 1, observations with younger children and parents included unstructured play and structured observations of parents and children, and observations of children in the school and in peer interactions. Information on marital, sibling, and parent–child relationships, as well as children's competence and behavior problems was obtained from a variety of informants, including children, parents, siblings, and teachers. In addition, data was collected on other variables outside the home, such as peer networks, social support, life events and stresses, and relationships with grandparents and nonresidential fathers (see Gunnoe, 1993; Hetherington, 1988, 1991a, 1991b, 1993; Hetherington & Clingempeel, 1992; Hetherington, Cox, & Cox, 1985; Reiss et al., 1994; for more details on methods).

Assessment of certain common areas or constructs were found in all studies. In the marital relationship, marital satisfaction, areas of conflict, family tasks and roles, warmth/support and conflict/negativity in the couple relationship were assessed. In the parent–child relationship, the child's negative/coercive/conflictual behavior, as well as warm, congenial behavior and feelings of closeness with the parent were assessed. Four parenting dimensions were central in these three longitudinal studies of marital transitions: warmth/involvement, negativity/conflict, and monitoring and control. In Study 3, monitoring and control were highly correlated and were combined into a single dimension (Hetherington, 1993; Hetherington & Clingempeel, 1992; Reiss et al., 1994).

Cluster analyses were used to develop parenting typologies. Among families with younger children, four types of parenting styles emerged, which included authoritative, permissive, authoritarian, and neglecting/disengaged parenting. With adolescent children, the clusters varied somewhat across studies, however, with the number of clusters used ranging from three to five. The three most common parenting types found in all studies of adolescents were authoritative, disengaged, and conflictual/authoritarian. An authoritative/harmonious parenting style was identified by higher levels of warmth/positivity and monitoring, moderate to high levels of control, and low negativity. Disengaged parents were characterized by moderate levels of negativity and lower levels of monitoring, control and positivity. Conflictual/authoritarian parents were identified by higher levels of conflict and monitoring and control attempts and low levels of positivity (Hetherington & Clingempeel, 1992). These authoritarian parents were characterized by less effective control and more conflict than the authoritarian parents of younger children.

Sibling relationships were described on dimensions of negativity and positivity based on observations of siblings' interactions and parents' and children's reports on Schaefer and Edgerton's (1981) Sibling Inventory of Behavior (SIB). A negativity factor was comprised of aggression (active unkindness/anger), avoidance/embarrassment, and rivalry; positivity was characterized by involvement/companionship, teaching/guidance, and empathy/support.

Measures of children's adjustment included measures of externalizing and internalizing, social and academic competence, and self-esteem.

Data Analysis.   Within-wave MANOVAs were performed to capitalize on sample size, as well as repeated-measure multivariate analyses involving wave, sex of child, family type, and when appropriate sex of parent were performed in these studies. Structural modeling, multiple regressions, and cross-lagged panel regressions were used in an attempt to identify functional and causal relationships contributing to changes in family relations and the adjustment of family members. Cluster analyses were used to identify types of parenting styles, types of sibling relations, and types of adjustment in parents and children, and, in Study 1, also types of schools. Observational measures were assessed through multiple ratings and coding systems. Molecular sequential coding was analyzed through sequential lag analyses for selected parts of the observational session in Studies 1 and 2.

Factor analyses and structural equation modeling were used to develop multimethod, multi-informant composite variables on the constructs of interest, with much of the information reported in this chapter based on these composites. However, reports of various informants were also examined and, at times, the different perspectives of family members are noted. We make little attempt to systematically report specific findings from the three studies. We use the three studies to present a comprehensive, replicated picture of changes in family relationships and child adjustment over time, as parents and children adapt to life in a stepfamily.

FAMILY RELATIONSHIPS

Remarriage impacts all family subsystems, including the marital relationship, parent–child relationshps, and sibling relationships. New family roles and relationships must be redefined and renegotiated in a family system which is structurally more complex than either the traditional, nondivorced, nuclear family or the divorced, single-parent household (Hetherington & Clingempeel, 1992).

The Marital Relationship

One of the most critical tasks confronting couples in reconstituted families is the establishment of a stable and enduring marital relationship. Spouses must construct a relationship in a ready-made family that often includes an extended network of ex-in-laws, noncustodial children, nonresidential parents, and grandparents (Albrecht, Bahr, & Goodman, 1983). Moreover, remarried family members bring to the newly reconstituted family, experiences, perspectives, expectations, and standards of comparison from an earlier marriage and family that can influence the adjustment to remarriage, either positively or negatively (Hetherington & Camara, 1984). The task of building a strong and enduring marital bond is thus not easily negotiated in the stepfamily.

In spite of these challenges, researchers typically find few differences in the marital satisfaction of couples in first marriages and those in remarriages (Anderson & White, 1986; Kitson, 1992; Pink & Wampler, 1985). Self-reports describing roles and relationships, however, suggest that second marriages are often viewed as more pragmatic, less romantic, more open with a greater willingness to confront conflict, and more egalitarian with respect to household chores and childrearing issues (Furstenberg, 1979, 1982; Giles-Sims, 1984, 1987). Furthermore, the findings from observational studies have not been consistent with the results of self-reports of marital relations in stepfamilies, sometimes identifying more negativity in interactions of remarried couples (Bray & Berger, 1993).

Our studies were in agreement with earlier studies indicating that once remarriages had stabilized, there were no differences in self-reports of marital satisfaction between remarried and longer-married, nondivorced couples. Although in the first 2 years of a remarriage, spouses typically reported greater satisfaction than those in longer-married first marriages, the satisfaction of the two groups gradually converged and declined over time. A decline in marital satisfaction was noted by couples in both nondivorced and remarried families as children moved into adolescence (Hetherington & Clingempeel, 1992).

Newly remarried couples also reported more positive and negative life events. Coping with their newly transformed family situation and life stresses while maintaining a satisfying marriage had psychological costs, because both husbands and wives in stepfamilies in the first 2 years of remarriage had higher scores on the Beck Depression Inventory than those in first marriages. These differences in depression were not found in longer, more stabilized remarriages. However, although remarried couples were satisfied with their marriages and reported more sharing in household tasks than spouses in first marriages, even those couples remarried for more than 2 years perceived their reconstituted families as less cohesive and more conflicted over issues of childrearing and finances. In the first 2 years of remarriage, no differences were observed between family problem-solving sessions in husbands' and wives' behavior in stepfamilies and first marriages. However, couples in stepfamilies became increasingly less positive and more negative in marital interactions over time, and differences between spouses in the two family types were most marked for longer-married families with adolescent children.

These findings suggest that stepfamily couples are committed to sustaining a satisfying marital relationship despite their changing life situation and problems in parent–child and sibling relationships. However, some of the problems in stepfamilies remain unresolved and, as the stresses in a remarriage are exacerbated by the normative challenges of adolescent children, marital interactions may deteriorate.

Parent–Child Relationships

Although stepfamilies can take many possible forms, most remarried households occur when a stepfather is added to the family through the remarriage of a divorced, custodial mother. It is therefore not surprising that most studies of parent–child relations in stepfamilies involve custodial mothers, their children, and stepfathers. A few examine custodial fathers, their children and stepmothers, and very few examine parenting in more complex stepfamily forms, such as blended families with children from the mother's and father's previous marriage, or families in which children from earlier marriages and children born to the remarriage are present. Although the families in Study 1 and 2 were stepfather families with children only from the mother's previous marriage, Study 3 did permit the examination of stabilized stepfamilies with varying forms and complexity. Overall, we have extensive information on custodial mothers and stepfathers, but more limited information on custodial fathers and stepmothers, and the latter only in restabilized blended stepfamilies with adolescent children.

In discussing parent–child relations, it is important to consider not only the length of time since remarriage and whether parents are in the early stages of a remarriage or are in a more established stepfamily, but also child gender and the child's age at remarriage and assessment. The major findings on parent–child relations from our three studies are listed below.

First, in the early stages of a marital transition, whether in divorce or remarriage, parent–child relations are more disrupted and conflictual and parenting is often less authoritative than in nondivorced families.

Second, over-time parenting of children in stepfamilies by their biological custodial parents becomes more similar to that in nondivorced families.

Third, even in restabilized stepfamilies, stepmothers and stepfathers remain more disengaged and less authoritative in the parenting of stepchildren than in parenting their own children. Stepparents are also less authoritative and more disengaged than are nondivorced parents.

Fourth, early adolescence is a difficult time in which to have a remarriage occur, with more sustained difficulties in stepfather–stepchild relations and child adjustment, than in remarriages when children are younger. In addition, family relationships and the adjustment of children in stepfamilies may be more vulnerable to the perturbations associated with entry into adolescence than are those in nondivorced families.

Fifth, early in a remarriage, adolescent children tend to behave more negatively and less positively to stepfathers than do children in nondivorced families. In longer established stepfamilies, however, many children are disengaged from their stepfamilies, and observed negativity is lower for children with stepmothers than it is for children with their own mothers, whether in nondivorced or remarried families. At all times in the remarriage, children report feeling less close to stepparents than to biological custodial parents.

Sixth, noncustodial mothers are more likely to remain involved with their children than are noncustodial fathers. Both noncustodial mothers and fathers are less authoritative in parenting than are custodial biological parents.

Custodial Parents

Although other studies (Zill et al., 1993) have not found sensitive periods in parents' and childrens' responses to remarriage, in these studies the age of the child at the time of remarriage was found to be a salient factor in the quality of parent–child relationships, as well as in children's adjustment. An initial period of conflict and low monitoring and control by custodial mothers followed remarriage when the children were any age. If the remarriage occurred when the children were preadolescents, the quality of the custodial mother's parenting gradually improved and showed few differences from those of nondivorced mothers. In the restabilized, remarried families with adolescent children in Study 3, neither custodial mothers nor custodial fathers in remarried families differed from their nondivorced family counterparts in warmth, conflict/negativity, or monitoring/control. In contrast, if the remarriage occurred when children were early adolescents, maternal monitoring and control stabilized at levels lower than that in nondivorced families.

Parents and children in divorced, remarried, and nondivorced families underwent realignments in family relations as children moved through the pubertal apex (Hetherington, 1993; Steinberg, 1988), reflected in decreases in parental monitoring, control, and warmth, and increases in conflict, especially with mothers. Our findings suggest that the conflict between adolescents and nonremarried, divorced custodial mothers is more severe and long-lasting, and temporary declines in monitoring and control triggered by adolescence may be more marked in remarried families than in nondivorced families. However, with the exception of those remarriages occurring in early adolescence, there are more similarities than differences in the parenting of custodial biological parents in remarried and nondivorced families.

Stepparents

Past research suggests that the course of adjustment to remarriage may be even more difficult for stepparents, especially stepmothers, than for custodial parents (Bray, 1990; Hetherington, 1989). Establishing a new close and constructive parent–child relationship may be particularly problematic.

Regardless of the child's age at remarriage, stepfathers initially reported lower levels of closeness and rapport with their stepchildren and made fewer attempts to monitor or control children's behavior than did fathers in nondivorced families. Early attempts to establish a positive stepfather–child relationship through self-disclosure, common interests, and shared activities were typically met with highly coercive reactions from stepchildren. Despite this resistance on the part of stepchildren, and in spite of expressing concerns about the lack of feelings of closeness or rapport with stepchildren, many stepfathers spent time with their stepchildren and remained relatively open to their stepchildren in the early stages of a remarriage (Hetherington, 1993; Hetherington & Clingempeel, 1992). Over time, however, the majority of stepfathers no longer attempted to engage in a warm and supportive relationship with their stepchildren as a result of continued resistance or distancing behavior, as well as the persistence of problem behaviors among stepchildren. It should be noted that differences in warmth and in control and monitoring were much more consistently found over the course of the stepfather's adaptation than were differences in negativity. In fact, it was often found that biological custodial parents were more affectively involved with their own children than stepparents were with stepchildren. They were not only more affectionate and supportive, but were also more willing to criticize their children for unacceptable behavior, such as untidy rooms, poor personal hygiene, and not doing their homework. An authoritative parenting style was less likely among stepfathers than among fathers in nondivorced families. Thus, the most common parenting style found among stepfathers was disengaged parenting, characterized by low levels of involvement and rapport, and a lack of control, discipline, and monitoring of the stepchild's behavior and activities (Hetherington & Clingempeel, 1992).

Little adaptation to remarriage occurred in stepfather–child relationships when a second marriage took place in early adolescence. Although stepfathers often manifested few signs of overt negativity, they were less positive and less involved in the monitoring and control of their children than were nondivorced fathers. Furthermore, adolescent children still displayed less positivity toward their stepfathers 2 years after remarriage (Hetherington & Clingempeel, 1992). Among more stabilized stepfamilies, stepfathers' control increased over time for stepsons, but not for stepdaughters, when remarriage occurred prior to adolescence. In the long run, a second marriage when children were younger was associated with a closer stepfather–stepson relationship. Unfortunately, even in the event of a remarriage during early childhood, adolescence created renewed conflict between stepfathers and stepdaughters (Hetherington, 1993; Hetherington & Clingempeel, 1992). Our evidence suggests that the development of a close stepfather–stepchild relationship is difficult at best, and may not occur at all if remarriage occurs when a child is entering adolescence (Hetherington & Clingempeel, 1992).

In remarriages that occurred prior to adolescence, stepfathers were most effective in building a positive stepfather–stepchild relationship when, initially, no independent attempts were made to control or discipline a child. Rather, a stepfather who was supportive of the custodial mother's efforts to discipline, who attempted to build a close relationship with the child, and who only gradually attempted to exert his authority was most effective (Hetherington, 1993;

Hetherington & Clingempeel, 1992). Otherwise, whether the stepfather had an authoritarian parenting style where control was accompanied by low warmth and high punitiveness and coercion, or an authoritative parenting style where control was accompanied by warmth and involvement, attempts to control and discipline from the outset seemed to trigger greater resistance on the part of the stepchild. Interestingly, more immediate authoritative stepparenting was associated with greater acceptance of the stepfather and more positive outcomes for children when a second marriage took place during adolescence (Hetherington & Clingempeel, 1992). Despite the difficulties inherent in stepfather–stepchild relationships, a close relationship with an authoritative stepfather eventually was able to partially buffer the effects of a hostile or neglecting mother in the development of antisocial, acting out behaviors in children, especially boys, in longer established remarriages (Gunnoe, 1993; Hetherington, 1993).

In Study 3, the degree of biological relatedness or "owness," rather than whether the family was a nondivorced family or a simple or complex stepfamily, was important to differences in parent–child relationships. There were no differences in the parenting of biological children in nondivorced families, or in any of the restabilized stepfamilies. Even in long-established, blended families, stepmothers and stepfathers were less warm and supportive with their stepchildren than were biological parents with their own children in either nondivorced or remarried households. Whether in nondivorced families or stepfamilies, or in simple or complex stepfamilies, biological fathers were more warm and supportive and involved in monitoring and controlling children's activities with their own children than were stepfathers with stepchildren. Biological mothers expressed more warmth, rapport, and closeness with their own children, regardless of family type or the complexity of the stepfamily system. In addition, children behaved more positively toward their biological parents and had more conflict with their biological mothers than their stepmothers, indicating, perhaps, greater emotional engagement.

These parenting findings are congruent with a sociobiological perspective that suggests there is a tendency to use reproductive and parenting strategies that will ensure the survival of genes into the next generation. Hence, more protective nurturant behavior might be expected with the parent's own offspring. The findings to be reported later on—the lack of contact and involvement of noncustodial parents, especially noncustodial fathers, do not seem to be in accord with evolutionary theory, although it has been argued that a quantity rather than quality strategy in procreation or parenting might be advantageous to males (Belsky, Steinberg, & Draper, 1991).

In summary, custodial parents and children who are biologically related are more likely to be involved and affectively engaged with each other, distance and disengagement with occasional explosive encounters are more characteristic of relationships between stepparents and stepchildren. Even in long established remarriages, authoritative parenting is more common with biologically related parents and children, whereas disengaged parenting is more common among stepparents. Adolescence seems to be an especially difficult time in which to have a remarriage occur, and in which to establish constructive parent–child relationships.

Noncustodial Parents

Although there is less research on noncustodial parents than on custodial parents or stepparents, our results supported and extended the findings of previous studies. Study 1 had extensive measures on the relationship with noncustodial fathers, whereas Studies 2 and 3 had more limited measures, but Study 3 also included noncustodial mothers in blended families. The work cited here on comparisons between noncustodial mothers and fathers from Study 3 is based on an unpublished dissertation by Gunnoe (1993).

Contact with the noncustodial parent declined rapidly over the first 2 years following divorce; however, noncustodial mothers in Study 3 were more likely than noncustodial fathers to maintain contact with their children, and this contact was twice as frequent as that of noncustodial fathers. In Study 3, 40% of adolescents in remarried families reported weekly contact with their noncustodial mothers and 22% reported weekly contact with noncustodial fathers. The quality of the father–child relationship before divorce did not predict continued involvement with the child, or the quality of the noncustodial father's post-divorce parenting in any of our studies (Hetherington & Clingempeel, 1992). Some fathers found intermittent parenting and the lack of control over their children's lives painful, and thus, withdrew. For other fathers who had previously not been involved parents, the divorce triggered a sense of loss that was sometimes associated with greater involvement and increases in parent–child contact. Mothers who were involved and competent before the divorce were more likely to remain so following the divorce and remarriage of the custodial parent (Hetherington, 1993). The maintainance of contact was associated with geographical proximity, remarriage, feelings of control over decisions in the child's life, and obstacles placed to visitation by custodial parents (Hetherington, 1993).

Noncustodial fathers became either more permissive and indulgent or more disengaged following divorce. Those who remained involved were more likely to assume a recreational, companionate role than an instrumental role of disciplinarian or teacher (Gunnoe, 1993; Hetherington, 1993). Adolescents reported less positivity toward and from noncustodial fathers than custodial fathers. In contrast, noncustodial mothers were more similar in parenting to remarried custodial mothers; however, they were also lower on monitoring and control. Noncustodial mothers, in contrast to noncustodial fathers, communicated better with their children, were more supportive in times of stress, and were more knowledgeable and interested in their children's activities. This greater involvement of noncustodial mothers, however, led to more problems in establishing a constructive, harmonious relationship between stepmothers and stepchildren, with children in stepmother families reporting more loyalty conflicts and feelings of being caught in the middle (Gunnoe, 1993).

Children's Behavior Toward Parents

Observations of parent–child interactions in stepfamilies in the early stage of a remarriage, showed children to be less warm and communicative, and more negative toward their custodial mother and stepfather than were children from nondivorced families (Hetherington, 1993; Hetherington & Clingempeel, 1992). More antagonistic, disruptive behavior toward both parents was found among younger girls, whereas increasingly noncommunicative, sullen, and avoidant behavior was more common among adolescent girls (Hetherington, 1993). However, relations between younger stepsons and stepfathers improved over time.

If the remarriage occurred when the children were adolescents, adolescent stepsons and stepdaughters remained less warm and responsive and more coercive toward stepfathers, even after 26 months of remarriage (Hetherington, 1993; Hetherington & Clingempeel, 1992). Adolescent girls were more withdrawn from their stepfathers than were boys. Adolescent stepdaughters were 30% less likely to talk to their stepfathers than were daughters and fathers in nondivorced families (Vuchinich, Hetherington, Vuchinich, & Clingempeel, 1991).

Although adolescent children in stepfamilies in the longer established Study 3 remarriages reported feeling less close to their stepparent than to their biological custodial parent, they also had more conflicts with their biological mothers than stepmothers, which suggests greater emotional involvement and less distancing. Furthermore, children in these stabilized stepfamilies felt closer and more positively toward their noncustodial mothers than toward their noncustodial fathers, perhaps because of the mothers' greater interest and involvement (Gunnoe, 1993).

About one third of adolescent boys and one quarter of adolescent girls in divorced and remarried families disengaged from their families. They spent little time at home and little time in family activities. They often became involved with a friend's family that became a surrogate family; with extracurricular activities or a job; and with peers. If this disengagement involved a close relationship with a caring, involved adult, it was sometimes a constructive solution to a difficult family situation. If disengagement involved associations with antisocial peers or no adult supervision, it was associated with substance abuse, low achievement, school dropout, sexual activity, and delinquency.

Interestingly, in terms of direction of effects, adolescent children in stepfamilies were more effective in altering the behavior of parents than parents were in shaping children's behavior in the early stages of a remarriage. Cross-lagged panel regressions indicated that externalizing behavior in early adolescent stepchildren was associated with subsequent increases in negative, punitive, and coercive behaviors in stepfathers. Similarly, adolescent social competence was associated with increases in later positivity directed toward children by custodial mothers and stepfathers (Hetherington & Clingempeel, 1992).

Links Between the Marital Relationship and Parent–Child Relationship

There is a complex association between the quality of the marital relationship in stepfamilies and the parent–child relationship that changes as a function of the age of the child. A strong marital relationship is often viewed as a firm foundation for positive family functioning that promotes both responsive, competent parenting and the psychological well-being of children (Hetherington, 1993). Although children's behavior problems and disrupted parent–child relationships have been frequently linked to difficulties in the marital relationship among nondivorced families (Emery, 1982; Hetherington, Cox, & Cox, 1982), less consistent associations between marital adjustment and children's adjustment have been found in stepfamilies (Bray & Hetherington, 1993). Subsystems within the context of a reconstituted family may thus be more independent than in a nondivorced household (Bray, 1992; Bray & Hetherington, 1993; Visher & Visher, 1988). As a result, the impact of marital relations on parent–child relations may be more limited in stepfamilies (Bray & Hetherington, 1993).

Our studies found that in younger children, especially preadolescent girls, a close marital relationship was associated with more negative behavior toward the custodial mother and the stepfather in the early stage of a remarriage (Hetherington, 1993). Moreover, the closer the mother–daughter relationship had been before remarriage, the more resistant girls were to parents with a satisfying marriage. Daughters may be particularly sensitive to the presence of a close marital relationship, because they may perceive the entrance of the stepfather as a threat to the often intimate, companionate mother–daughter relationship formed in the mother-headed, single-parent family after the divorce. Stepfathers may be viewed by stepdaughters as potential competitors for the affection of the mother and by both children as threats to the precocious power and autonomy they have attained in the single-parent household. In contrast, relations between custodial mothers and their sons often involved high levels of reciprocal coercion and conflict following a divorce. As a result, boys may have nothing to lose and something to gain in establishing a relationship with a warm and caring stepfather. The quality of the marital relationship was also differentially related to the adjustment of preadolescent stepchildren. A satisfying marital relationship was associated with a higher incidence of internalizing and externalizing behavior in preadolescent stepdaughters and lower levels of externalizing in preadolescent stepsons (Hetherington, 1993).

When the remarriage occurred in adolescence, a close marital relationship was associated with more acceptance of the remarriage and more harmonious parent–child relations for both boys and girls (Hetherington, 1991a, 1991b; Hetherington & Clingempeel, 1992). What is it about adolescence that precipitates this change in the response of stepdaughters to the quality of the marital relationship? Adolescence is associated with marked physical changes and increasing sensitivity to issues of intimate relations and sexuality. Even biologically related fathers may be disconcerted by their adolescent daughters burgeoning sexual development. Our fathers in nondivorced families showed a decrease in expressions of physical affection, physical contact, and in the direct orientation of their bodies when conversing with their daughters at this time. Confusion about appropriate expressions of affection and how to deal with issues of sexuality may be more marked for girls and their nonbiologically related stepfather. Thus, a close marital relationship may be seen by daughters and parents in stepfamilies as a protective buffer against the threat of inappropriate intimacy between stepdaughters and stepfathers.

Adolescence as a Sensitive Period for Stepfamilies

As we have noted, the normative changes and stresses associated with the transition to adolescence may be magnified for children experiencing a marital transition (Hetherington & Anderson, 1987). This period is typically marked by an adolescent's bid for greater autonomy, and by increased parental disengagement and distancing (Baumrind, 1991), and heightened levels of conflict as children enter the pubertal apex (Steinberg, 1988). Children in divorced families have already attained precocious independence and the entrance of a stepfather may be seen as a threat to their autonomy. The introduction of a stepfather may further stress a family system which is unstable or in transition, because of normative changes in adolescence leading to more rapid or inappropriate disengagement of the child from the family unit (Hetherington, 1989).

Earlier studies of divorce and remarriage involving younger children demonstrated substantial adaptation in children's behavior and family relationships in the first 2 years following a marital transition (Bray, 1987; Hetherington, 1988, 1989, 1993). In contrast, more recent findings suggest that a child's adaptation in the context of a stepfamily may be particularly problematic during adolescence (Bray & Berger, 1993). Disruptions in family functioning with minimal improvements in either adolescent adjustment or stepfather–stepchild relations were found 2 years after a remarriage that occurred when children were early adolescents (Hetherington & Clingempeel, 1992). Although children in both nondivorced and remarried families displayed increasingly more negative behavior as they moved into adolescence, over time these children declined in negativity and became more positive toward all parents except stepparents. As parents distanced themselves and granted greater autonomy to their adolescent children, conflict between parents and children seemed to decline (Hetherington & Clingempeel, 1992).

When a remarriage occurred early in adolescence, measures of children's adjustment indicated a sustained, high level of internalizing and externalizing disorders and low social responsibility and academic competence, over the course of 26 months, with none of the adaptation found in younger children (Hetherington & Clingempeel, 1992). Even among stabilized divorced and remarried families, such behavior problems seemed to resurface when children entered adolescence (Bray & Berger, 1993; Hetherington, 1993). The transition to adolescence may, therefore, act as a catalyst for latent problems of adjustment in families who have gone through the stresses and changes associated with marital transitions and disrupted attachments. Studies of older adolescents and young adults suggest that, as achievement and the formation of intimate relations become increasingly central areas in development, the offspring of divorced and remarried families show more problems in these domains (Amato & Keith, 1991; Zill et al., 1993).

Children's Adjustment in Stepfamilies: Relationship to Parenting

Although it used to be said that divorce and life in a household headed by a custodial mother was more damaging to boys and that remarriage was more detrimental to girls, these effects are related to the age of the child and the era in which the study was conducted. Gender differences in response to parents' marital transitions are more frequently found in preadolescents and rarely found in adolescents (Hetherington, 1993; Zaslow, 1989). In addition, larger effects of divorce and remarriage on the adjustment of children and more frequent gender effects are found in older rather than newer studies of divorce and remarriage (Amato & Keith, 1991; Zaslow, 1989). In general, temperament, intelligence, self-esteem, and locus of control were stronger correlates of the adjustment of children, especially adolescent children, in response to their parents' remarriage than was gender (Hetherington, 1989, 1991a; Hetherington & Clingempeel, 1992). However, in our work with preadolescent children, there were initial declines in social and academic competence, and increases in externalizing and internalizing among both boys and girls following the remarriage of their custodial mother. After 2 years, preadolescent boys growing up in a stepfamily with a warm, supportive, authoritative stepfather showed no more behavior problems than boys in nondivorced families. In contrast, in spite of adaptation over the course of two years, preadolescent girls from stepfamilies demonstrated more acting out, antisocial behaviors than girls from either divorced or nondivorced families (Hetherington, 1993). As has been found in other studies (Baumrind, 1989; Zill et al., 1993), most of the gender differences in adjustment in response to divorce and remarriage observed in younger children were not apparent by early adolescence (Hetherington, 1993; Hetherington & Clingempeel, 1992). That is not to say there were no main effects for gender. In all of our studies, girls were perceived as more socially and academically competent and as having fewer behavior problems than adolescent boys (Hetherington, 1993; Hetherington & Clingempeel, 1992). However, gender X family type interactions in child outcomes commonly found among younger children were rarely found in adolescence.

At all ages, children growing up in stepfamilies and divorced, single–mother households tended to be viewed as less well-adjusted, and as exibiting more behavior problems than children from nondivorced households, and in the early stage of a remarriage, stepchildren were less well-adjusted than children in stabilized families headed by a divorced, custodial mother (Hetherington & Clingempeel, 1992; Hetherington, Cox, & Cox, 1985).

The results of Study 3 with longer established remarriages indicate that problems in social responsibility, cognitive agency, school achievement, and conduct disorders are more sustained than those in internalizing, self-worth or sociability. The perceptions of children's adjustment in stepfamilies varied across informants, with parents and observers being more likely than teachers to view children in stepfamilies as being higher in externalizing and lower in competence than children from nondivorced families whereas teachers viewed children with divorced, nonremarried mothers as most disturbed. In contrast, the children reported greater antisocial behavior and internalizing, but not lower social competence or self-worth. In addition, remarried, custodial mothers reported more behavior problems in boys, whereas stepfathers perceived both boys and girls as having high levels of behavior problems.

There was an indication in Study III that custodial arrangements may make a difference in child adjustment. Adolescents who had spent some time in a mother-custody home had the most conduct problems, whereas those with custodial fathers had the most academic difficulties. Furthermore, an interesting interaction between sex of parent and sex of child occurred in these established remarriages. The parenting of custodial or noncustodial parents of the same sex as the child was more strongly associated with child adjustment than was parenting by custodial or noncustodial parents of the opposite sex (Gunnoe, 1993).

Evidence is accumulating that, although children in divorced or remarried families have problems exacerbated by the stresses associated with their parents' marital transitions, children whose parents later divorced are more likely to also have had problems in adjustment before these transitions occurred (Block, Block, & Gjerde, 1986; Cherlin et al., 1991). Thus, individual predispositions and problems in family relations preceding divorce and remarriage are already contributing to problem behavior.

It must be underscored that most children in remarried families are not demonstrating severe or enduring behavior problems. If we use clinical cutoffs on such measures as the Child Behavior Checklist (Achenbach, 1978; Achenbach & Edelbrock, 1979) and the Center for Epidemiological Studies' Depression Scale (CES-D; Garrison, Schluchter, Schoenbach, & Kaplan, 1988) about 10% of children from nondivorced families, and one quarter to one third of children in stepfamilies, score above the clinical cutoff. Therefore, two-thirds to three-quarters are not exibiting serious emotional and behavioral problems, and the rate above the cutoffs in our longer, established remarriages are even lower. Thus, although children in remarried families are at risk for adjustment problems, in the long run, the response of most children to the challenges of life in a stepfamily is characterized by resiliency and adaptability.

Siblings, Peers, and the School as Risk or Protective Factors

As we have noted, members of divorced and remarried families encountered more stresses than those in nondivorced families. Although authoritative residential parents served as the most effective protection against adverse effects of these stresses on children, children with authoritative parents in divorced and remarried families still showed more problems than those with authoritative nondivorced parents (Hetherington & Clingempeel, 1992). Furthermore, the amount of variance in children's adjustment explained by parenting declined as children grew older (Miller, Cowan, Cowan, Hetherington, & Clingempeel, 1993) and relationships with siblings, peers, and the school environment became increasingly salient.

Siblings. Conflictual or ambivalent sibling relationships characterized by negative, rivalrous, aggressive interchanges have been commonly associated with parents' marital transitions (Hetherington, 1989, 1993). The results of Study 1 and Study 2 indicate that younger siblings and early adolescent siblings in newly remarried stepfather families demonstrated lower positivity and greater negativity toward their siblings than did children from nondivorced families (Hetherington & Clingempeel, 1992). Male sibling relations in stepfamilies were more likely to be characterized by coercive cycles of reciprocal, aggressive behavior than those in nondivorced households. In addition, boys growing up in reconstituted families were also less likely to receive support and positive feedback from their female siblings (Hetherington, 1988, 1993). Girls displayed more empathy, support, involvement, and teaching behavior than boys in stepfamilies (Hetherington & Clingempeel, 1992); and poor relations between female siblings in remarried families tended to improve as they moved through adolescence (Hetherington, 1993). Few gender differences were indicated for such negative behaviors as aggression and sibling rivalry (Hetherington & Clingempeel, 1992).

Preliminary analyses of sibling relations in more established stepfamilies in Study 3 yielded results we had not expected on the basis of findings from the other two studies. There were no differences in positivity and negativity in sibling relations among nondivorced families or full or half siblings in remarried families. There was, however, less aggression and rivalry among unrelated siblings in blended families than in any of the biologically related siblings in the other three groups. Again, it was owness (in this case, the child's own sibling) rather than being in a nondivorced family or stepfamily that was important. It may be that biologically related siblings are more likely to compare their performance and their relationships with each other than are nonbiologically related siblings.

More negative, contentious sibling interactions had a greater impact on the development of problem behaviors than did positive, supportive sibling relationships on fostering positive adjustment among children experiencing a marital transition. Moreover, positive sibling relations were more likely to serve as a buffer when both siblings were female, and during adolescence, rather than during preadolescence (Hetherington, 1993).

A pattern of increasing distance and disengagement similar to that in parent–child relations was observed among siblings as they entered adolescence (Hetherington & Clingempeel, 1992). Unlike parent–child interactions in early adolescence, however, a decrease rather than an increase in conflict was found among siblings as they moved through early adolescence. These adolescents may become embarrassed by their younger siblings and, therefore, may more actively distance themselves from parents and siblings to form bonds outside the stepfamily system (Hetherington & Clingempeel, 1992). As adolescents distance themselves from parents and siblings, they become more actively engaged with peers.

Peers.   Peer relations play an increasingly salient role in the adjustment of children as they grow older. Divorce and remarriage are followed by perturbations in peer relationships that are manifested in increases in aggressive, impulsive interactions and withdrawn behavior.

Adolescents in divorced and remarried families are often more vulnerable to peer influences than are children in nondivorced families (Hetherington, 1993; Steinberg, 1988). We found that early maturing girls who became involved with older peers were more likely to become involved in norm-breaking, externalizing behaviors and that these effects were stronger in divorced and remarried families than in nondivorced families. Both the absence of a biological father and the presence of a stepfather in the home were associated with earlier onset of menarche (Hetherington, 1993). Thus, girls in remarried families were at risk because of precocious puberty and vulnerability to peer influences.

Schools.   The school environment may also serve as a risk or protective factor in the adjustment of children to remarriage. In Study 1, it was found that an authoritative school that provided a structured, predictable environment was related to greater social and academic competence and a lower incidence of behavior problems among children (Hetherington, 1993). However, the largest effects of an authoritative school environment were found among early adolescent children as opposed to younger children, and were more marked in adolescents in divorced and remarried families. Structure, control, responsiveness, warmth, and demands for maturity on the part of teachers were associated with greater social and academic competence in both boys and girls from remarried families. Teacher warmth, responsiveness, and demands for maturity were more critical for girls, whereas structure and control within the school setting were more salient for boys (Hetherington, 1993).

These main effects of school environment were qualified by a significant interaction between an authoritative parenting style and an authoritative school. No enhancing effect of an authoritative school environment was demonstrated at age 15 when both residential parents (in the case of stepfamilies, the custodial mother and stepfather), were authoritative. However, if only one residential parent was authoritative, or if neither parent was authoritative, a school classified as authoritative contributed to increased academic achievement, social responsibility, and a lower incidence of behavior problems in children growing up in a stepfamily (Hetherington, 1993).

SUMMARY AND CONCLUSION

Remarriage imposes challenges for all family members, involving changes in established roles and relationships and the building of new or altered family relationships. Remarriage involves temporary perturbations in the relationship between the custodial parent and child, as well as in sibling relationships, and more enduring problems in stepparent–stepchild relations.

The stresses and changes in family functioning found in remarried families are associated with problems in children's adjustment. The literature on marital transitions suggests that children growing up in divorced families and in stepfamilies experience greater difficulties in social relations, achievement, and behavioral adjustment, including both internalizing and externalizing behaviors (Amato & Keith, 1991; Bray & Berger, 1993; Zill et al., 1993). In the long run, however, children who have experienced a marital transition are only slightly more troubled than children from intact households (Emery, 1992), although their problems may increase in adolescence and young adulthood (Amato & Keith, 1991; Bray & Berger, 1993; Hetherington, 1993). Despite the significant challenges associated with remarriage, most children eventually adapt to life in a stepfamily, and emerge as reasonably competent individuals (Hetherington, 1991a, 1991b).

Only recently has the focus of research on divorce and remarriage switched from a pathogenic model to one that emphasizes diversity of outcomes and changes in the family system associated with marital transitions. The move toward using a developmental, contextual, family systems perspective has been

an important advance in understanding factors that moderate and mediate short-
and long-term outcomes of marital transitions. Adaptation to remarriage is influenced not only by the balance of risk and protective factors in the individual and
the family, but also the larger social milieu. The next generation of studies needs
to explore the complex interactions among these factors in different types of
stepfamilies. A developmental, contextual approach to risk and resiliency in
coping with family transitions will promote greater understanding of the diverse
developmental trajectories and variations in the timing of the emergence of
sequelae associated with divorce and remarriage.

REFERENCES

Achenbach, T. M. (1978). The child behavior profile: I. Boys aged 6–11. *Journal of Consulting and Clinical Psychology, 46*, 478–488.

Achenbach, T. M., & Edelbrock, C. S. (1979). The child behavior profile: II. Boys aged 12–16 and girls aged 6–11 and 12–16. *Journal of Consulting and Clinical Psychology, 47*(2), 223–233.

Albrecht, S., Bahr, H., & Goodman, K. (1983). *Divorce and remarriage: Problems, adaptations, and adjustments*. Westpoint, CT: Greenwood.

Amato, P. R., & Keith, B. (1991). Parental divorce and the well-being of children: A meta-analysis. *Psychological Bulletin, 110*, 26–46.

Anderson, J. Z., & White, G. D. (1986). Dysfunctional intact families and stepfamilies. *Family Process, 25*, 407–422.

Baumrind, D. (1989, April). *Sex-differentiated socialization effects in childhood and adolescence in divorced and intact families*. Paper presented at the meeting of the Society for Research in Child Development, Kansas City, MO.

Baumrind, D. (1991). Effective parenting during the early adolescent transition. In P. A. Cowan & E. M. Hetherington (Eds.), *Family transitions* (pp. 111–163). Hillsdale, NJ: Lawrence Erlbaum Associates.

Belsky, J., Steinberg, L., & Draper, P. (1991). Childhood experience, interpersonal development, and reproductive strategy: An evolutionary theory of socialization. *Child Development, 62*, 647–670.

Block, J. H., Block, J., & Gjerde, P. F. (1986). The personality of children prior to divorce: A prospective study. *Child Development, 57*, 827–840.

Bray, J. H. (1987, August). *Becoming a stepfamily*. Paper presented at the meeting of the American Psychological Association, New York.

Bray, J. H. (1988). Children's development during early remarriage. In E. M. Hetherington & J. D. Arasteh (Eds.), *Impact of divorce, single parenting and stepparenting on children* (pp. 279–298). Hillsdale, NJ: Lawrence Erlbaum Associates.

Bray, J. H. (1990). *Developmental issues in stepfamilies research project* (final report). Un-published manuscript.

Bray, J. H. (1992). Family relationships and children's adjustment in clinical and nonclinical step-father families. *Journal of Family Psychology, 6*, 60–68.

Bray, J. H., & Berger, S. H. (1993). Developmental issues in Stepfamilies Research Project: Family relationships and parent–child interactions. *Journal of Family Psychology, 7*(1), 7–17.

Bray, J. H., & Hetherington, E. M. (1993). Families in transition: Introduction and overview. *Journal of Family Psychology, 7*(1), 1–6.

Bumpass, L., & Sweet, J. A. (1989). Children's experience in single–parent families: Implications of cohabitation and marital transitions. *Family Planning Perspectives, 6*, 256–260.

Cherlin, A. J. (1981). *Marriage, divorce, remarriage: Changing patterns in the postwar United States.* Cambridge, MA: Harvard University Press.

Cherlin, A. J. (1992). *Marriage, divorce, remarriage* (rev. ed.). Cambridge, MA: Harvard University Press.

Cherlin, A. J., Furstenberg, F. F., Jr., Chase-Lansdale, L. P., Kiernan, K. E., Robins, P. K., Morrison, D. R., & Teitler, J. O. (1991). Longitudinal effects of divorce in Great Britain and the United States. *Science, 252,* 1386–1389.

Depner, C. E., & Bray, J. H. (Eds.). (1993). *Nonresidential parenting: New vistas in family living.* Newbury Park, CA: Sage.

Emery, R. E. (1982). Interparental conflict and the children of discord and divorce. *Psychological Bulletin, 92,* 310–330.

Emery, R. E. (1992). Parental divorce and children's well-being: A focus on resilience. In R. J. Haggerty, N. Garmezy, M. Rutter, & L. Sherrod (Eds.), *Risk and resilience in children.* London, England: Cambridge University Press.

Furstenberg, F. F., Jr. (1979). Recycling the family: Perspectives for researching a neglected family form. *Marriage and Family Review, 2,* 12–22.

Furstenberg, F. F., Jr. (1982). Conjugal succession: Reentering marriage after divorce. In P. B. Baltes & O. G. Brim (Eds.), *Lifespan development and behavior* (Vol.4). New York: Academic Press.

Furstenberg, F. F., Jr. (1990). Divorce and the American family. *Annual Review of Sociology, 16,* 379–403.

Garrison, C. Z., Schluchter, M. D., Schoenbach, V. J., & Kaplan, B. K. (1988). Epidemiology of depressive symptoms in young adolescents. *Journal of the American Academy of Child and Adolescent Psychiatry, 28,* 343–351.

Giles-Sims, J. (1984). The stepfamily role: Expectations, behaviors, and sanctions. *Journal of Family Issues, 5,* 116–130.

Giles-Sims, J. (1987). Social exchange in remarried families. In K. Pasley & M. Ihinger-Talman (Eds.), *Remarriage and stepparenting today: Current research and theory* (pp. 141–163). New York: Guilford.

Glick, P. C. (1989). The family life cycle and social change. *Family Relations, 38,* 123–129.

Gunnoe, M. L. (1993). *Noncustodial mothers' and fathers' contribution to the adjustment of adolescent stepchildren.* Unpublished doctoral dissertation. University of Virginia, Charlottesville.

Hetherington, E. M. (1988). Parents, children and siblings six years after divorce. In R. Hinde & J. Stevenson-Hinde (Eds.), *Relationships within families* (pp. 311–331). Cambridge: Cambridge University Press.

Hetherington, E. M. (1989). Coping with family transitions: Winners, losers, and survivors. *Child Development, 60,* 1–14.

Hetherington, E. M. (1991a). The role of individual differences in family relations in coping with divorce and remarriage. In P. Cowan & E. M. Hetherington (Eds.), *Advances in family research: Vol. 2. Family transitions.* Hillsdale, NJ: Lawrence Erlbaum Associates.

Hetherington, E. M. (1991b). Presidential address: Families, lies, and videotapes. *Journal of Research on Adolescence, 1*(4), 323–348.

Hetherington, E. M. (1993). An overview of the Virginia Longitudinal Study of Divorce and Remarriage: A focus on early adolescence. *Journal of Family Psychology, 7,* 39–56.

Hetherington, E. M., & Anderson, E. R. (1987). The effects of divorce and remarriage on early adolescents and their families. In M. D. Levine & E. R. McAnarney (Eds.), *Early adolescent transitions* (pp. 49–67). Lexington, MA: Heath.

Hetherington, E. M., & Camara, K. A. (1984). Families in transition: The process of dissolution and reconstitution. In R. D. Parke (Ed.), *Review of child development research* (pp. 398–439). Chicago: University of Chicago Press.

Hetherington, E. M., & Clingempeel, W. G. (1992). Coping with marital transitions: A family systems perspective. *Monographs of the Society for Research in Child Development, 57*(2–3, Serial No. 227).

Hetherington, E. M., Cox, M. J., & Cox, R. (1982). Effects of divorce on parents and children. In M. E. Lamb (Ed.), *Nontraditional families* (pp. 233–288). Hillsdale, NJ: Lawrence Erlbaum Associates.

Hetherington, E. M., Cox, M. J., & Cox, R. (1985). Long-term effects of divorce and remarriage on the adjustment of children. *Journal of American Academy of Psychiatry, 24*(5), 518–530.

Kitson, G. C. (1992). *Portrait of divorce*. New York: Guilford.

Miller, N. B., Cowan, P. A., Cowan, C. P., Hetherington, E. M., & Clingempeel, W. G. (1993). Externalizing in preschoolers and early adolescents: A cross-study replication of a family model. *Developmental Psychology, 29*, 3–18.

Norton, A. J. (1991 April). *Marriage behavior of women: 1990 and beyond*. Paper presented at symposium in honor of P. C. Glick, "The American family on the eve of the twenty-first century: A demographic perspective," Tempe, AZ.

Papernow, P. L. (1984). The stepfamily cycle: An experimental model of stepfamily development. *Family Relations, 33*, 355–363.

Pink, J., & Wampler, K. (1985). Problem areas in stepfamilies: Cohesion, adaptability and the stepparent–adolescent relationship. *Family Relations, 34*, 327–335.

Reiss, D., Plomin, R., Hetherington, E. M., Howe, G., Rovine, M., Tryron, A., & Stanley-Hagen, M. (1994). The separate worlds of teenage siblings: An introduction to the study of the non-shared environment and adolescent development. In E. M. Hetherington, D. Reiss, & R. Plomin (Eds.), *Nonshared environment*. Hillsdale, NJ: Lawrence Erlbaum Associates.

Schaefer, E., & Edgerton, M. (1981). *The sibling inventory of behavior*. Chapel Hill: University of North Carolina.

Steinberg, L. (1988). Pubertal maturation and family relations: Evidence for the distancing hypothesis. In G. R. Adams, R. Montemayor, & T. P. Gullotta (Eds.), *Advances in adolescent development*. Beverly Hills, CA: Sage.

U. S. Bureau of the Census (1989). Studies in marriage and the family: Married couples and families with children. In *Current Population Reports* (Series P-23, No. 162). Washington, DC: U. S. Government Printing Office.

Visher, E. B., & Visher, J. S. (1988). *Old loyalties, new ties: Therapeutic strategies with stepfamilies*. New York: Brunner/Mazel.

Vuchinich, S., Hetherington, E. M., Vuchinich, R. A., & Clingempeel, W. G. (1991). Parent–child interaction and gender differences in early adolescents' adaptation to stepfamilies. *Developmental Psychology, 27*(4), 618–626.

Zaslow, M. J. (1988). Sex differences in children's response to parental divorce: 1. Research methodology and postdivorce family forms. *American Journal of Orthopsychiatry, 58*, 355–378.

Zaslow, M. J. (1989). Sex differences in children's response to parental divorce: 2. Samples, variables, ages and sources. *American Journal of Orthopsychiatry, 59*, 118–141.

Zill, N. (1988). Behavior, achievement, and health problems among children in stepfamilies: Findings from a national survey of child health. In E. M. Hetherington & J. D. Arasteh (Eds.), *Impact of divorce, single parenting, and stepparenting on children* (pp. 325–368). Hillsdale, NJ: Lawrence Erlbaum Associates.

Zill, N., Morrison, D. R., & Coiro, M. J. (1993). Long-term effects of parental divorce on parent–child relationships, adjustment, and achievement in young adulthood. *Journal of Family Psychology, 7*(6), 1–13.

6

The Implications of Research Findings on Children in Stepfamilies

Paul R. Amato
University of Nebraska—Lincoln

Hetherington's studies of divorce and remarriage have become classics in the field of child development. Based on longitudinal data derived from multiple methods and sources, the research of Hetherington and her colleagues during the last two decades provided much of what we know about the effects of divorce and remarriage on children. Her chapter, co-authored with Kathleen Jodl, is a lucid summary of the results of three separate studies. My comments focus on their findings about differences between stepchildren and children in other family forms and, in particular, the implications that we draw from these data.

Hetherington and Jodl describe many differences between children in step-families and continuously intact two-parent families. They note that, as a group, children in stepfamilies are less well-adjusted and exhibit more behavior problems. And depending on the source and subgroup of children, children in step-families are rated as less competent, have more internalizing problems, and score lower on measures of cognitive ability and academic achievement. In his chapter, Popenoe cites several other studies that yielded similar findings to make the point that stepfamilies are a problematic setting for children's development. And in White's chapter, we find that when stepchildren become adults, their families form comparatively weak support networks.

These results paint a consistently negative picture of stepfamily life for children. But even though the differences between children in stepfamilies and other family types are statistically significant and well-replicated, we should not over-interpret these findings. Indeed, we need to be careful about the conclusions that we draw from these data.

In 1991, Bruce Keith and I published a meta-analysis based on 92 studies of children of divorce. As part of this larger project, we combined the results of 21

TABLE 6.1.
Mean Effect Sizes Comparing Children in Three Family Types
on Measures of Well-Being and Development

	Stepfamily Versus Intact Two-Parent	Stepfamily Versus Single-Parent
Academic achievement	−.07#	−.01
Conduct/behavior problems	−.32***	−.09#
Psychological adjustment	−.37***.	−.16**
Self-esteem	−.16***	−.06
Social relations	−.14**	−.04
All outcomes	−.17***	−.03

Note. Data are derived from 21 independent studies. The number of studies on which particular mean effect sizes are based range from 9 (psychological adjustment) to 12 (conduct).
$#p < .10.$ $*p < .05.$ $**p < .01.$ $***p < .001.$

studies that reported data on children's well-being and development in step-families, divorced single-parent families, and continuously intact two-parent families (Amato & Keith, 1991). We expressed each reported difference between family groups in terms of an effect size, that is, the mean difference between groups divided by the standard deviation of the outcome. We then aggregated these effect sizes both within and across studies. The results of our procedures, as they pertain to stepfamilies, are summarized in Table 6.1.

The sign of the coefficient shows how the first group listed in each column compares with the second, with negative signs indicating a poorer outcome. For example, the mean effect size of −.07 in column 1, row 1 indicates that children in stepfamilies scored .07 of a standard deviation below children in continuously intact two-parent families on measures of academic achievement and cognitive ability (when averaged across all measures reported in all studies). Note that children in stepfamilies scored below children in continuously intact two-parent families across all outcomes, with an average difference of .17 of a standard deviation. Also, note in column 2 that children in stepfamilies scored below children in single-parent families across all outcomes, although this difference was only significant for psychological adjustment and marginally significant for conduct. (Although not shown in the table, children in single-parent families scored consistently below those in two-parent families on all outcomes.)

What does this tell us? Simply that divorce and remarriage (or some factors associated with divorce and remarriage) increase the risk of poor academic, behavioral, and psychological outcomes for children enough to shift group averages significantly downward. These results cannot be denied or ignored, no matter how unpalatable they may be to some people.

But let us explore the issue further. A difference of .17 of a standard deviation

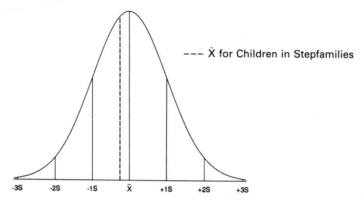

FIG. 6.1. Distribution of scores on a typical measure of well-being for children in intact two-parent families.

between two groups on some outcome is not a large difference. Figure 6.1 presents a normal distribution. Assume that this is a distribution of scores on some measure of well-being for a large sample of children in continuously intact two-parent families. Solid vertical lines mark the mean and points representing 1, 2, and 3 standard deviations above and below the mean. The broken vertical line marks .17 of a standard deviation below the mean—the point where the average child in a stepfamily scores. Note that the two averages are not far apart.

Figure 6.2 superimposes the distribution for stepchildren (which is also as-

Region 1: Children in Two-Parent Families Who Score Below the Mean of Children in Stepfamilies
Region 2: Children in Stepfamilies Who Score Above the Mean of Children in Two-Parent Families

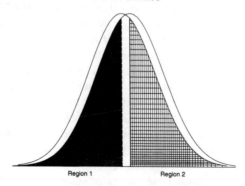

FIG. 6.2. Distribution of scores on a typical measure of well-being for children in intact two-parent families (right) and stepfamilies (left).

sumed to be normal) onto the first distribution. Notice the substantial overlap in the two sets of scores. In particular, I draw your attention to two regions of these overlapping distributions. The first represents children in intact two-parent families who score below the average of children in stepfamilies. In this figure, 43% of children in two-parent families are worse off than the average child in a stepfamily. The second region refers to children in stepfamilies who score above the average child in a continuously intact two-parent family. Because of the symmetry of the normal curve, this figure is also 43%.

If we take the most extreme difference—the effect size of .37 from studies of psychological adjustment, then 36% of children in stepfamilies score higher than the average child in an intact two-parent family. Although the difference is larger than the one just described, substantial overlap still remains.

The overlap in outcomes reflects, to a large extent, the variability in children's circumstances within family types. Some children grow up in dysfunctional, intact families in which they encounter abuse, neglect, poverty, parental mental illness, and parental substance abuse. Other children grow up well-functioning stepfamilies and have caring stepparents who provide affection, effective control, and economic support. There is by no means a one-to-one correspondence between family structure and the quality of children's home environments.

The point is that we get a very different picture depending on whether we emphasize central tendency (which leads us to conclude that children in stepfamilies are worse off) or dispersion (which leads us to conclude that substantial overlap exists in the outcomes for children in different family structures). This is not merely a statistical issue. In discussions and debates about family structure that I have seen, traditionalists consistently focus on the differences in central tendency, whereas nontraditionalists consistently focus on the overlap in distributions. Both are correct interpretations of the data, but focusing on one or the other, rather than both, leads to a distorted, one-sided interpretation of what the data indicate.

To further explore the implications of data on group averages, I would like to pose three questions. First, should we use information on children's outcomes in making individual decisions about divorce and remarriage? In answering this question, I begin by agreeing with Popenoe that, all things being equal, children are better off living with both biological parents than with a single parent or a stepparent. Most Americans would also agree with this position. The majority of people, when they first marry, want their marriages to succeed and for their children to be raised by both parents. Given a choice between living in a happy, close, mutually supportive nuclear family and living as a single parent or as a stepparent, most people would certainly opt for the former.

The problem is that for some people, living in a happy, close, mutually supportive, two-parent family is not an option. Consider a mother who contemplates ending a highly conflicted marriage to a belligerent and abusive husband. For her, the choice is between two less-than-ideal outcomes: maintaining the status quo, or living as a single parent. Given the circumstances of some dysfunctional two-parent families, children may be better off living with a single parent, or later, in a stepfamily—a conclusion with which most experts have agreed (Amato, 1993; Emery, 1988; Furstenberg & Cherlin, 1991; Hetherington, 1989). Our meta-analysis also supported this conclusion (Amato & Keith, 1991). Of course, not all instances of divorce are preceded by intense overt conflict or abuse. But divorce is a reasonable choice for at least some parents—not only to ensure their own happiness, but also that of their children.

Many single parents wish to remarry following divorce. Should single parents sacrifice their own chance of happiness because living in a stepfamily might further increase the risk that their children will experience problems? Given the variability noted above, this conclusion would not be warranted—not when so many children in stepfamilies are "better off" than the average child in an intact family. The odds are not that bad. The point I wish to make here is that predictions about children's outcomes based on information on family structure contain a substantial degree of error; consequently, no matter how statistically significant and widely replicated are differences in central tendency, they are not a useful basis for making individual decisions.

Now I turn to a second question: Based on information on children's outcomes, is it worthwhile to consider policies that decrease the number of single-parent and stepparent families? If the differences in central tendency noted above are real—and I believe they are—then increasing the proportion of children living in intact two-parent families could favorably affect the overall level of children's well-being at the societal level. This is because, given the large number of children involved, even small differences in group averages could translate into improvements in the lives of many children. Rather than make it difficult for single parents to enter stepfamilies, it would be more practical and humane to consider policies that decrease the rate of nonmarital birth, and improve the quality of marriages so that they result less often in divorce. It may be possible, for example, to lower the divorce rate by making family life education and counseling more widely available, or by increasing tax credits to poor working families with children. Given that economic hardship is a major cause of divorce (U. S. Bureau of the Census, 1992), one thing that government can do to strengthen nuclear families is to ensure that every adult has access to a well-paying job.

On the other hand, policies that attempt to increase the proportion of two-parent families by making divorce more difficult to obtain (e.g., by restricting access to no-fault divorce) could do more harm than good. It is true that the divorce rate was lower in the past, when the legal system was less favorably disposed toward divorce, but the rate of marital separation and desertion was higher—especially among the poor and some minority groups (Glendon, 1989; Sweet & Bumpass, 1987). From a child's perspective, there is probably little difference between informal separation and legal divorce. Furthermore, making divorce less readily available would increase the proportion of children trapped in high conflict marriage—an outcome that would decrease children's well-being. Given that parents cannot be forced to live together or to be happily married, placing restrictions on divorce is unlikely to improve the overall well-being of children.

Now for my third question: Given the small effect sizes and the diversity in outcomes noted above, should social scientists continue to investigate family structure differences in children's outcomes? My answer is that comparative studies continue to provide a useful function in allowing us to hone our theoretical understanding of the relations between children's social environments and their development. For example, several studies showed that some children who live with a single parent exhibit fewer problems if an additional adult resides in the household, especially if the person is a grandparent (Dornbusch et al., 1985; Kellam, Ensminger, & Turner, 1977; Stolba & Amato, 1993). Residential grandparents can promote children's development by providing emotional support, assisting the parent with supervision and discipline, and taking over childrearing responsibilities when the parent is overburdened.

Another example involves comparing children in single-parent families formed through divorce with those formed through parental death. The fact that children of divorce reveal more problems than children who lose a parent through death tells us something about the role of interparental conflict in decreasing children's well-being (Amato & Keith, 1991).

A third example would be comparing children in stepmother and stepfather families. Hetherington's research indicates that children in stepfamilies feel closer to noncustodial mothers than to noncustodial fathers—a finding that tells us something about the special resiliency of the maternal role, as well as the special difficulty of the stepmother role.

Thus, the search for group differences provides a useful scientific function: It allows us to test hypotheses, to formulate and revise theories, and to come to a better understanding of how children's social environments affect their development. Although the effect sizes generated by these studies tend to be small, this is not surprising, given the large number of social and environmental factors that impact children's development. Each piece of the puzzle is important, no matter how small.

Unfortunately, people trying to make their stepfamilies work who hear about research that reports poorer outcomes for children in stepfamilies, must surely be dishearted and annoyed. Nevertheless, it may be useful for stepparents, and for single parents contemplating remarriage, to be informed about the problems that frequently occur within stepfamilies. If nothing else, it may lead people to be aware of problems before they become too large, to try a little harder to reach compromises, and to be less reluctant to seek out counseling if problems appear to be intractable.

Let me conclude by returning to the Hetherington and Jodl chapter. The authors note that children's adaptation to remarriage is influenced by the balance of risk and protective factors in the individual, the family, and the larger social milieu. It is probably fair to say that, on average, single-parent households and stepfamilies offer greater risks and fewer protective factors to children than do continuously intact two-parent families. But there is considerable variation in the balance of risk and protective factors within these family structures. Even if one accepts the sociobiological premise that parents are genetically predisposed to invest resources in their own biological children, one must also acknowledge that biological systems do not involve strict determinism. Many biological parents invest little in their children, and many stepparents invest a great deal in their stepchildren. Indeed, some neglectful and abusive parents act in a manner that decreases the chances of their genes surviving into the next generation. For many stepparents and stepchildren, biology is not destiny.

As Hetherington and Jodl point out, stepfamilies contain winners as well as losers. Their research takes us a long way in understanding the diversity of outcomes within stepfamilies. As they note, outcomes vary with the child's age at the time of parental remarriage, the child's sex, the length of time in a stepfamily, and other factors. We need more studies that focus on the circumstances under which children are more or less successful in stepfamilies. But as long as stepfamilies represent a chance for a better life for many parents and children, it makes little sense to condemn them or to discourage their formation.

REFERENCES

Amato, P. R. (1993). Children's adjustment to divorce: Theories, hypotheses, and empirical support. *Journal of Marriage and the Family, 55,* 23–38.

Amato, P. R., & Keith, B. (1991). Parental divorce and the well-being of children: A meta-analysis. *Psychological Bulletin, 110,* 26–46.

Dornbusch, S., Carlsmith, J. M., Bushwall, S. J., Ritter, P. L., Leiderman, H., Hastorf, A. H., & Gross, R. T. (1985). Single parents, extended households, and the control of adolescents. *Child Development, 56,* 326–341.

Emery, R. E. (1988). *Marriage, divorce, and children's adjustment.* Newbury Park, CA: Sage.

Furstenberg, F., & Cherlin, A. (1991). *Divided families: What happens to children when parents part.* Cambridge, MA: Harvard University Press.

Glendon, M. A. (1989). *The transformation of family law.* Chicago: University of Chicago Press.

Hetherington, E. M. (1989). Coping with family transitions: Winners, losers, and survivors. *Child Development, 60,* 1–14.

Kellam, S. G., Ensminger, M. E., & Turner, R. J. (1977). Family structure and the mental health of children. *Archives of General Psychiatry, 34,* 1012–1022.

Stolba, A., & Amato, P. R. (1993). Extended single-parent households and children's behavior. *Sociological Quarterly, 34,* 543–549.

Sweet, J. A., & Bumpass, L. L. (1987). *American families and households.* New York: Russell Sage Foundation.

U. S. Bureau of the Census. (1992). *Current population reports, series P23–179, studies in household and family formation.* Washington, DC: U. S. Government Printing Office.

7

"Settings" and "Development" From a Demographic Point of View

Elizabeth Thomson
University of Wisconsin—Madison

Hetherington and Jodl present a comprehensive, densely packed summary of an extremely important body of stepfamily research. Taking a demographer's perspective, I focus this comment on the two key concepts in the title—settings and development. I conclude that the research reviewed by Hetherington and Jodl provides a rich set of hypotheses that may or may not be supported for stepfamilies in more diverse settings. I also raise questions about the extent to which we can distinguish effects of developmental stages (for children or families) from the cumulative effects of parents' marital and residential histories.

In the Hetherington and Jodl chapter, the term *settings* refers primarily to relationships among family members. Their chapter briefly comments on schools, communities, and kin networks as part of the setting. For a sociologist, especially a family demographer, family settings also include the social and economic conditions of life. The research reported by Hetherington and Jodl purposefully limits variation in the socioeconomic settings in order to focus on relational settings. Whether similar results and conclusions would be drawn from a more diverse population of stepfamilies is an open question.

Socioeconomic differences between original families and stepfamilies pale by comparison to those between single- and two-parent families. But they do exist, and may underlie, or at least exacerbate, the complexities of stepfamily life. Table 7.1 summarizes information from the National Survey of Families and Households (NSFH; Sweet, Bumpass, & Call, 1989) for married couples with children under 19 living in the household. Stepfamilies include those in which either the mother, father, or both has a resident stepchild under 19, while original

TABLE 7.1.
Socioeconomic Settings—Stepfamilies Versus Original Two-Parent Families

	Stepfamilies		Original Two Parents	
	M	SD	M	SD
Annual family income ($1,000s)	43.0	46.9	44.8	48.5
Own home	64.7%		74.9%	
Home equity ($1,000s) (if own home)	58.8	44.1	78.7	65.0
Any savings, investments	71.1%		79.1%	
Mother employed	66.5%		62.1%	
Hours (if employed)	37.2	10.5	33.4	12.4
Father employed	91.2%		91.9%	
Hours (if employed)	45.6	10.7	45.5	10.3
Mother's education (years)	12.7	3.8	13.1	3.5
Father's education (years)	12.8	2.8	13.5	3.2
European–American (both parents)	79.9%		87.2%	
Religion				
None (both parents)	3.7%		2.9%	
Same	67.0		78.2	
Different	29.4		18.9	
Children < 19 at home	2.2	1.2	2.0	1.0
Age youngest child	7.8	5.4	7.1	5.7
Age oldest child < 19	12.4	4.2	10.0	5.8
Any Children > 19	27.4%		21.7%	

Note. From 1987–1988 National Survey of Families and Households. Married couples with child under 19 living in the household: 2,913 original two-parent families, 718 stepfamilies. Statistics estimated with weighted data.

two-parent families report no stepchildren under 19, either in or out of the household.[1]

Although differences between families are relatively small, they are impressively consistent, and in most respects, favor original two-parent families. Current annual family incomes are virtually identical, but parental education is lower in stepfamilies than in original two-parent families. Noticeable differences also exist in home ownership, home equity, and savings or investments, with stepfamilies less economically secure. Other structural strains in stepfamily life are evident in the higher employment rates and longer work hours of remarried versus originally married mothers, the higher likelihood of minority status for at least one of the parents or differences in religious identification, and the larger numbers and older ages of children, compared to original two-parent families.

These differences stem in part from the selection processes into and out of

---

[1] NSFH data are ambiguous with respect to the step status of children 19 and older living outside the household; some of the original two-parent families in this analysis may have older stepchildren.

single parenthood. Stepfamilies are formed after nonmarital births or divorces, so the population of stepparents is already selected for younger age at marriage or first birth, lower education, and so on. Even if selection out of single parenthood into stepfamilies works in opposing directions (e.g., selection of the better educated single parents), the combined selection processes are likely to leave stepfamilies at a socioeconomic and structural disadvantage when compared with original two-parent families.

From a demographer's point of view, the definition of stepfamily used in Table 7.1 excludes a considerable proportion of stepfamily experience. First, nonresident stepfamilies (those defined by a nonresident parent's marriage) are excluded. Nonresident parents' financial contributions to children are included in the resident stepfamily's income. But a full description of stepfamily settings would include information on the nonresident parent's whereabouts, socioeconomic and family status. Among NSFH resident stepfamilies, almost one quarter are also nonresident stepfamilies; that is, at least one of the resident parents reported a minor child living with the child's other parent. If these children were taken into account, differences in sibship size would be even larger than that shown in Table 7.1. Financial obligations to nonresident children might also put stepfamilies at an even greater economic disadvantage than is suggested by their income and assets.

The second type of stepfamily experience missing from Table 7.1 is cohabiting couples. In the NSFH, cohabiting stepfamilies represent only 3% of all families with children under age 19 living at home. But they constitute almost one quarter of all families in which at least one of the children is not the child of both partners. Parent–partner families live in much more disadvantaged socioeconomic settings than do marital stepfamilies, again due in large part to the selection of parents into cohabitation. Recent research indicates that such families also differ in relational settings and child outcomes (Thomson, Hanson, & McLanahan, in press; Thomson, McLanahan, & Curtin, 1992).

Most studies with diverse and large samples statistically control for some differences in socioeconomic settings when estimating differences between stepfamilies and original two-parent families in family relationships or child outcomes. They rarely, however, include measures of economic security, and data are limited on the extent of financial obligations or expenditures across, as well as within, stepfamily households. Only recently have data become available to illuminate the increasing proportion of children in parent–partner settings. The studies summarized by Hetherington and Jodl were designed to eliminate much of the economic and structural variation between families in order to focus on relationship variation. This means, however, that the conclusions are generalizable to a shrinking proportion of stepfamilies.

The second key concept in the Hetherington and Jodl chapter—development—is closely linked to two fundamental demographic concepts, age and duration. Hetherington and Jodl report that many of the differences between original

original families and stepfamilies are reduced over time as family relationships develop, and that differences may be more pronounced when children enter stepfamilies at early adolescence, a vulnerable developmental stage. Since parent–child relationships and children's behavior also change with the child's current age, we are presented with a classic age–period–cohort problem: How do we disentangle effects of the child's age at entry into a stepfamily (cohort), his or her current age (period), and the duration of stepfamily experience (family age)?

This problem is exacerbated by the limits imposed by the duration of childhood—18 years—which means that the timing of family events in children's lives is strongly linked to differences in their parents' marital histories. For example, among recent cohorts, children whose parents separated before their fifth birthday had a 59% chance of acquiring a stepfather before age 16. The chances were reduced to 35% for separations occurring at ages 5–9, and to 14% when parents separated during the child's adolescence (Bumpass & Sweet, 1989). The earlier a stepfamily forms, the longer the remarriage is exposed to the risk of divorce, and the greater likelihood the family will not be included in a sample of stepfamilies when the child is an adolescent. Further, children who live with single mothers from birth are an increasing proportion of children who will ever live with a single mother (Bumpass & Raley, 1993). This increases the likelihood of entering a stepfamily at younger ages. Thus, a child's age at entry into a stepfamily will be associated with differences in birth status, number of family changes, and types of changes, each of which may be a source of spurious interactions between the child's age and stepfamily entry.

What makes this problem even worse for understanding stepfamily effects is that unobserved differences between parents and families may lead to nonmarital versus marital births, earlier versus later divorce, cohabitation versus remarriage, and earlier versus later stepfamily formation. With longitudinal data, we might be able to sort out the extent to which children's outcomes are consequences of family disruption and change, or can be attributed to socioeconomic or relational settings preceding the stepfamily experience. Of the studies reviewed by Hetherington and Jodl, only the Virginia study has information on children and parents in original families who subsequently divorced and remarried. From their chapter and other reports (e.g., Hetherington, 1993), fewer than 70 such families were studied, with perhaps 30 families divorcing by the time the children were last observed at age 15. If this sample were further divided according to the ages of children at remarriage, the number of cases would be too few for good estimates of remarriage effects. The recent study of siblings described by Hetherington and Jodl provides a different way to control for unobserved family differences, but is limited to the study of adolescents. No data, however, can overcome the the conceptual issue of the 18-year constraint on combinations of divorce and remarriage at different ages, and with different durations. We must be extremely careful when interpreting analytic differences as consequences of either time and adjustment, or of particular developmental stages in children's lives.

The development of stepfamily relationships over time, or the effects of stepfamily formation at different developmental stages in the child's life, are further complicated by cohabitation. Bumpass and Raley (1993) have recently examined children's experience in single-mother households under two definitions of two-parent families: married couples only versus married and cohabiting couples. While cohabitation does not change the likelihood of children ever living in a single-mother family, it markedly changes estimates of duration. For example, if we classify children born to cohabiting couples as living in original two-parent families, and if we specify a cohabiting relationship as the point at which a stepfamily is first formed, the median length of time for a child's first spell in a single-mother family is cut in half—from about 7 to 3.5 years for children born in the early 1980s. Most of this difference is due to divorced mothers cohabiting before remarrying or returning to singlehood (R. K. Raley, personal communication, October 12, 1993).

Table 7.2 shows that more than half of the marital stepfamilies in the NSFH had experienced cohabitation, and half of those had cohabited for more than 1 year before the remarriage. The average cohabitation period was about 10 months. Table 7.2 also shows how cohabitation alters the distribution of stepfamilies by duration. The first column is based on married couples in stepfamilies, with time in the stepfamily beginning at marriage. The second column includes the same families, but uses the year of cohabitation as the marker for stepfamily formation. By comparing columns 1 and 2, we see that the proportion of families observed in the critical 2-year period is reduced by almost one third, from 27% to 18%. If this is to be the cutting point for family recovery, cohabitation has a relatively large effect on the distribution of families. A parallel increase occurs in the proportion of stepfamilies formed when the oldest child was younger than age 5.

The third column in Table 7.2 combines the married stepfamilies and parent– partner families, with both families' formation begun at cohabitation. Column 3 shows that including current cohabiters puts more families into the crisis period. This is consistent with the high rates of cohabitation before remarriage (longer term relationships are likely to exit cohabition by remarriage), and with the higher dissolution rates of cohabiting versus marital relationships. Bumpass and his colleagues (Bumpass, Sweet, & Raley, 1994) found that the median duration of a first stepfamily was reduced from almost 6 to less than 4 years, when cohabiting unions were included in the definition.

The proportion of oldest children who entered the family before age 5 does not differ between columns 2 and 3, because cohabiters are younger and bring younger children to the union than do persons who remarry, with or without having cohabited. Using life table estimates, the chance of entering a stepfamily

TABLE 7.2.
Time in Unions, Stepfamilies and Parent–Partner Families

Cohabitation	Married Couples in Stepfamilies
Did not cohabit	46.4%
1–11 months	27.6
12–23 months	11.7
24–35 months	5.4
≥36 months	8.8

	Married Stepfamilies		All Stepfamilies
	Marriage	Union	Union
Year in Union			
<2	26.8%	18.0%	25.0%
2–4	30.8	30.1	30.2
5–9	29.3	34.4	30.6
>10	13.1	17.5	14.2
Age Oldest Child at Union*			
<5	24.5%	31.1%	30.1%
5–8	41.8	41.7	40.3
9–13	25.1	19.9	21.4
≥14	8.7	7.2	8.2

Note. 1987–1988 National Survey of Families and Households, couples with at least one stepchild or partner's child under 19 living in the household (718 married couples, 260 cohabiting couples). Estimates based on weighted data.

[a]Respondents reporting child or stepchild age 19 or older were excluded from these estimates.

before age 5 is more than doubled when cohabiting unions are defined as stepfamilies (Bumpass et al., 1994).

These differences could alter our conclusions about changes in stepfamily relationships over time. In previous analyses of the NSFH data, I found that stepfathers and stepmothers, as well as remarried mothers living with stepfathers, reported lower frequencies of several activities with children than did parents in original two-parent families, net of socioeconomic and sibship characteristics. When we divided these stepfamilies into those who had been married less than 2 years versus 2 years or more, we found virtually no differences (Thomson et al., 1992). Similar findings were reported for child outcomes (Thomson et al., in press). It could be, however, that some of our crisis period families should have been in the stabilized group because the couple had lived together for some time before marriage. Incorrect assignment of families to the crisis period would decrease differences between the two groups of families.

I reanalyzed these data, dividing married stepfamilies according to time since cohabitation. Results were consistent with earlier analyses. Remarried mothers and stepfathers reported less frequent activities with children than parents in original families, and there were no statistically significant differences between families formed within the past 2 years and longer term families.

Of course, these results are based on cross-sectional data. Amato and Keith (1991) reported that duration effects of divorce were more likely to be found in longitudinal than in cross-sectional studies. It is possible that longitudinal data would show a different pattern of adjustment during periods of cohabitation and subsequent remarriage than what we observe during the first 2 years after marriage. It is also possible that time in cohabiting unions is not as influential as time in marital stepfamilies. Cohabitation may signal a lower commitment than remarriage, leading to lower investments in family relationships, particularly that between children and cohabiting partners. We do not yet know enough to determine when and how to start the relational clock.

The past and ongoing research of Hetherington and her colleagues provides a very rich description of stepfamily relationships. It demonstrates the centrality of marital and stepparental relationships, and the active participation of children in constructing their stepfamily lives. I do not think this could have been accomplished without limiting other sources of variability, such as socioeconomic diversity and cohabitation. In fact, when the Virginia study was begun in the early 1970s, I doubt even demographers anticipated the extent to which parents would choose to cohabit before, or instead of, remarrying. But we can no longer ignore socioeonomic diversity and the complexity of parental histories associated with stepfamily formation. Hypotheses generated from research by Hetherington and her colleagues must be rigorously evaluated with the full spectrum of stepfamily experiences.

REFERENCES

Amato, P. R., & Keith, B. (1991). Parental divorce and the well-being of children: A meta-analysis. *Psychological Bulletin, 110*, 26–46.

Bumpass, L., & Raley, R. K. (1993). *Trends in the duration of single-parent families* (NSFH Working Paper No. 58). Madison: University of Wisconsin, Center for Demography and Ecology.

Bumpass, L., & Sweet, J. A. (1989). *Children's experience in single-parent families: Implications of cohabitation and marital transitions* (NSFH Working Paper No. 3). Madison: University of Wisconsin, Center for Demography and Ecology.

Bumpass, L., Sweet, J. A. & Raley, R. K. (1994, January). *The changing character of stepfamilies: Implications of cohabitation and nonmarital childbearing.* Paper presented at the Rand Corporation conference, Reshaping the Family: Social and Economic Changes and Social Policy, Los Angeles.

Hetherington, E. M. (1993). An overview of the Virginia Longitudinal Study of Divorce and Remarriage with a focus on early adolescence. *Journal of Family Psychology, 7*, 39–56.

Sweet, J., Bumpass, L., & Call, V. (1989). *The design and content of the National Survey of*

Families and Households (NSFA working paper no. 1). Madison: University of Wisconsin, Center for Demography and Ecology.

Thomson, E., McLanahan, S. S., & Curtin, R. B. (1992). Family structure, gender, and parental socialization. *Journal of Marriage and the Family, 54*, 368–378.

Thomson, E., Hanson, T., & McLanahan, S. S. (1993). Family structure, parental socialization, and child well-being. *Social Forces*

8

Understanding Why Ch in Stepfamilies Have M Learning and Behavior Problems Than Children in Nuclear Families

Nicholas Zill
Westat, Inc., Rockville, MD

By way of commenting on Hetherington's excellent chapter, I apply a family resources perspective to the question of how stepfamilies function as childrearing organizations. This perspective begins with the proposition that the more resources a family can apply to the task of raising a child, the better will be the outcomes for the child, all other things being equal. Family resources include such things as the number of adults who are available to interact with and supervise the child, the time each devotes to childrearing activities, the fewer siblings with whom the child has to compete for parental time and attention, the ability and education level of the parents, family income, and the number of books and other educational resources in the home.

There is extensive evidence that the proposition just stated is true on a general level, although we have a lot to learn about the relationship between specific kinds of resources and different aspects of children's development and well-being, such as physical health and growth, economic well-being, academic achievement, emotional well-being, and social development. There are also at least three different explanations of how family resources operate to enhance children's development and well-being. One account might be called the *liberal–additive viewpoint*. This position sees family resources as substitutable for one another, the important thing being the total amount of resources available to the child. For example, if a single mother has a reasonable education and adequate income, she can do a perfectly good job of raising a child. The problem is that single parenthood is often associated with low parent educational attainment and poverty-level income.

A contrasting outlook might be called the *conservative–interactive viewpoint*. This position posits that family resources are not interchangeable and that a certain combination of resources is optimal for healthy child development. Proponents of this viewpoint usually argue, as Popenoe does in his chapter, that the nuclear family, with both biological parents present in the household, is the best environment for children's well-being.

Still another viewpoint is the *behavior genetic position*. In extreme form, this view considers the observed relationship between parental resources and child outcomes as partly artifactual. Parents with favorable genes earn more education and money and have children who do well in school. But the mechanism by which they transmit their social advantage is largely genetic, not environmental. A minimal level of resources is needed to ensure the child's survival and adequate nutrition and supervision. Beyond that, the story is in the genes.

Now let us apply the family resources perspective to the stepfamily situation. At first glance, it would appear that moving from a single-parent, mother-only family to a two-parent, mother–stepfather family is a major resource gain for the child. Remarriage usually bolsters family income through the addition of another wage earner to the household. Even though average incomes of mother–stepfather families are somewhat lower than the incomes of two birth-parent families, they are dramatically higher than those in mother-only families. Remarriage also makes another parent available to supervise, instruct, and provide emotional support for the child. Although indifferent or exploitive stepparents certainly exist, the evidence is that most stepparents have good intentions and try to do well by their stepchildren. The question is why these additional resources do not have more of a beneficial impact on children's development.

As Hetherington states in her chapter, research with large survey databases failed to show a beneficial effect of remarriage on children's achievement or behavior. Children's emotional, behavioral, and academic problems are typically found to be as frequent in stepfamilies as in single-parent families, with problem rates for both types of families being significantly greater than those found in intact two-parent families (Dawson, 1991; Zill, 1988). This is true despite the fact that the financial advantages stepchildren enjoy over those in mother-only families are clearly evident in the survey data (Zill, 1988). When rates of behavioral and learning problems are adjusted for differences in average parent education and income levels, children in stepfamilies are sometimes found to have higher rates than those in single-parent families.

National survey data illustrate the kinds of findings I have just summarized. Figure 8.1 shows how the percentage of children experiencing problems in school varies across students from three different types of families: mother–father families, mother-only families, and mother–stepfather families. The specific problems examined are: ever having to repeat a grade in school; ever having been suspended or expelled from school; being in the bottom half of the class in the current school year; and the child's parents being contacted by the child's teacher during the current school year, because of the child's problematic behavior in school. The determination as to whether or not a given child had each of

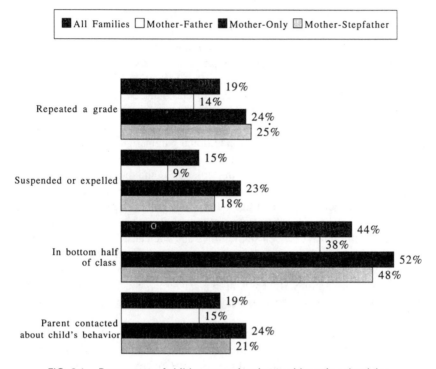

FIG. 8.1. Percentage of children experiencing problems in school, by family type.

these problems is based on the reports of a parent respondent, usually the child's mother.

The children in the sample were 10,117 students in Grades 6–12 from communities across the United States. The data are from the National Household Education Survey conducted by Westat, Inc. for the National Center for Education Statistics (NCES). There were 5,510 children in mother–father families in the random sample, 2,399 in mother-only families, and 1,144 in mother-stepfather families. For simplicity, estimates for children from the less common family types, such as father-only or father–stepmother families, are not shown separately, but were included in the "all families" totals.

Looking first at the frequencies of learning and school behavior problems in the general student population, we see that 19% of all 6th–12th graders had to repeat at least one grade, 15% had been suspended or expelled at some point, 44% were described as being in the middle to the bottom of their class, and 19% had had a conduct problem at school during the current school year that led to the teacher or principal contacting the child's parents.

Comparing the frequency of these problems across the three family types, we see that children in mother-only and in mother–stepfather families were significantly more likely to exhibit each type of problem than were children from mother–father families. Students from mother–stepfather families were 80% more likely to have repeated a grade, and twice as likely to have been suspended or expelled, than were those from mother–father families. They were one quarter more likely to be in the bottom half of their class, and 50% more likely to have had their parents contacted about school behavior problems in the last year. Problem frequency is rather similar in the stepfamilies and the single-parent families, despite the presence of an additional parent figure in the stepfamilies and other differences in life circumstances that were previously discussed.

The differences between children in stepfamilies and those in nuclear families remained significant after controlling for related differences in child and family characteristics, such as age of child, parent education level, and racial and ethnic composition of the two groups. Note that though the beta coefficients and effect sizes for the difference between stepfamilies and nuclear families were relatively modest (as Amato points out in his comments), these coefficients meant sizable differences in the risk that children in stepfamilies faced when compared with those in nuclear families. In epidemiological terms, the doubling of a risk is hardly trivial. Many well-known medical risk factors are far weaker in their impact.

As I mentioned, these findings are from a recent national survey, but very similar results have been obtained in several previous national studies, including the National Survey of Children (Allison & Furstenberg, 1989; Peterson & Zill, 1986), and the National Health Interview Surveys on Child Health conducted in 1981 (Zill, 1988) and 1988 (Dawson, 1991; Zill & Schoenborn, 1991). Consistent evidence has been found in longitudinal, as well as cross-sectional studies (Zill, Morrison, & Coiro, 1993).

Although coming from a stepfamily significantly increases the relative risk that a child will experience problems in school, it is important to note that these findings can be seen in a positive light. One can correctly say, for example, that three quarters of children from stepfamilies have not had to repeat a grade, more than 80% have never been suspended or expelled from school, and a majority are in the upper half of their classes. This is true despite the fact that these children have experienced marital conflict and parental divorce, or birth outside marriage and the entrance of a new, and perhaps, unwelcome adult into the family constellation.

We are still faced with the dilemma of explaining why the additional family resources do not exert more of a protective or ameliorative effect on the young people in stepfamilies. Certainly, the magnitude of additional resources single-parent families obtain through remarriage is far greater than, for example, the $1,000 child allowance that the Rockefeller Commission proposed. Part of the answer may lie in the history of marital conflict and other family stress that some stepchildren have experienced before the stepfamily was formed. Such a history of conflict and stress may leave long-term emotional scars that additional resources cannot overcome.

Another possible explanation is individual differences—either in the children, or in the parents, or both. There may be some children who, for constitutional or other reasons, are especially vulnerable to the repeated family upheavals that divorce, remarriage, and possible redivorce represent. Likewise, there may be some adults who are especially prone to early divorce and remarriage whose overall behavior pattern as marital partners and parents increases the risk of emotional difficulties in their children.

Still another possible explanation is that there is something about the way in which some stepfamilies function as childrearing organizations that puts the children in those families at greater risk. Hetherington discussed nonsupportive or dysfunctional family patterns at some length. Further evidence from the same national survey we examined a moment ago indicate that there are differences in the support that many parents in stepfamilies give to their children's schoolwork. Do these differences help to account for the differences in student outcomes we have just seen?

Many educators believe that children are more likely to do well in school if their parents are involved in school activities than if the parents are uninvolved. It is not that having a parent attend PTA meetings leads to higher test scores or better conduct marks for the child. Rather, parent participation in school activities is likely to mean closer parental monitoring of what is happening in the school and in the child's classroom, in particular. Parent participation can lead to better coordination of teacher and parent efforts, to greater personal attention for the child from the teacher, and to problems detected and corrective action taken before difficulties become too serious. The fact that the parent bothers to get involved communicates to the child that he or she considers school important. In addition, parental participation in organized school activities is usually an indication that the parent provides other forms of encouragement and support for the learning process outside of school.

In the National Household Education Survey, the parents of students in Grades 6–12 were asked three relatively simple questions that could be used to gauge their school involvement, namely:

"Since the beginning of the school year, have you or [child's other parent] . . .

1. Attended a general school meeting, for example, back to school night or a meeting of a parent–teacher organization?"

2. Attended a school or class event such as a play, sports event, or science fair?"

3. Acted as a volunteer at the school or served on a school committee?"

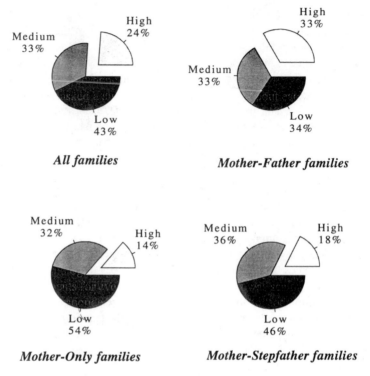

FIG. 8.2.   Level of parental involvement in school activities, by family type.

Parents who had done none of these things, or only one of them, were categorized as displaying a low level of involvement in school-related activities. Those who answered "yes" to two of the questions were classified as having a moderate level of involvement, while those who had done all three were said to have a high level of involvement.

As shown in Fig. 8.2, only about one quarter of all U.S. students in Grades 6–12 have parents who are highly involved in their schools, as gauged by this index. About one third more have parents who show a moderate level of involvement. A sizable minority of students' families have only a low level of involvement in their teenager's school.

As also shown in Fig. 8.2, parent involvement shows significant variation related to the number and type of parents present in the household. Families in which both of the child's biological or adoptive parents are present show higher levels of parent involvement than do single-parent families, stepfamilies, or families in which neither parent lives with the child. In the national survey, parent involvement was found to be low for about half of all students from mother-only or mother–stepfather families, versus one third of students from mother–father families. Parent involvement was high for only 14% of students from mother-only families and 18% of those from mother–stepfather families, as opposed to one third of students from mother–father families.

The differences in parent involvement by parents present in the household are partly attributable to the lower education and income levels that characterize single-parent families and stepfamilies. However, even when education, income, and other related factors were controlled, single parent and especially, stepfamilies, showed lower levels of involvement than did mother–father families.

As stated previously, many educators believe that students are more likely to succeed in school if their parents participate in the schooling process. Do children whose parents are highly involved in school activities in fact do better in school? The national survey findings indicate that they do. In the National Household Education Survey, students with parents who were relatively uninvolved in school activities were more likely to have experienced problems in school, whereas students whose parents reported high levels of school involvement tended to have a low incidence of learning and behavior problems.

As shown in Fig. 8.3, the National Household Education Survey found that 19% of all U.S. students in Grades 6–12 had to repeat a grade at some point in

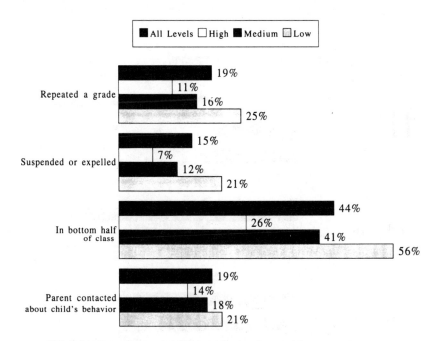

FIG. 8.3. Percentage of children experiencing problems in school, by parental involvement.

their academic careers. Among students whose parents showed low levels of school involvement, 25% had repeated a grade, whereas among those whose parents showed high involvement, only 11% repeated.

Further, 15% of all students in Grades 6–12 had been suspended or expelled from school at some point. Students with parents who had little involvement in school were three times as likely to have been suspended as those whose parents were highly involved (21% vs. 7%). Students whose parents showed moderate involvement fell in between; 12% of them had been suspended at some point.

Parental involvement was also related to the child's current academic standing and classroom conduct. Students from low-involvement families were twice as likely to be in the lower half of their classes as students from high-involvement families. Parents from low-involvement families were half again as likely as parents from high-involvement families to have been contacted by the child's teacher during the current school year because of a problem with the child's classroom behavior—21% of students from the former group had a teacher contact, versus 14% of students from the latter group.

Does the lower average level of parental involvement in stepfamilies help to explain the higher incidence of school problems that children from these families experience? As shown in Figs. 8.4 and 8.5, it partly does so, but is not the whole explanation. Figure 8.4 shows the percentage of students suspended or expelled from school by both parents present in household and level of parental involve-

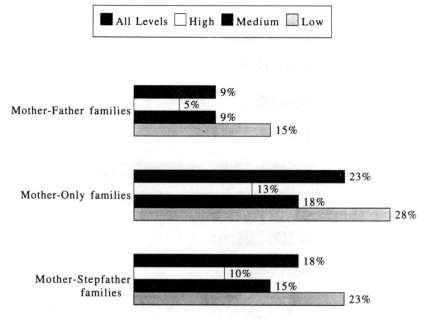

FIG. 8.4. Percentage of children suspended or expelled from school, by family type and level of parental involvement.

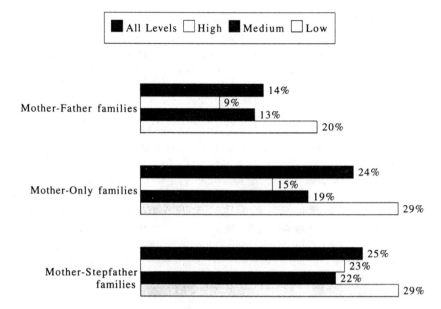

FIG. 8.5.   Percentage of children who repeated a grade, by family type and level of parental involvement.

ment. We see that within each of the three family types, there are significant differences in rate of suspension by level of parent involvement. Thus, children from stepfamilies whose parents are highly involved in school have a rate of suspension that is no different from that of the average child from a mother–father family. This suggests that if all parents in stepfamilies were highly involved, their children would not be at increased risk of school behavior problems.

However, at each involvement level, the children from the stepfamilies still have a higher rate of suspension than those from the mother–father families. In other words, high involvement does not totally ameliorate the negative effects of marital conflict, divorce, and remarriage. Indeed, when a multiple logistic analysis of these data were done, it showed that there was a significant main effect of stepfamilies on suspension, and a significant main effect of parental involvement, but an insignificant interaction of parent involvement by stepfamily status.

A slightly different picture emerges when we look at grade repetition, which is shown in Fig. 8.5. Although children in all three types of families show a lower incidence of grade repetition in high- or moderate-involvement families than do those in low-involvement families, the differences are less pronounced in stepfamilies. Again, however, the multiple logistic analysis here did not show a significant interaction between stepfamily status and parental involvement, but only main effects of each.

Obviously, because these are cross-sectional data, one must be cautious about making causal inferences from them. However, this is the kind of research that is needed if we are to better understand how stepfamilies operate as childrearing environments, and if we are to derive some practical lessons for stepfamilies on how some of their problems and pitfalls might be avoided. We must move beyond showing differences by family type to finding out what these differences mean in the way of family functioning. Further, we must discover what the differences in family functioning imply for children's development and well-being.

Hetherington's chapter gave us many insights and suggestions about what some of the significant differences in stepfamily functioning might be. My only caution would be that many of the findings she described were based on relatively small subsamples from larger studies. For now, those observations should be treated as promising leads that should be replicated and verified with larger and more representative groups similar to the national survey samples I described. I do not doubt, however, that pursuing these leads will result in rich rewards regarding our understanding of stepfamilies and their strengths and difficulties.

REFERENCES

Allison, P. D., & Furstenberg, F. F., Jr. (1989). How marital dissolution affects children: Variations by age and sex. *Developmental Psychology, 25*, 540–549.

Dawson, D. A. (1991). Family structure and children's health and wellbeing: Data from the 1988 National Health Interview Survey on Child Health. *Journal of Marriage and the Family, 53*, 573–584.

Peterson, J. L., & Zill, N. (1986). Marital disruption, parent–child relationships, and behavioral problems in children. *Journal of Marriage and the Family, 48*, 295–240.

Zill, N. (1988). Behavior, achievement, and health problems among children in stepfamilies: Findings from a national survey of child health. In E. M. Hetherington & J. Arasteh (Eds.), *The impact of divorce, single parenting and stepparenting on children*. Hillsdale, NJ: Lawrence Erlbaum Associates.

Zill, N., Morrison, D. R., & Coiro, M. J. (1993). Long-term effects of parental divorce and parent–child relationships, adjustment, and achievement in young adulthood. *Journal of Family Psychology, 7*(1), 91–103.

Zill, N., & Schoenborn, C. A. (1991). Health of our nation's children: Developmental, learning, and emotional problems. United States, 1988. *Advance Data from Vital and Health Statistics, 190*, 1–18.

III HOW DO STEPFAMILIES FUNCTION AS SOURCES OF SUPPORT?

9 Stepfamilies Over the Life Course: Social Support

Lynn White
University of Nebraska—Lincoln

Most of the research on stepfamilies rightly focuses on the stepfamily with young children. Childrearing and social replacement are clearly the most important functions of families in any society, and knowing how well stepfamilies perform these functions is crucial to understanding how children and society will fare under this increasingly common family form.

Families are much more than childrearing organizations, however. Relationships between parents and children remain important long after co-residence ends and the children are grown. Although the actual quantity of goods and services exchanged between generations may be rather small under routine conditions, family members remain important sources of identity and perceived social support. In the the National Survey of Families and Households (NSFH), for example, 80% of adults listed a family member as their first source of assistance in at least one of three emergencies. This perceived supportiveness has been found to be more important than actual exchange for mental health outcomes (House, Umberson, & Landis, 1988).

Thus, one question we need to ask about stepfamilies is whether they will provide these sorts of services to their members. Do people feel confident about relying upon their stepmothers or stepfathers in emergencies? Do stepchildren provide the same kinds of social integration and assistance as biological children?

There has been much speculation on these questions, but few definitive answers. Some scholars have taken a positive stance, arguing that remarriage and stepfamilies enrich the kinship network and provide us with an enlarged pool of potential kin (Furstenberg & Spanier, 1984; Wald, 1981). Others suggest that stepfamily bonds will be weaker than those in biological families, with a resulting shortfall in social support (Bartlema, 1988). In 1979, Troll, Miller, and Atchley (1979), wrote that "we know so little about kinship relations among reconstituted families that we cannot even speculate about them" (p. 69). In the ensuing 15 years, modest steps were taken to fill this gap.

In this chapter, I review theoretical frameworks for stepfamily support, and then examine empirical findings. Because few previous studies have been published, I rely largely on my own NSFH research to answer questions about stepfamily support.

THEORETICAL FRAMEWORKS

I briefly review sociobiological, social psychological, social network, and institutionalization perspectives on stepfamilies as support networks. Each leads to the prediction that stepfamilies will be less supportive than biological families.

Sociobiology: They're Not Carrying My Genes

The sociobiological argument (taken from Daly & Wilson, 1978) suggests that animals are reproductive strategists who maximize the survival of their genes into the next generation, in part by focusing nurturance on their own offspring. Not only is there no genetic predisposition to nurture another's children, such children may be seen as rivals who endanger one's own children's survival. In many species (including some primates), males will kill a mate's young from former unions, increasing the chances that her attention and resources will be devoted to bearing and nurturing his offspring. This argument was noted by some scholars as an explanation for the higher likelihood that stepchildren will be abused or killed (Dobash, Dobash, Wilson, & Daly, 1992; Finkelhor, 1979).

From a sociobiological perspective, not all conflict in stepfamilies will be between stepparent and stepchild. Van den Berghe hypothesized (personal communication, March 5, 1986) that as stepchildren reach puberty, they will become sexual competitors to their parents. In the usual structure of stepfamilies— biological mother/stepfather—his model implies that post-pubertal stepdaughters will be the most troublesome element in stepfamilies and that this family configuration will be most unstable.

Although sociobiology is controversial, I do not introduce it as a straw man. To paraphrase Alice Rossi (1984), failure to recognize the extent to which biology shapes our lives cripples our efforts to understand the role that social structures play. It may be that, given biological predispositions, human stepfamilies are amazingly successful.

Social Psychological Perspectives

Taking a very different approach, scholars who approach the family from a social–psychological orientation argue that what sets parent–child relationships apart from others is the long-term, cumulative nature of the affective bond (Atkinson, 1989). The issue is not whether you like or love your parents/children, but the extent to which your relationship to these persons is a defining characteristic of your identity.

Turner (1970) introduced the concept of *crescive bonds* to describe incrementally built bonds that "link irreplaceable individuals . . . into a continuing relationship" (p. 89). According to Turner, the development of such bonds requires that the relationship: (a) have a long history and an open-ended future orientation, (b) be a label others use to identify you (e.g., "you are John's father"), (c) be a label you use to identify yourself, and (d) provide rewards, particularly enhanced self-esteem. When all criteria are met, the relationship becomes an integral part of identity, and it is maintained even if it ceases to be rewarding.

Empirical evidence about family identities tends to focus on parents rather than children. Research suggests that "parent" is a defining role, a role that sits at or near the top of men's and women's identity salience hierarchies. Parenthood is, after all, an incredibly time-consuming role that, for many years, shapes and constrains lifestyle choices. It would be surprising, indeed, if parenthood was not nearly as important as age and gender in determining our sense of "Who am I?" Stepparenting, however, should be substantially less important to our identities: Stepparenting takes fewer years of our lives, we can walk away, identification is incomplete and tentative ("No, I'm not John's father; I'm his stepfather"), and social recognition is weak and inconsistent. As a result, we would anticipate weaker role performance.

In recent research, Thoits (1992) documented the difference in role salience for parenting and stepparenting. Although her results must be tentative because of the small number of stepparent respondents, differences in role salience are more dramatic than those found in behavioral domains. Thoits asked her respondents to rank each of 17 roles (if occupied) on a scale of 0 (respondent held the role but did not list it as one of his or her nine top role identities) to 3 (most important identity). Although parenthood received ratings of 2.7–2.9 (the highest ratings of any role), the stepparent role ranged in salience from only 0.2–0.6. Nearly a dozen roles—including neighbor, churchgoer, in-law, relative, friend—intervened between parenthood and stepparenthood, and in general, being a stepparent was about as important as belonging to voluntary associations or having a hobby.

Thus, social psychological theory and evidence suggest that stepfamily roles are less salient to parents than are biological family roles. We might expect that this salience would be significantly greater when the stepfamily relationship had lasted longer and been formed earlier in the child's life. It is startling in Thoits' data, however, to note that stepparent roles were only marginally more salient for married than for divorced respondents.

The consequences of low role salience remain to be established. It seems likely that social support to stepchildren will be far higher than these salience rankings suggest—at least as long as the marriage creating the stepfamily lasts. Stepparents may aid stepchildren in order to please their spouse, rather than because of their own relationship to the stepchildren; likewise, stepchildren may maintain cordial relationships with the stepparent in order to please their parent. In the face of such very low role salience, the enactment of role obligations must depend on external forces—in this case, the biological parent.

Social Network Perspectives

In the last decade, a body of work has developed around the notion of social network—an interacting group whose exchanges are regulated by the density and duration of social relationships. Although the family is distinct from voluntary groups in many ways, the structural factors that operate to make other groups cohesive also apply to the family. Briefly, social network characteristics may partly explain why the family is more cohesive than other social groups: The family has high levels of density (everyone knows one another) and so has higher social control capacity (Fischer, 1982); long and open-ended interaction, and so greater likelihood of cooperation and diffuse reciprocity (Axelrod, 1984; Carley, 1991; Ekeh, 1974); and strong similarity, which reduces the cost of exchange (Carley 1991; Knoke, 1990). In every case, the stepfamily is structurally weaker than the biological family. The uniformly dense network of the biological family breaks into cliques where stepchildren and stepparent may have nonoverlapping sets of ties (to noncustodial fathers, noncustodial children, former affines), ties are of shorter duration and not so open-ended (stepparents can walk away), and genetic and, perhaps, even social similarity is less.

The structural weakness of the stepfamily implies that stepfamilies will be less able to maintain and enforce obligations to one another. They may be more apt to operate as a voluntary group, characterized by demands for immediate as opposed to diffuse reciprocity, and more dependent on affect. This line of reasoning leads to the direct hypothesis that stepfamilies will be weaker support mechanisms than biological families. It also leads to subsidiary hypotheses that exchange within stepfamilies will be greater when the stepfamily has lasted longer and when there are fewer competing ties (stepparent has no own children, noncustodial parent is dead or absent); it also implies that affect will have a greater effect on exchange within stepfamilies than biological families.

Institutionalization Perspectives

Many family scholars argue that what sets the family apart from other collections of individuals is not genetics, crescive bonds, or density of networks, but institutionalized norms of obligation—norms that hold us reponsible for our children or parents even if we don't like them (Finch, 1989).

Norms of family obligation are weakening in contemporary society for blood relatives. Certainly, many fathers have found ways to walk away from their children without being, apparently, overwhelmed with guilt or ostracized by polite society. As Cherlin (1978) noted, these norms are even weaker for stepfamilies, and it is not at all clear how much obligation stepparents and stepchildren owe one another. How much guilt do stepparents/children impose on themselves if they fail to meet a need in the other? How much censure will others impose on the individual? Two kinds of evidence can be brought to bear on these questions: evolving legal obligation among stepfamily members and survey evidence about perceived normative obligation.

Legal Obligations.   Laws about family obligation reflect, sustain, and create behavior. Thus, laws about stepfamilies are informative about how our society views these obligations. Two issues are of particular relevance: child support and inheritance. Fine and Fine (1992) provided important insight into stepparent/stepchild relationships by reporting on legal rights and responsibilities in these areas.

In 45 states, stepparents have no obligation to support minor stepchildren even while they live with the child's parent; in no state are they required to continue providing support if their marriage to the child's parent ends or they cease to live with the child.

In regard to inheritance, stepparents *may* choose to specify that their stepchildren receive a share of their estate, but in cases where they die without a will, the courts will assume that they intended to omit their stepchildren. If a will directs that the estate is to be divided among "my children," the courts will interpret that phrase as excluding stepchildren. No evidence exists to support or refute the assumption of such an intention on the part of stepparents.

California has recently permitted stepchildren to inherit if "the relationship of parent and child [began] during the person's minority and continued throughout the parties' joint lifetimes [and if] it is established by clear and convincing evidence that the foster parent or stepparent would have adopted the person but for a legal barrier" (Waggoner, Wellman, Alexander, & Fellows, 1991, p. 131). The problem with this doctrine is that very few stepparents formally adopt their stepchildren, even though (in the many cases where the noncustodial parent disappears from the child's life and provides no support) such adoptions could probably be achieved even over the noncustodial parent's objections (Waggoner et al., 1991). Failure to adopt signals to the courts an absence of commitment. Does it carry the same signal to the child or the child's parent? Social science research could make a useful contribution, here.

From their review of statutes and judicial findings, the Fines deduce a judicial assumption that "stepfamily status entails no rights or obligations" (Fine & Fine, 1992, p. 335). If this assumption accurately reflects the feelings of stepfamily members—and little evidence exists one way or the other—then it is an inescapable conclusion that stepfamilies are seriously weak organizations whose roles lack substance.

Normative Obligations to Stepfamily Members. Bartlema (1988) argued that as serial monogamy replaces monogamy, we will find kinship networks filled with "all kinds of affinal kin of varying degree of relationships" (p. 218). In many cases, we may not even be sure that these people are, in fact, relatives or what we should call them (Day, 1988). Such confusion "leaves the individual free to fill in the nature and degree of affinity of such relationships according to his or her own needs and preferences" (Bartlema, 1988, p. 218). The result is less normative pressure and more dependence on individual characteristics, such as affection, affluence, and proximity.

Rossi and Rossi's (1990) study of three-generational family relationships in the Boston area provided unique information about norms of stepfamily obligations. Rossi and Rossi gave each of their respondents a set of 32 vignettes that randomized hundreds of combinations of situation, relationship, and gender. For each vignette, respondents were asked how obligated they would feel to provide the assistance specified to the kin member named. Stepparents and adult stepchildren were among the relationships examined.

The vignettes represented hypothetical situations, and the vast majority of respondents reporting on kinship obligations to adult stepchildren and stepparents had no such relatives in their own families. Evidence that those with stepfamily experience are less likely to carry negative stereotypes about stepchildren/parents than others (Fine, 1986; Fluitt & Paradise, 1991) suggests that these hypothetical reports may underestimate actual feelings of obligation among stepfamily members. On the other hand, Thoits' data showing extraordinarily low salience of stepparent roles suggests that stepparents may distance themselves from their stepchildren even more than the public anticipates. Because generalized norms affect the degree to which stepfamily members will be sanctioned for failing to meet obligations, however, they are important.

Rossi and Rossi (1990) showed that normative obligations to stepchildren fall very materially below those to own children, but they are nevertheless substantial.[1] Obligation was rated on an 11-point scale, where 0 represented *no obligation at all* and 10, *a very strong obligation*. Averaging obligation ratings across the four crisis situations for which the Rossis provide tabular data (p. 173), the average obligation rating was 8.3 for own children and 6.4 for stepchildren. These figures suggest a public perception that stepparents ought to feel a moderate obligation to assist adult stepchildren, and that, although the obligation to assist stepchildren falls materially below the obligation to help own children, obligations to stepchildren are rated higher than those to nieces/nephews, aunts/

---

[1]The same general finding is reported in Schwebel, Fine, and Renner's (1991) small study of college students' perceptions of stepparent obligations to school-age children. Averaging across several vignettes in which the child needed some sort of assistance or support, 80% of the students thought stepparents ought to provide assistance, compared to 83% of biological parents—a significant, but quite small difference. These authors note that standard deviations differ more across categories than do the means, suggesting less consensus on norms about stepfamily obligations.

uncles, cousins, friends, and neighbors. Stepparents fared somewhat less well than stepchildren, and the gap between biological and stepparents was greater than that between biological children and stepchildren. Stepparents rated below friends, but ahead of neighbors, nieces/nephews, aunts/uncles, and cousins. Average obligation to stepparents was 5.8, compared to 8.3 for own parents.

The Rossi and Rossi data suggest that public opinion (presumably reflected in internalized normative pressure) would support giving less to stepparents and stepchildren than to biological parents and children. Public opinion would condemn those who failed to provide comfort or support in times of crisis, or who failed to keep up normal intercourse with stepfamily members.

A question unanswered by the Rossis' hypothetical data is whether obligations to the two types of kin might be more or less determined by circumstances. It seems likely that the normative obligations between stepchildren and stepparent like the very modest legal obligations discussed earlier, depend on an intact marriage between parent and stepparent. Normative obligations probably also depend on such factors as duration of the stepfamily relationships, the age of the child when the stepfamily was formed, length of co-residence with the stepparent, and whether one has relatives in the higher ranked categories (e.g., whether one has own children).

Whether normative and legal obligations extend beyond the marriage between stepparent and parent brings up an even more basic question: Does the relationship itself extend beyond the marriage? Is John still your stepson if you divorce his parent? Day (1988) noted that we have no readily agreed-upon terms to refer to such people, and that the vagueness of the role relationship is likely to be paralleled by the vagueness and ambiguity of the role expectations. In this regard, however, it is interesting that Thoits' research on role identities found that 11% of divorced men and 3% of divorced women (compared to 19% of married women and men) reported being a stepparent—and that the majority of these divorced stepparents claimed the role by saying they thought of themselves as stepparents. These data imply that role relationships, and perhaps, role obligations between stepparents and stepchildren may have a lasting quality not entirely embedded in the marriage between parent and stepparent.

The extent and determinants of normative obligation in stepfamilies are empirical questions worth further study. Both theory and the limited existing evidence, however, suggest that members of stepfamilies will feel less normative obligation (internal and external) to provide social support.

Conclusion

From each of the theoretical perspectives reviewed here, we come to the hypothesis that stepfamilies will not be as effective as biological families in providing social support to members. The extent of supportiveness in stepfamilies is likely to be enhanced by longer duration of childhood co-residence, weakness of competing ties, and especially by the continued marriage of the stepparent to the biological parent. In the absence of this last critical link and the absence of strong institutionalized support, exchange among stepparents and stepchildren is likely to be fragile. We now turn to an examination of the empirical evidence to find out how well these predictions are supported.

EMPIRICAL FINDINGS

The following sections provide evidence about four areas of family support in grown-up stepfamilies: (a) parental support during launching and the transition to adulthood, (b) sibling relationships during adulthood, (c) children's reports of exchange with their parents, and (d) parents' reports of exchange with their children. For the first two areas, I rely on published research reports. In the case of exchange and relationships among adult stepfamily members, review of previous work is heavily supplemented by unpublished analyses of NSFH data.

Stepchildren During the Launching Phase

Parental support is an important resource for young adult children. Continuing in school is rare without parental backing; fewer than 20% of college freshmen receive no support from parents (Astin, Korn, & Berg, 1989). Whether in or out of school, young adult children rely on parental support via continued residence in the parents' home. Approximately 50% of unmarried children ages 18–24 live with their parents, and another significant proportion uses their parents' home as an occasional base. Recent reports suggest that 10%–15% of unmarried children are still living with their parents into their 30s and even 40s (Speare & Avery, 1993). Children return home during role transitions (e.g., leaving school or military, job changes, divorce), in times of need (e.g., unemployment), and sometimes just for company and comfort.

Beginning with a report by White and Booth (1985), a substantial body of research in the United States, Australia, and the United Kingdom demonstrates that stepchildren leave home earlier than children from intact biological families. Controlling for a dozen background variables, Aquilino (1991a) reported that 65% of stepchildren leave home before age 19, compared to 50% of children raised in intact families. This effect is roughly doubled if there are also stepsiblings in the home.

Children's reports of home-leaving are paralleled by parental reports of co-residence. Aquilino (1991b) found that if all children are stepchildren, parents are significantly and substantially less likely to include adult children in their home. Remarried parents with unmarried adult children are only about half as likely to include children in their home (29% vs. 50%) as are once-married parents (Aquilino, 1990).

British data from the National Child Development Study, which has followed all members of the March 1958, birth cohort for over 30 years, allow us to compare the reasons of stepchildren and biological children for leaving home. Kiernan (1992) reported that not only did stepchildren leave home substantially earlier than those in intact families, but they more often cited family conflict as the reason. Twenty-six percent of the women and 19% of the men raised in stepfamilies after their own parents divorced cited conflict as the reason for leaving home, compared to 5%–6% of children in intact families.

Stepchildren not only leave earlier, they leave with less support. A variety of United States and British reports confirmed that, while controlling for family income and other background factors, stepchildren are less likely than others to leave home to attend college (Aquilino, 1991a; Kiernan, 1992). If they do attend college, they are less likely than others to be doing so with financial support from their parents (Goldscheider & Goldscheider, 1991).

Two factors have been found to interact with stepfamily status in its effect on young adults—child's sex and race. In two pieces, Goldscheider and Goldscheider (1991, 1993) demonstrated that the effect of stepfamily status is stronger for Whites and Asians than for African Americans, with Hispanics somewhere in between. This suggests that the negative effects of stepfamily status are strongest where it is the rarest and least institutionalized.

Both Aquilino and Goldscheider and Goldscheider (1993) showed that the stepfamily effect on early home-leaving was much stronger for daughters than sons. Although consistent with van den Berghe's hypothesis, the data are not consistent across all studies. Kiernan's (1992) study of home-leaving in the United Kingdom showed no substantial gender difference in the effect of stepfamilies on home-leaving before age 18, leaving school before age 16, or entering the work force before age 16, and Mitchell, Wister, and Burch (1989) showed that, among firstborn Canadian children, the stepfamily effect was stronger for sons than daughters.

In almost all of these reports, dummy variables indicating stepfamily membership and perhaps other family structures, are compared against an omitted category of intact biological families. An equally compelling question is how stepfamilies compare to disrupted families. Does remarriage improve or worsen intergenerational support relationships compared to the immediate alternative of remaining in a single-parent family? Perhaps half of the studies that examine stepfamily effects also include a measure of single-parent families, so that one can compare the size and direction of the coefficients (albeit without significance tests). Such a comparison yields a mixed picture. With all control variables included, Kiernan (1992) showed that stepfamilies were consistently more likely than single-mother families to lead to early school leaving, labor force entry, and home-leaving, and to leaving home on account of conflict. Working with the dependent variable for early home-leaving, Aquilino (1991a) showed almost identical coefficients for stepfamilies and for single-parent families formed after divorce for girls, but stronger effects of single-parent than stepfamily homes for boys. The strongest evidence of a difference between the two family structures came from Goldscheider and Goldschedier's (1993) report that stepchildren are significantly more likely, and children from single-mother families significantly less likely than children from intact families to marry early.

Perhaps not coincidentally, the only report to directly compare remarried families with single-parent families finds no significant difference. McLanahan and Bumpass (1988), using the National Survey of Family Growth, asked whether growing up in a remarried household affects early family formation: marriage before 20, birth before 20, premarital birth, divorce, remarriage. Although they found significant, negative effects of living in a single-parent home during childhood, they find no significant difference between those who did and did not also experience parental remarriage during childhood. They suggested that the advantages and disadvantages of remarriage (more money, but also more conflict) may balance one another. Although surprised by their findings, they raised the possibility that "parental remarriage is irrelevant to later family experiences" (p. 147).

Summary.   Research established that stepchildren leave home earlier and are less likely to attend college than comparable children from intact biological families. They are more likely to have left the family home on account of conflict. Therefore, stepchildren may be disadvantaged both in the status attainment process and in the level of comfort and security they experience in young adulthood. The extent to which stepchildren's disadvantage is due to parental remarriage rather than their previous experience in single-parent households is inadequately understood. Kiernan's (1992) evidence showing stepchildren leave more often because of conflict, and Aquilino's (1991a) finding that stepsiblings significantly increase the odds of early home-leaving are the strongest pieces of evidence that parental remarriage may lead to problems over-and-above the deficits associated with the single-parent experience. It seems likely, however, that a portion of the disadvantage experienced by stepchildren in the transition to adulthood is more properly attributed to their parents' marital disruption or even to marital conflict than to the remarriage.

Stepsiblings

Family research tends to focus on vertical relationships, and we know much less about siblings than we do about parents and children. Nevertheless, siblings are an important part of the family support network. In NSFH, 29% of the respondents listed a sibling as their first source of emergency assistance in at least one scenario, and 63% said that at least one of their siblings was a "best friend." Fifty percent said they had monthly or more contact with a sibling (White & Riedmann, 1992b).

Given the salience of siblings as friends and sources of support, how well do stepsiblings fill these shoes? My own research with Riedmann (White & Riedman, 1992a) provides the only empirical evidence on this issue. In our analysis, we were restricted to analyzing only one measure of stepsibling relationships: Frequency of contact was the only measure for which NSFH asked separately about stepsiblings and full siblings.

Respondents reported significantly less contact with step-/half siblings than they did with full siblings. Contact averaged one to three times a month for full siblings, but only several times a year for step-/half siblings. Although contact was significantly and substantively less with stepsiblings, it remained substantial, and only 0.5% of stepsiblings were so estranged that they did not at least know where their step-/half siblings lived. Contact with stepsiblings was strongly related to characteristics of the childhood family. Respondents reported more contact with their step-/half siblings when they had no full siblings, spent more childhood years with a stepparent, and lived with a stepfather rather than a stepmother. Contact with step-/half siblings was more contingent upon proximity than contact with full siblings.

Drawing on the literature that suggests African Americans have a more embracing approach to defining kin, we tested the hypothesis that African Americans would make less distinction between full siblings and half/stepsiblings than others. This hypothesis was not supported. African Americans have more contact with both their step-/half and full siblings than do others, but this differential is similar across both types of sibship. Thus, African Americans, like other U.S. groups, are less close to their stepsiblings than to full siblings.

Summary.   In the NSFH sample of nearly 11,000 adults with siblings, 4% had only stepsiblings and 9% had both step- and full siblings. This number is likely to rise substantially as recent cohorts move into adulthood. People who have only stepsiblings are more apt to treat them as full siblings, but claims for support may go unmet if the stepsibling has full siblings as well. Thus, I think we must treat these data as evidence that the sibling support network will be weaker in the future than it has been. Stepsiblings are more likely to function as weak ties—people we could call on for information or with whom we could stay for a few days if we were traveling through their town, but not people about whom we could feel confident if we called on them for emergency assistance.

Relationships Among Adult Stepchildren and Stepparents

In the following sections, I use unpublished NSFH analyses to look at relationships between adult stepchildren and stepparents from two perspectives. First, I ask how stepchildren feel about their stepparents: how much contact they report, how they evaluate their relationships, and how much exchange they report. Second, I asked how parents feel about their stepchildren compared to their own children. In neither case does the data set provide information on everything we might wish, but it does provide basic descriptive information. In addition to comparing stepfamilies to intact biological families, the analysis compares intact and disrupted stepfamilies and examines determinants of outcomes within stepfamilies. (The Methodological Appendix on pp. 132–135 provides details of study design.)

Children's Report on Parents/Stepparents. The analysis reported here is based on nearly 4,000 individuals who have at least one living parent (biological or step), who do not live with any parent, and who fall into one of four categories based on both current and childhood family structure:

1. Intact biological families: The respondent spent his or her entire childhood living in an intact family; both parents are still alive and living together (N = 3,277).

2. Intact stepfamilies: The respondent spent part of his or her childhood living with a stepparent; that marriage is still intact and both partners are living (N = 370).

3. Stepfamilies broken by divorce: The marriage between the respondent's parent and stepparent was ended by divorce; the stepparent is still alive (N = 168).

4. Stepfamilies broken by own parent's death: The marriage between the respondent's parent and stepparent was broken by the death of the parent; the stepparent is still alive (N = 47).

Two types of dependent variables are available in the data set for children's reports on parents. Relationship quality and amount of contact are available for each living parent and one stepparent. In addition, we have information about exchange with "parents," a vague category that may include noncustodial parents, stepparents, and even in-laws, as well as custodial, biological parents.

The hypothesis is that relationships with stepparents will be weaker than those with biological parents; within stepfamilies, relationships with stepparents should be weaker after the death of own parent and weakest where the marriage between parent and stepparent is broken by divorce. Exchange with parents is expected to show weaker effects, but exchange is hypothesized to be greatest in intact biological families. Among stepfamilies, exchange should be lowest after the death of one's own parent, and intermediate in cases where the marriage between parent and stepparent is broken by divorce. In all stepfamily types, theory suggests relationships with stepparents will be stronger when the stepfamily was formed earlier in the child's life and when child gets along well with the intermediary—his or her own parent. Previous research also suggests that absence of stepsiblings will strengthen stepfamily bonds. The van den Berghe hypothesis, that relationships will be stronger when the child and stepparent are the same sex, will also be tested. We begin with simple descriptive analyses.

Table 9.1 compares relationship quality and amount of contact across the four family types, dividing the stepfamily types into those with a stepmother and those with a stepfather. The results are consistent with expectations. Adults with intact stepfamilies generally report lower contact and relationship quality with their stepparent than with the comparable biological parent in an intact family. In intact stepfather families, stepfathers are rated much higher than noncustodial fathers, whereas in stepmother families, stepmothers and noncustodial mothers fare about equally.[2]

The results for disrupted stepfamilies provide evidence of the fragility of stepfamily relationships. When the stepfamily is broken by divorce, both relationship quality and contact with the stepparent are lower. In a large proportion of cases, the relationship ends entirely. In stepfamilies broken by divorce, 57% of the respondents never see their stepparent and 57% never talk to him or her. Among those whose stepfamily is broken by the parent's death, the contact and quality are less affected than when the remarriage ends with divorce, but 47% never see and 34% never talk to the stepparent. Thus, in nearly half of all cases, the relationship between stepparent and stepchild is effectively broken when the marriage with the respondent's parent ends. The large proportion who end the relationship entirely shed a different light on the modest averages reported in Table 9.1, suggesting that a minority must maintain quite close relationships with former stepparents.

The data allow us to compare these four family types on perceived social support from parents (whether respondent would call on parent in an emergency) and a variety of specific kinds of help given and received. Table 9.2 provides a general description of social support across the four family types, again dividing intact stepfamilies into those with a stepmother and a stepfather. Means are adjusted for respondent's age, sex, race, and ethnicity. F tests were used to compare intact biological with intact stepfamilies, intact stepfather to intact stepmother families, and disrupted with intact stepfamilies.

On 13 separate items and 2 summed indexes of giving and receiving support, about half showed significant differences between intact biological and intact stepfamilies. All differences were in the direction hypothesized: Respondents with intact stepfamilies were less likely to perceive their parents as emergency helpers or to provide help to or receive help from parents. Although statistically significant and probably important, most of the differences are not dramatic. For example, 47% of respondents from intact biological families reported receiving at least some help from their parents, compared to 41% from intact stepfather families, and 38% from intact stepmother families. The differences between step- and biological families are greatest for the two items on which stepmother and stepfather families differ significantly: Respondents from stepmother fami-

---

[2]Although the relatively high contact with intact stepfathers may be an artifact of the study design (the assumption that contact with mother's husband is the same as with mother), relationship quality was assessed independently and shows the same pattern.

TABLE 9.1.
Mean Relationship Quality and Contact with Parents and Stepparents by Parent's Marital Status and Respondent's Childhood Living Arrangements

Family Type While R Growing Up	Relationship Quality				Contact Frequency			
	Family Type Now				Family Type Now			
	Natural Parents Together	Stepparents Together	Stepfamily Broken by Divorce	Stepfamily Broken by Parent's Death	Natural Parents Together	Stepparents Together	Stepfamily Broken by Divorce	Stepfamily Broken by Parent's Death
Mother	6.0 (1.3)	5.9 (1.3)	5.3 (1.6)	—	4.4 (1.2)	4.3 (1.3)	4.2 (1.4)	—
Stepfather	—	5.0 (1.7)	3.1 (2.0)	3.7 (2.3)	—	4.3 (1.3)	1.8 (1.2)	2.3 (1.7)
Father	5.8 (1.3)	3.5 (2.2)	2.9 (2.0)	*	4.4 (1.2)	2.5 (1.4)	2.2 (1.4)	*
Father	5.8 (1.3)	5.2 (1.9)	4.5 (2.1)	—	4.4 (1.2)	3.5 (1.3)	3.6 (1.7)	—
Stepmother	—	4.4 (1.5)	3.4 (2.2)	4.5 (2.3)	—	3.5 (1.3)	2.3 (1.3)	2.8 (1.6)
Mother	6.0 (1.3)	4.6 (2.3)	4.8 (2.2)	*	4.4 (1.2)	3.5 (1.6)	3.1 (1.2)	*
N^a	3,277	254 116	119 49	22 25				

Note. SDs are given in parentheses.
[a]Top row is number of stepfather, and bottom row, number of stepmother families.
*Too few cases ($n < 10$).

TABLE 9.2.
Percentage of Adult Children's Report of Exchange With Parents,
Adjusted for Respondent's Age, Sex, Race, and Ethnicity

	Natural Parents Together	Stepparents Together/ Stepfather	Stepparents Together/ Stepmother	Stepfamily Broken by Divorce	Stepfamily Broken by Parent's Death
Perceived support	71**[a]	67	47**[b]	51	27**[c]
Received from parent					
Any	47*	41	38	38	28
Child care	18*	14	11	14	7
Transportation	12	10	15	12	10
Repairs	9	6	10	6	6
Household	9**	6	1*	7	5
Advice	34	30	30	25	19
Given to parents					
Any	46**	41	41	33	28
Child care	2	3	3	3	2
Transportation	15*	11	10	10	2
Repairs	14	14	14	8	11
Household	24	20	18	17	15
Advice	28	24	22	21	12
N	3,277	254	116	168	47

[a]F test comparing intact biological families to intact stepfamilies (stepmother and stepfather combined).
[b]F test comparing intact stepfather to intact stepmother families.
[c]F test comparing all stepfamily types.
*$p < .05$.   **$p < .01$.

lies are much less likely to receive help with work around the house and to perceive their parents as sources of emergency assistance.

What happens when the stepfamily breaks up through death or divorce? Columns 4 and 5 provide a partial answer. Few comparisons are significant, but disrupted stepfamilies—especially those where own parent has died (mostly stepmother families)—provide substantially less perceived support. Even this small level of support may be overestimated, as respondent may have referred to a living noncustodial parent, rather than the stepparent.

From the children's perspective, individuals raised by their biological mothers appear to receive and perceive about the same amount of social support, whether they lived with a biological father or a stepfather. Respondents raised by fathers and stepmothers perceive signicantly and substantially lower social support than those raised by their mothers, but deficits in actual exchange are quite small.

Finally, I turn to multivariate analysis of intact stepfamilies to examine hypotheses about factors that determine solidarity within stepfamilies. Isolating the

370 intact stepfamilies, four dependent variables are examined: relationship with stepparent, perception of parental support, giving support to parents, and receiving support from parents (Table 9.3). Each analysis begins with a general model that regresses the relationship measure on respondent and stepfamily characteristics: respondent's age, sex, race and ethnicity, age at acquiring stepparent, whether respondent also lived with stepsiblings while growing up, and stepparent's sex. In the second stage, two contemporary measures of respondent's relationship with own parent—relationship quality and frequency of contact—are added.

When relationship with the stepparent is the dependent variable (columns 1 and 2), presence of stepsiblings and having a stepmother rather than a stepfather are associated with lower relationship quality. Surprisingly, age at acquisition of the stepparent is not related to current relationship with the stepparent. These respondents (average age of 31) acquired their stepparents at the average age of 9, so that the stepparent/stepchild relationships reported here average more than 20 years duration. A test for interaction showed no difference between younger and older respondents in the effect of age of stepfamily formation. Age of respondent itself, however, is significant and positive, indicating that competition and strain in stepchild/stepparent relationships may decline with greater maturity and as the period of co-residence recedes farther into the background.

After control for two measures of respondent's current relationship with own parent—variables that are strongly related to quality of relationship with stepparent—the effect of stepmothers virtually disappears, suggesting the reason stepmother families look weaker than stepfather families is a weaker relationship with the biological parent. Stepsiblings continue to mar the relationship with the stepparent, however, even after these factors are controlled.

Turning to measures of exchange between stepchild and the parental dyad, no stepfamily measure is significantly related to amount of exchange in intact stepfamilies. Presence of stepsiblings, stepparent's sex, or age at which stepfamily was formed have no effect on children's report of giving or receiving help—surprisingly, neither does relationship with one's own parent. Children do, however, report significantly greater perceived support from mother/stepfather families than from father/stepmother families. This effect is reduced, but not eliminated, by control for relationship with own parent. Again, it seems likely that the key here is gender of one's own parent, rather than that of the stepparent. My own interpretation is that it is the availability of the child's own mother that is critical to the sense of perceived support.

The Parental View: Children and Stepchildren. What happens when we ask parents about their relationships with children and stepchildren? Before beginning the report of my own analysis, I review three pertinent studies, all of which also draw on NSFH data.

In a design much like mine, Kulis (1992) analyzed parents' ratings of their

TABLE 9.3.
Multivariate Analysis: Determinants of Relationships and Exchange for Adult Children From Intact Stepfamilies

	OLS				Logistic Regression			
Respondent	Relationship With Stepparent		Perceive Support From Parents		Any Help From Parents		Any Help to Parents	
Age	.032** (.010)	.023* (.010)	−.070** (.013)	−.060** (.014)	−.079** (.014)	−.068* (.014)	−.046** (.013)	−.034** (.013)
Female	−.041 (.184)	−.025 (.192)	.197 (.240)	.067 (.259)	.246 (.230)	.063 (.244)	−.109 (.225)	−.311 (.240)
African American	−.131 (.324)	−.016 (.349)	−1.170** (.416)	−1.343** (.437)	−.733 (.448)	−.842 (.459)	−.298 (.421)	−.369 (.436)
Hispanic	−.228 (.389)	−.004 (.420)	−1.950** (.558)	−2.185** (.595)	−.976 (.560)	−1.038 (.585)	−1.050 (.590)	−1.132 (.612)
Age at step	−.022 (.019)	−.026 (.021)	−.015 (.027)	−.007 (.028)	.006 (.025)	.015 (.026)	.037 (.025)	.048 (.025)
Stepsiblings (0,1)	−.603** (.197)	−.602** (.212)	−.087 (.269)	−.085 (.280)	.166 (.252)	.174 (.261)	.017 (.248)	.007 (.254)
Stepparent female	.078 (.179)	−.413* (.208)	−.879** (.258)	−.569* (.275)	−.189 (.252)	.103 (.262)	.189 (.247)	.056 (.262)
Contact own parent		.170* (.077)		.342** (.111)		.410** (.105)		.380** (.104)
Relationship own parent		.399** (.062)		.216* (.086)		.039 (.086)		.009 (.083)
R^2/χ^2	.05	.19	61.23	24.75	48.12	19.34	22.43	16.19
Constant	4.94	1.52	3.33	.37	1.98	−.36	.81	−1.26
N	368	368	432	432	432	432	432	432

Note. SEs are given in parentheses.
$*p < .05.$ $**p < .01.$

relationships with each of their children. Net of 2 dozen control variables, he found that parents rate their relations with their adult stepchildren significantly and substantially worse than those with their biological children. Although he included indicators of actual exchange as predictors of relationship quality, the beta for stepchild was stronger than for any other variable in the equation except for parent's age.

Eggebeen (1992) did not look at individual parent–child dyads, but analyzed exchange when parents have no stepchildren versus one or more stepchildren. After controlling for background factors, he found no difference between parents with and without stepchildren in the likelihood that they will receive help from their children. He did find, however, that parents with stepchildren reported giving significantly less to their children. He found no evidence that this effect depended on child's or parent's sex or marital status.

Finally, in an earlier piece (White, 1992), I compared divorced and remarried parents to parents in intact first marriages in their support for adult children. This analysis focused on parental aid to children in general, and did not distinguish among individual children by step status. The results showed a significant support deficit for children whose parents had divorced, a deficit that characterized both mothers and fathers, and that was neither increased nor decreased by parental remarriage. That study concluded that divorce is associated with a reduction in the parent–child bond (perhaps occurring due to parental conflict rather than the divorce itself), a rift that is not repaired by remarriage.

NSFH provided detailed data on parents' relationships with each of their children and stepchildren: distance, contact, relationship quality, and exchange. In the analysis that follows, a separate case record was created for each adult child not living in the respondent's home. After missing data were taken into account, the analysis included approximately 7,600 cases, of which 867 (11%) were stepchildren.

Again, we begin with simple descriptive analysis, reporting differences between parents' relationships with own and stepchildren, controlling for parent's age, sex, race, and ethnicity, and child's age and sex. First, own and stepchildren were compared for the entire sample of parent–child pairs, including divorced and widowed, as well as still-married parents. Because divorce and widowhood were expected to affect relationships with stepchildren more than with biological children, the sample was then divided into respondents who were currently married and those who were not. We assumed that married respondents' stepchildren were from the current union.[3] The results are tabulated in Table 9.4.

On nearly every dimension investigated, parents reported a statistically signif-

---

[3]Both Thoits' data (1992) and our own show that individuals continue to claim stepchildren even after their marriage to the child's parent has ended. In our case, 6% of formerly married parents report having stepchildren, compared to 15% of the currently married. It is possible that people carry claims to stepchildren even into a new union.

TABLE 9.4.
Means: Parent's Relationship with Individual Children, Adjusted
for Parent's Age, Sex, Race, Ethnicity and Child's Age and Sex

	All Parents		Married Parents		Unmarried Parents	
	Own	Step	Own	Step	Own	Step
Contact	4.30	3.35**	4.40	3.64**	4.23	2.48**
Distance	234.17	313.06**	234.26	285.89**	236.38	372.80**
Relationship quality	6.45	5.56**	6.52	5.77**	6.36	4.90**
Received from child						
Any	78%	55**	79%	58**	77%	45**
Advice	47	19**	44	19**	52	24**
News	60	39**	63	40**	58	39**
Household help	26	13**	23	12**	29	10**
Financial assistance	10	7*	8	6	13	7
Company	56	30**	57	30**	54	31**
Given to child						
Any	82%	63**	84%	65**	79%	62**
Advice	64	45**	65	47**	61	40**
News	69	47**	74	51**	64	43**
Household help	19	11**	21	12**	15	10
Financial assistance	22	20	26	20	18	23
Company	53	33**	55	34**	51	32**
Child care	21	13**	23	13**	17	14**
N Dyads[a]	6,523	834	3,623	651	2,900	183
	5,722	528	3,100	440	2,622	88

Difference between own and stepchild dyads significant: *$p < .05$. **$p < .01$.
[a]Top row is number of cases when contact and distance are the dependent variables; bottom is number of cases for all other analyses.

icant, and substantively large bias in favor of their own children. These differences were smaller among married parents than unmarried parents (compare columns 3 & 4 with columns 5 & 6), but the conclusion is the same: Parents reported more contact with their own children, closer distances, higher quality relationships, and substantially more exchange. Overall, 78% of own children were reported by parents to give help to parents, but only 55% of stepchildren were reported to give such help. Approximately the same level of difference existed for parental aid to the child—stepchildren got less. These differences were apparent in nearly every component of exchange assessed, except financial assistance. Because the questions about help given to children specified "by you or your spouse," these results suggest that stepchildren not only receive less from their stepparent, but also from their biological parent.

Finally, I turn to multivariate regression analysis to test hypotheses about factors that may modify the stepfamily deficit. Four dependent variables are included: relationship quality, contact, and any help received from or given to the child. The first step of the analysis regresses each dependent variable on background factors, parent's marital status, and whether the child is a stepchild. OLS regression was used for relationship quality and contact (both continuous variables) and logistic regression for the two dummy variables measuring exchange. Step 2 of the analysis adds interaction effects, testing the hypotheses that step status would be less important when stepparent had no biological children, less important if the stepparent was married, and more important when stepparent was a female.

As expected from the analysis in Table 9.4, child's step status was significantly and strongly related to each dependent variable. The second stage of the analysis, however, shows that this negative effect is often modified by other characteristics. For all four of the dependent variables, the negative effect of being a stepchild was approximately doubled if the reporting parent was a female. For the variables of relationship quality and contact with child, the negative effect of being a stepchild was reduced if the stepparent was married (presumably to child's biological parent). This interaction term, however, had a surprising negative effect on parents' giving aid to the stepchild. Having no competing own child had a positive effect on stepparent/stepchild relations for only one dependent variable—quality of the relationship. Analysis showed no consistent interactions by race or ethnicity. Relationship quality was entered into the equations for the three behavioral dependent variables to test the hypothesis that relationship quality would matter more for stepchildren/stepparent relationships. Only one interaction was significant; for the dependent variable of parents giving to children, relationship quality matters less for stepchildren. To test the van den Berghe hypothesis, an interaction effect was added to test the combination of male stepparent and female child. None of the coefficients reached significance.

Combining the interaction effects in Table 9.5 suggests that the best-case scenario is where the stepparent is a stepfather who is still married to the biological mother, and has no children of his own. In this case, there is no deficit for stepchildren in relationship quality or aid received from parents, and deficits in contact and aid given to parents are sharply reduced. The worst-case scenario is a stepmother family where the stepmother has children of her own and is no longer married to the biological father. In this case, the deficit for stepchildren is raised 50%–100%.

Summary.   Viewed from either the parent's or the child's perspective, relationships between stepchildren and stepparents are weaker than those between biological parents and children. The stepfamily is not a monolithic entity, however, and evidence presented here suggests relationships among steprelatives are better when the stepparent is a male, there are no stepsiblings, stepparent has no own children, stepchild's relationship with biological parent is good, and the marriage between biological and stepparent is intact.

TABLE 9.5.
Multivariate Analysis: Parent's Reports of Relationships With Individual Children by Step Status, Unstandardized Regression Coefficients

	OLS				Logistic Regression			
	Relationship with Child	Relationship with Child	Contact with Child	Contact with Child	Exchange C to P	Exchange C to P	Exchange P to C	Exchange P to C
C's age	−.003 (.003)	−.002 (.003)	−.011** (.003)	−.009** (.003)	−.003 (.005)	−.003 (.005)	−.016 (.005)	−.016 (.005)
C female	.049 (.031)	.042 (.031)	.231** (.031)	.225** (.031)	.260** (.064)	.254** (.065)	.163* (.064)	.153* (.065)
P's age	.021** (.002)	.020** (.002)	.012** (.002)	.011** (.002)	.014** (.005)	.013** (.005)	.005 (.005)	.004 (.005)
P female	.245** (.036)	.348** (.036)	.346** (.034)	.441** (.035)	.342** (.064)	.446** (.068)	.326** (.070)	.526** (.074)
P married (0,1)	.329** (.034)	.304** (.035)	.369** (.034)	.318** (.035)	.230** (.065)	.243** (.065)	.377** (.070)	.447** (.073)
P Black	.038 (.046)	.041 (.046)	.021 (.046)	.025 (.046)	−.016 (.089)	−.016 (.089)	−.174 (.093)	−.170 (.094)
P Hispanic	−.113 (.075)	−.093 (.074)	−.039 (.075)	−.017 (.074)	−.627** (.143)	−.622** (.143)	−1.011** (.143)	−1.003** (.144)
C step	−.797** (.051)	−.749** (.121)	−1.007** (.050)	−1.127** (.118)	−.974** (.098)	−.502** (.145)	−.898** (.104)	.478 (.289)
X step only		.353** (.102)		ns		ns		ns
X P female		−.868** (.100)		−.861** (.099)		−.856** (.190)		−1.568** (.212)
X P married		.443** (.117)		.800** (.115)		ns		.586* (.267)
R^2/χ^2	.068	.082	.081	.098	196.136	20.430	177.849	60.084
Constant	4.880	4.831	3.359	3.357	.065	.026	1.344	1.256
N	7,627		7,670		6,635		6,334	

Note. SEs are given in parentheses.
$*p \le .05$ $**p \le .01$.

A critical issue in thinking about these findings is whether we are discussing stepfamilies or stepparents vis-à-vis their stepchildren. If steprelationships are weaker than biological relationships, without damaging relationships between biological parents and children, an individual with a combination of step- and biological relatives will have a smaller support network. If the introduction of stepfamily members weakens ties among biological relations (perhaps, by introducing more jealousy and competition), then the support network will be more seriously damaged. The evidence suggests both factors operate. Stepparents reporting on aid given by themselves and their spouses say that stepchildren receive consistently and significantly less. Children from stepfamilies say they give less to their parents, receive less from them, and perceive less support from them. Thus, although relationships between stepparent and stepchild are those most directly affected by the steprelationship, the evidence suggests that support relations among biological kin may also be damaged. As noted earlier, however, at least some of this damage may be traced back to the original marital disruption and the processes surrounding it.

DISCUSSION

The analysis presented here provides merely a broad outline, and many details remain to be filled in. Nevertheless, I think it is unlikely that more detailed analysis and more control variables will change the general picture outlined previously. Stepfamilies are weaker support networks than intact families. The effects are not simply statistically significant, they are of substantive magnitude. Thus, I think we can set aside the view that stepfamilies mean more relatives, broader networks, and more support. This potential is generally not realized.

Overall, I think stepfamily members are best viewed as affines, much like parents-in-law or children-in-law. The relationship is created and sustained by a marriage; although affectionate relationships may develop, the primary impetus for exchange with the affine is to benefit or please the biological relative. When the marriage ends, the relationship falters or dies.

The fact that stepfamily ties are not interchangeable with biological ties does not mean that stepfamily ties are useless as sources of support. As Rossi and Rossi's (1990) data on perceived normative obligation to stepparents and stepchildren suggest, people in stepfamilies have weaker, but still important, family ties. Stepfamily members continue to keep track of one another and to exchange at above minimum level. Ties may be weak rather than strong, but a growing literature shows that we should not underestimate "the strength of weak ties" (Granovetter, 1973).

The question remains as to whether or not the proliferation of stepfamilies in contemporary society actually reduces family support. I think the general answer is yes, but that the strength of effect differs substantially by gender. Fathers and stepfathers are probably seriously disadvantaged. Divorced fathers tend to lose contact with their own children, yet fail to form enduring bonds with their stepchildren. In general, stepfathers will remain a part of their stepchildren's lives only as long as they remain married to the children's mother.

Stepmothers and their stepchildren are probably the most serious losers in stepfamily relationships. From both child's and parent's points of view, the family with a stepmother fares worse than that with a stepfather. Several explanations can be offered for this finding. Stepmother families may have a weaker foundation because of the generally poorer relationship between the child and the custodial parent.

A second possibility is that it is harder to fill the role of mother than father. Although one can be a decent father by being a good provider and a nice guy, filling an absent mother's shoes requires establishing gut-level empathy and attachment that may be more difficult to develop or fake. I would also like to raise the possibility that, although sociobiologists have focused on stepfathers because female animals seldom inherit their mates' offspring from previous unions, it is females more than males for whom the distinction between own and step is most critical.

Those least affected by stepfamily proliferation are biological, custodial mothers and their own children. Mothers who have remarried report moderately weaker bonds to their own adult children than mothers in intact marriages (White, 1992; see also Table 9.1), but their relationships are least affected by marital disruption and remarriage.

IMPLICATIONS FOR RESEARCH AND THEORY

The problem of social support in stepfamilies is not an insignificant one. Glick (1990) estimated that 14% of all U.S. children under 18 live with a stepparent at the present time, and that 30%–40% of today's children will live in a stepfamily sometime before they reach 19 (Glick, 1989). Another significant portion will experience parental remarriage in middle age after the parent is widowed.

This chapter has scratched the surface of some of the most critical areas of stepfamily support in adult stepfamilies. Much more needs to be done, and several areas of stepfamily relationships have not been touched upon at all. For example, a small literature exists on relationships between grandparents and their children's stepchildren, but no research has examined relationships between the senior generation and their stepchildren's children. Similarly, a review of social science journals on aging found almost no studies that distinguished between step- and own children. Although there is a growing concern that falling fertility may reduce the number of potential helpers (e.g., Brody, 1990), no attention has been addressed to the issue that stepfamilies may reduce support availability.

An important group that has not been touched upon here is stepfamilies formed after the child has grown up, sometimes by late remarriage after divorce, but more often by parental remarriage following widowhood. Is your elderly father's new wife your stepmother? How does a parent's remarriage restructure ties to his or her own children? Are the effects dependent on whether the new spouse has biological children or on the gender of the parent? Based on the analysis reviewed here, it seems likely that late-life stepfamilies face serious dilemmas. At this end of the life course, the issue often revolves around the age-old problem of inheritance (Collins, 1991), with children worried that their inheritance will go to the new spouse, or even the new spouse's children, rather than themselves. It is an issue that is fraught with opportunities for significant intergenerational conflict (Sussman, 1985).

Although it is correct to focus our most immediate research on young children, stepfamilies form and reform across the entire life course. Perhaps we can spare some attention to focus on the issues of stepchildren ages 18–80.

METHODOLOGICAL APPENDIX

Sample Information

The analysis of parent–child exchange is drawn from the National Survey of Families and Households conducted in 1987–1988. This survey was funded by grant no. DH 21009 from the Center for Population Research of the National Institute of Child Health and Human Development. A detailed description of design and results is found in Sweet, Bumpass, and Call (1988). The fieldwork was done by the Institute for Survey Research at Temple University.

This study includes personal interviews with a national probability sample of 13,017 respondents, representing the noninstitutionalized population of the United States. The response rate was 73.5%. The survey oversampled minority groups, single parents, cohabitors, persons with stepchildren in the household, and the recently married. The analysis reported here is weighted to compensate for differential probabilities of selection due to oversampling, household size, and differential response rates. (Because the analysis focuses on adult stepchildren no longer living in their parents' households, the standard weight— adjusting for the oversampling of households with stepchildren in them—is used.) The sample has also been weighted to make it match the age, race, and sex composition of the U.S. sample reported by the Current Population Survey.

The analysis of children's reports on relationships with parents is restricted to respondents with at least one living parent (step or biological) who were not living in a household containing any type of parent at the time of interview. In addition, analysis was restricted to respondents whose experiences could be organized into one of the four family structure types noted in the text.

Questions about family experiences while growing up occurred in both the main questionnaire and the self-enumerated booklet, and the answers do not always agree. Of 1,047 persons who reported having lived with a stepparent prior to age 19 in the family history chart, 5% denied it in the self-enumerated booklet, and another 3% recorded "don't know" or "refuse." Another 125 persons reported in the self-enumerated booklet that they had lived with a stepparent despite having no record of same in the family history chart. These may be individuals who lived with a stepparent after the age of 19 or individuals who lived with a stepparent for fewer than 4 months (the time frame used on the family history chart). Because the analysis includes information from both the family history chart (age at which stepparent acquired, sex of stepparent) and the self-enumerated booklet, only individuals who reported a stepparent in both places can be included in the analyses.

For the analyses of parents' reports on individual children, a separate file was created for each adult child not living with the parent who was listed as a child on the main interview, and for whom information on step status was available. The resulting file contained 8,691 children, of whom 967 (11%) were stepchildren. Only 2% of the children had no usable data on contact with parents, but nearly 20% were missing data for relationship quality and exchange, measures which came from the self-enumerated booklet, rather than from the main questionnaire. Due to an error in the NSFH questionnaire, approximately 15% of the sample were missing data on child's sex. Because the number of cases is large and because child's sex is important in parent–child exchange, these cases were excluded. On measures of contact and relationship quality, the rate of missing data was not higher for stepchildren than for biological children. On the two measures of exchange, however, missing values were more than twice as high for stepchildren (40% vs. 16%). Given that all questions explicitly instructed the respondent to include stepchildren in the listings, it is surprising to find such a high level of missing data.

Measures

Dependent Variables. For both parents and children, *relationship quality* was assessed by a single-item measure that asked respondents to describe their relationship on a 7-point scale ranging from *very poor* (1) to *excellent* (7). This question was asked for each child and stepchild, for each biological parent, and, if respondent had ever lived with a stepparent, for one stepparent. Instructions specified that, in cases of more than one stepparent, the respondent should choose the stepparent lived with the longest. The same criteria carried through questions about stepparent contact.

Contact was the mean of two questions asking about frequency of seeing the other and frequency of talking to the other. Both were 6-point scales varying from *not at all* (1) to *several times a week* (6) When only one question was answered, this answer was used as the measure. In the case of fathers and stepparents, contact may be overestimated. Apparently on the assumption (perhaps supported by pretests) that contact is similar for all household members, the questionnaire did not ascertain contact for biological fathers living with biological mothers or for stepparents who were still living with the biological parent. In analyses reported here, contact with the mother/biological parent was substituted in the appropriate places. The assumption of similar contact is probably much weaker for stepfamilies.

Perceived social support was a dummy variable indicating whether respondent volunteered that "a parent" was who he/she would call in any of three types of emergencies: "an emergency in the middle of the night and [you] needed help," "you had to borrow $200 for a few weeks because of an emergency," or "you had a problem, and you were feeling depressed or confused about what to do."

Respondents were asked about *support given* and *support received* from "parents." No instructions were given about who to include as parents. Individual questions asked about help with baby-sitting or childcare, transportation, repairs, work around the house, or advice and emotional support in the last month, and whether a loan or gift of $200 or more had been given or received in the last 2 years. In addition to looking at each type of support individually, dummy variables indicated those who gave any support or received any support versus those who gave or received none.

Parents were asked a similar set of questions, but about each of their children and stepchildren separately. Parents were asked whether the child did any of the following on a regular basis: listens to parent's problems, provides news about mutual friends and family, helps out with household tasks (including transportation), provides financial assistance, or provides companionship. Parents were asked whether they or their spouse: listen to problems, provide news, help with household tasks, help with childcare, financial assistance, or companionship. Again, dummy variables were used to distinguish exchangers from those who gave/received nothing.

Stepfamily Characteristics.   For respondents who reported that they did not live with both biological parents through age 19, a family history chart recorded living arrangements for every year of age. The chart was scanned to find the first year in which respondent lived with a stepparent to code age at stepfamily formation. Sex of stepparent was determined by counting number of years lived with a stepmother and a stepfather (in almost all cases, there was only one stepparent) and assigning the sex of the stepparent with whom the respondent lived the longest. Presence of step-/half siblings was a direct yes/no question asking whether respondents had "any stepbrothers or stepsisters of half-brothers or half-sisters who lived with you while you were growing up?" For children's reports, *step status* was assigned if they recorded any stepparent living on the family history chart or they gave an affirmative to the direct question, "Have you ever lived with a stepparent?" When parental reports were analyzed, step status was determined by answers to the direct question, "Is (CHILD) your child or a step-child?"

Control Variables. Race and ethnicity were coded through two dummy variables identifying African-Americans and Latinos; nonHispanic Whites were the omitted group. Sex of child and parent was coded 1 = female, 0 = male. Ages of child and parent were coded as continuous variables.

ACKNOWLEDGMENTS

I would like to thank Naomi Lacy for providing bibliographic assistance.

REFERENCES

Aquilino, W. S. (1990). The likelihood of parent–adult child coresidence: Effects of family structure and parental characteristics. *Journal of Marriage and the Family, 52,* 405–419.

Aquilino, W. S. (1991a). Family structure and home-leaving: A further specification of the relationship. *Journal of Marriage and the Family, 53,* 999–1010.

Aquilino, W. S. (1991b). Predicting parents' experiences with coresident adult children. *Journal of Family Issues, 12,* 323–342.

Astin, A., Korn, W., & Berg, E. (1989). *The American freshman: National norms for Fall 1989.* Los Angeles: University of California, Los Angeles, American Council on Education.

Atkinson, M. (1989). Conceptualizations of the parent–child relationship: Solidarity, attachment, crescive bonds, and identity salience. In J. Mancini (Ed.), *Aging parents and adult children* (pp. 81–97). Lexington, MA: Lexington.

Axelrod, R. (1984). *The evolution of cooperation.* New York: Basic Books.

Bartlema, J. (1988). Modeling step-families: Exploratory findings. *European Journal of Population, 4,* 197–221.

Brody, E. M. (1990). *Women in the middle: Their parent-care years.* New York: Springer.

Carley, K. (1991). A theory of group stability. *American Sociological Review, 56,* 331–354.

Cherlin, A. (1978). Remarriage as an incomplete institution. *American Journal of Sociology, 84,* 634–649.

Collins, S. (1991). British stepfamily relationships, 1500–1800. *Journal of Family History, 16,* 331–344.

Daly, M., & Wilson, M. (1978). *Sex, evolution, and behavior.* North Scituate, MA: Duxbury.

Day, A. T. (1988). Kinship networks and informal support in the later years. In E. Grebenik, C. Hohn, & R. Mackensen (Eds.), *Later phases of the family cycle: Demographic aspects* (pp. 184–207). Oxford, England: Clarendon.

Dobash, R. P., Dobash, R. E., Wilson, M., & Daly, M. (1992). The myth of sexual symmetry in marital violence. *Social Problems, 39,* 71–91.

Eggebeen, D. J. (1992). Family structure and intergenerational exchanges. *Research on Aging, 14,* 427–447.

Ekeh, P. (1974). *Social exchange theory: The two traditions.* Cambridge, MA: Harvard University Press.

Finch, J. (1989). *Family obligations and social change*. Oxford, England: Polity Press.

Fine, M. A. (1986). Perceptions of stepparents: Variation in stereotypes as a function of current family structure. *Journal of Marriage and the Family, 48*, 537–543.

Fine, M. A., & Fine, D. R. (1992). Recent changes in laws affecting stepfamilies: Suggestions for legal reform. *Family Relations, 44*, 334–340.

Finkelhor, D. (1979). *Sexually victimized children*. New York: The Free Press.

Fischer, C. (1982). *To dwell among friends: Personal networks in town and city*. Chicago: University of Chicago Press.

Fluitt, M. S., & Paradise, L. V. (1991). The relationship of current family structure to young adults' perceptions of stepparents. *Journal of Divorce and Remarriage, 15*, 159–173.

Furstenberg, F. F., Jr., & Spanier, G. (1984). *Recycling the family: Remarriage after divorce*. Beverly Hills, CA: Sage.

Glick, P. C. (1989). Remarried families, stepfamilies, and stepchildren: A brief demographic profile. *Family Relations, 38*, 24–27.

Glick, P. C. (1990). American families: As they are and were. *Sociology and Social Research, 74*, 139–145.

Goldscheider, F. K., & Goldscheider, C. (1991). The intergenerational flow of income: Family structure and the status of black Americans. *Journal of Marriage and the Family, 53*, 499–508.

Goldscheider, F. K., & Goldscheider, C. (1993). *Leaving home before marriage: Ethnicity, familism, and generational relationships*. Madison: University of Wisconsin Press.

Granovetter, M. (1973). The strength of weak ties. *American Journal of Sociology, 78*, 1360–1380.

House, J. S., Umberson, D., & Landis, K. R. (1988). Structures and processes of social support. *Annual Review of Sociology, 14*, 293–318.

Kiernan, K. (1992). The impact of family disruption in childhood on transitions made in young adult life. *Population Studies, 46*, 218–234.

Knoke, D. (1990). Networks of political action: Toward theory construction. *Social Forces, 68*, 1041–1063.

Kulis, S. S. (1992). Social class and the locus of reciprocity in relationships with adult children. *Journal of Family Issues, 13*, 482–504.

McLanahan, S., & Bumpass, L. (1988). Intergenerational consequences of family disruption. *American Journal of Sociology, 94*, 130–152.

Mitchell, B. A., Wister, A. V., & Burch, T. K. (1989). The family environment and leaving the parental home. *Journal of Marriage and the Family, 52*, 605–613.

Rossi, A. S. (1984). Gender and parenthood. *American Sociological Review, 49*, 1–18.

Rossi, A. S., & Rossi, P. H. (1990). *Of human bonding: Parent–child relations across the life course*. Hawthorne, NY: Aldine de Gruyter.

Schwebel, A. I., Fine, M. A., & Renner, M. A. (1991). A study of perceptions of the stepparent role. *Journal of Family Issues, 12*, 43–57.

Speare, A., Jr., & Avery, R. (1993). Who helps whom in older parent–child families? *Journal of Gerontology, 48*(2), S64–73.

Sussman, M. B. (1985). The family life of old people. In R. S. Binstock & E. Shanas (Eds.), *Handbook of aging and the social sciences* (2nd ed., pp. 415–443). New York: Van Nostrand.

Sweet, J., Bumpass, L., & Call, V. (1988). *The design and content of the National Survey of Families and Households* (Working Paper No. NSFH-1). Madison: University of Wisconsin, Center for Demography and Ecology.

Thoits, P. A. (1992). Identity structures and psychological well-being: Gender and marital status comparisons. *Social Psychology Quarterly, 55*, 236–256.

Troll, L., Miller, S. J., & Atchley, R. C. (1979). *Families in later life*. Belmont, CA: Wadsworth.

Turner, R. H. (1970). *Family interaction*. New York: Wiley.

Waggoner, L. W., Wellman, R. V., Alexander, G. S., & Fellows, M. L. (1991). *Family property law: Cases and materials on wills, trusts, and future interests*. Westbury, NY: Foundation Press.

Wald, E. (1981). *The remarried family: Challenge and promise*. New York: Family Service Association of America.

White, L. K. (1992). The effect of parental divorce and remarriage on parental support for adult children. *Journal of Family Issues, 13*, 234–250.

White, L. K., & Booth, A. (1985). The quality and stability of remarriages: The role of stepchildren. *American Sociological Review, 50*, 689–698.

White, L. K., & Riedmann, A. C. (1992a). When the Brady Bunch grows up: Relations between fullsiblings and stepsiblings in adulthood. *Journal of Marriage and the Family, 54*, 197–208.

White, L. K., & Riedmann, A. C. (1992b). Ties among adult siblings. *Social Forces, 71*, 85–102.

10

Conceptual and Methodological Issues in the Study of Stepfamilies Over the Life Course

Teresa M. Cooney
University of Delaware

White's chapter reviews a comprehensive array of theoretical perspectives, all leading to the conclusion that supportive exchanges in step relationships are fewer and weaker than those occurring in intra- and intergenerational biological relationships. I found the introductory discussion quite provocative, and the empirical questions it raised were exciting to consider. Unfortunately, existing data do not permit a thorough testing of several of the issues raised in White's introduction. In light of this, I begin my comments with a discussion of some data problems that exist in the NSFH study and that underlie White's analysis. Following these comments, I move on to address, more extensively, a few conceptual issues her chapter raises, or, in some cases, skims over.

A CALL FOR BETTER DATA AND MORE DESCRIPTION

Although I commend White for her competent use of the NSFH data on stepfamily relationships, her analyses reflect the dearth of good data pertaining to adult members of stepfamilies. Certainly, the NSFH data are some of the best available for pursuing the questions posed, yet it is clear from the analyses that these data lack some much-needed specificity, and that their use requires the acceptance of some questionable assumptions.

My first concern centers on the issue of documenting respondents' experiences with a given stepparent over time. The NSFH required respondents to report, for each single year of age from birth until 19, whether they lived for over 4 months with both biological parents, a single parent and/or a stepfather or stepmother. Knowing nothing more about the marital history of the respondents' parents, these data are particularly limiting, since they place too much emphasis on shared residence of stepfamily members.

Specifically, this method fails to document the presence of a given stepparent in a child's life unless the two coresided for more than 4 months of any year. Clearly, one lesson that we have learned in our study of family life is that family relationships and family influences operate across household boundaries. Thus, for a child to have a relationship—either good or bad—with a stepparent, does not require that the two parties coreside. Children who maintain contact with their absent parents are likely to be exposed to any new partners who enter the picture, even cohabiting partners, as Thompson discussed previously. These contacts with the stepparent may be very influential even if they do not occur daily, or even in person. Thus, it is not surprising that White finds no connection between step relationship duration (indexed by the child's age when the two parties first began living together as step relations) and relationship quality or exchanges in stepfamilies, because by measuring relationship duration merely in terms of coresidence completely neglects a wide array of potentially important, nonresidential experiences that stepparents and children may share.

The importance of nonresidential step relationships is particularly salient to the specific questions raised in White's chapter because most adult offspring whose parents are remarried do not live within the stepfamily household. Whether one considers adult offspring whose parents remarried prior to their leaving home, or those for whom the remarriage occurred later in adulthood, it is the duration of the step relationship that is probably more influential than whether and how long the stepparent/stepchild ever lived together. Interestingly, White excludes from her analyses those cases in which a stepfamily situation appears to have been initiated after the child turned 20. Given the topic of the chapter, I think this was an especially unfortunate analytic decision, and I would have preferred to see this group in the analyses, as I suspect that their situation may be different than that of the groups that were included.

Aside from these issues pertaining directly to White's chapter, I want to raise a few more preliminary, descriptive questions that deserve research attention before much more hypothesis testing and theory building is undertaken. For example, I believe that research is needed that more clearly describes the typical experience of adult stepchildren and their stepparents, including such issues as: What percent of adults are stepchildren, or have been stepchildren at some point in adulthood? What is the average duration of the stepchild/stepparent relationship in adulthood? What is the average age at which individuals become stepchildren when the event occurs after childhood? What percent of adult stepchildren assume this status because of parental death versus divorce? What percent of adults have more than two parental figures in their lives because of parental remarriage?

Although these preliminary questions are certainly not very intriguing, their answers are extremely important, because as Bumpass (1984) pointed out, "An understanding of the demography of family life is an essential prerequisite for the sociology of the family, and of the life course of individuals as well as for the formulation of social policy" (p. 71).

It seems to me, that in some ways we have prematurely moved ahead to try and understand the sociology of older stepfamilies and consider policy issues that pertain to them, without having a good grip on what these families look like, demographically. In my opinion, before moving on to further investigation and policy development in this area, we need to discuss the demographic foundation that is needed to address this topic, and where relevant descriptive data can be found.

REMARRIAGE AS A SPECIAL CASE
OF ROLE TRANSITIONS

For the remainder of my comments, I want to shift to some conceptual issues, and in so doing, focus on remarriage as a special case of role transitions. In this section, I raise some conceptual issues that were glossed over in White's chapter, and try to highlight some of my points with data from my current 3-year, longitudinal study of young adults, ages 18–25, who have experienced recent parental divorce.[1]

In some of the earliest thinking on role transitions, van Gennep (1960) described the assumption of new social roles, or rites of passage, as involving three distinct phases: rites of separation, rites of transition, and rites of incorporation. Considering these specific stages of social transitions in regard to remarriage and stepfamily formation, highlights some of the central problems facing stepfamilies today. I limit my discussion to the first of these three phases—rites of separation—because consideration of this aspect of social transitions provides some particularly important insights for White's analyses.

The rites of separation that we recognize in stepfamily formation apply primarily to the marital couple. Before remarrying, formerly married persons legally, socially, and emotionally separate from the spousal role with their former partners. This process of separation, or role relinquishment, may be difficult for individuals because of the feelings of loss that often accompany it (Riley & Waring, 1976). However, this process is essential to the successful acquisition and acceptance of a new role. For, as Riley and Waring (1976) noted in regard to role transitions, "each time a new role must be taken on, an old one given up" (p. 381).

A central problem with step relations today, even more so than in the past, because remarriage is now more commonly the result of divorce rather than

---

[1]This research is supported by Grant #1 R29 MH46946 awarded to the author from the National Institute of Mental Health.

spousal death (Uhlenberg & Chew, 1986), is that the parent and child roles that accompany this transition are not replacement roles but, rather, additional roles for most people. For both stepparents and stepchildren, the task to be accomplished during the separation phase of this role transition is not learning to give up rewards and responsibilities that were part of past roles now discarded, but to make room for new, added responsibilities and relationships.

Consequently, to understand the dynamics occurring in a particular step relationship, one needs to consider the entire set of additional biological family relationships, because they constitute competing roles for the step relationship. In my view, White's analyses fall short in doing this. The analysis she reports in Table 9.5 is the only one in which we see some aspect of additional biological relationships considered in predicting the support exchanged in current step relationships. In line with the theorizing I just presented about competing roles, the analysis reported in Table 9.5 seems to suggest that having biological children, in addition to stepchildren, inhibits stepparents' supportive exchanges with their stepchildren. It is puzzling to me why none of the other tabled analyses include predictor variables that refer to other important, competing, biological relationships. The most obvious variables missing from these analyses are those that refer to the stepchild's relationship with the outside noncustodial parent.

Given the theorizing about the necessity for role relinquishment when assuming new roles, I think White should have looked more directly at factors competing against the step relationship by examining stepchildren's relationship quality and contact with their biological parent in the respective relationship. My hunch is that these outside relationships may have a significant, negative influence on the step relationships of interest. For example, adult children who have little contact with their biological, divorced fathers and low levels of affective closeness to them, may be more accepting of a new stepfather and more willing to establish an active, caring relationship with him, than would adult offspring who are close to and actively involved with their biological fathers. The former group may find it easier to relinquish their roles and relations with the respective biological parent as they adopt their new roles of stepchildren. The same may apply for stepparents; in fact, the findings I mentioned earlier from Table 9.5 offer preliminary support for this notion.

Another role-related concept that I find particularly useful in thinking about divorce and stepfamily formation, is that of countertransitions. Originally referred to as counterpart transitions by Riley and Waring (1976), countertransitions are role transitions that occur to individuals involuntarily, as the result of more voluntary role transitions made by someone with whom they are closely associated.

Parental divorce and remarriage constitute important countertransitions for offspring. These parental transitions demand children to adjust to many new roles in their own lives, as well as to make room for their parents' newly chosen roles and commitments. The involuntary nature of countertransitions is especially important. With regard to parental divorce and remarriage, it is this aspect of countertransitions that often leaves children—even adult ones—feeling like helpless victims of their parents' actions. These feelings of helplessness are likely to be acted out in subsequent family interactions and relationships.

Parental divorce, followed by remarriage, is likely to have even more serious consequences for parent–child relationships than just parental divorce, because of the added number of countertransitions offspring are forced to confront. Because of this, I want to emphasize how important it is not to downplay the added effects of remarriage (in addition to divorce) on family relationships. Although it is true, as White notes, that some of the problems observed in stepfamilies result from the initial divorce and from living in a single-parent household, many other outcomes are very specific to the remarriage situation, including problematic aspects of the parent–child relationship.

My data reveal some fairly clear differences between the parent–child relationships of youth with married, divorced and remarried parents, particularly in the period immediately following remarriage. In Table 10.1, mean parent–child intimacy scores are separated by parents' marital status, for each of the two waves of my study. The first wave was conducted within 15 months of parental divorce (when the youth were ages 18–23), and the second wave followed 2

TABLE 10.1.
Wave 1 and 2 Parent–Child Intimacy Scores, by Parents' Marital Status

		Wave 1	Wave 2
Mother's marital status			
Continuously married	M	56.05 ($n = 227$)$_a$	56.32 ($n = 199$)
	SD	4.52	4.20
Divorced	M	55.63 ($n = 215$)$_a$	56.14 ($n = 192$)
	SD	6.08	5.83
Remarried	M	53.89 ($n = 38$)$_b$	54.72 ($n = 25$)
	SD	6.69	6.31
F		2.55*	1.06
Father's marital status			
Continuously married	M	54.83 ($n = 227$)$_a$	55.10 ($n = 199$)$_a$
	SD	5.68	5.44
Divorced	M	50.85 ($n = 197$)$_b$	50.71 ($n = 163$)$_{b,c}$
	SD	9.83	10.65
Remarried	M	48.03 ($n = 59$)$_c$	52.77 ($n = 48$)$_{a,c}$
	SD	11.87	6.69
F		20.68**	13.12**

Note. Means having the same subscript are not significantly different from one another at $p = .05$.
*$p < .10$.   **$p < .001$.

years later. In terms of mother–child intimacy, youth with remarried mothers reported significantly lower intimacy scores than youth whose mothers were either continuously married or divorced (Wave 1, $p < .08$). At Time 2, the significance of this finding no longer held with mothers, although the ordering of group means still placed relations with remarried mothers lowest on the scale. Of course, these results might be due to the comparatively small n for the remarried group.

The negative effects of remarriage are more impressive with regard to fathers. According to the figures for Wave 1, youth with continuously married fathers report the closest relationships with them, followed by those with divorced fathers, and then by those with remarried fathers. Differences between each of the groups are significant ($p < .05$). At Time 2, youth with divorced and remarried fathers do not report significantly different levels of intimacy with them, although those with divorced fathers do score significantly lower than those with continuously married fathers.

In an open-ended, follow-up question to this scale, I asked my respondents to describe the major changes they had experienced in relationships with their mothers and fathers since high school. Some of the specific problems that emerge from remarriage and stepfamily formation were evident in their responses. One respondent reported that the father, "has a new family [and] I am not important." Another reported that "his wife won't (let) him contact his kids, and he's accepted this." Comments pertaining to maternal remarriage tended to focus on unfavorable qualities of the mother's new partner. One young woman reported that her mother's new boyfriend has "hands for me," and although her mother had not yet remarried, this man already was creating problems in the mother–daughter relationship.

One gets the sense from these qualitative accounts that not only parental divorce, but subsequent remarriage, forces new situations and people into the lives of these youth, and many of them are not readily accepting of such changes. Thus, it is not surprising that studies like White's find weaker and less positive relationships between stepchildren and stepparents when the perspective of the stepchild is taken. The stepchild has much less choice in the assumption of the step role than does the stepparent. Stepparents voluntarily enter into marriage, fully aware of the presence of stepchildren. And, although they might prefer not to blend their new marital role with a new stepparental role, in marrying a particular partner they have made an active choice to do so. On the other hand, for stepchildren, there is no choice in assuming the new step status, and thus the only way for them to express their feelings about this transition is through the role behavior they adopt. Refusing to get involved with the new stepparent is surely one way to make known one's displeasure with the countertransition, as is distancing oneself physically and emotionally from the remarried parent.

Children of divorce and remarriage, even adult ones, seem willing to punish their parents if they feel their parents have wronged them. We see this in their reports of weakened closeness to the parents, like those I just presented, and also through reduced obligation to their parents, which White also discusses in her chapter.

Table 10.2 illustrates the markedly different levels of association that exist between contact and intimacy (or affect) for youth and their parents in intact versus divorced families. Based on the reports of my respondents, one gets the clear sense that intimacy and contact are, for the most part, unrelated in intact families, as the top panel of Table 10.2 demonstrates (sons above the diagonal,

TABLE 10.2.
Correlations (& Ns) Between Intimacy and Contact[a] Dimensions,
Within Parent–Child Dyads[b], and Between Mother–Child (MC)
and Father–Child (FC) Dyads, by Parents' Marital Status

	Parents Married			
	MC Intimacy	MC Contact	FC Intimacy	FC Contact
MC intimacy		.398** (51)	.254** (109)	−.040 (52)
MC contact	.227 (51)		−.196 (51)	.547** (52)
FC intimacy	.451** (110)	−.123 (51)		−.014 (52)
FC contact	.209 (53)	.401** (51)	.120 (53)	

	Parents Divorced			
	MC Intimacy	MC Contact	FC Intimacy	FC Contact
MC intimacy		.355** (77)	.197* (110)	.100 (90)
MC contact	.533** (106)		−.014 (77)	.011 (58)
FC intimacy	−.058 (151)	.012 (109)		.507** (90)
FC contact	.006 (134)	.109 (96)	.572** (136)	

Note. From "Young Adults' Relations with Parents: The Influence of Recent Parental Divorce" by T. M. Cooney (1994) *Journal of Marriage and the Family, 56,* 45–56.

[a]Correlations involving a contact variable are only computed for those not living with that particular parent.

[b]Sons above the diagonal and daughters below the diagonal.

*p < .05.   **p < .01.

daughters below). That suggests to me that obligation is still a driving force behind interaction in intact families, as sociologists and anthropologists have argued. But, the bottom panel of this table tells a very different story for divorced families (and the same holds true in remarried families, although the data are not shown here). In these families, intimacy and contact are highly correlated, which suggests that forced association due to obligation is not at work in most divorced families. Intimacy, or affect, seems to be the driving force behind contact.

I end with a quote from a college student I interviewed 10 years ago, when I first began to study divorce while in graduate school here at Penn State. In interviewing this student about his parents' recent divorce, I asked him about his feelings of obligation to his father. This young man's comments illustrate how parental divorce can hurt intergenerational relations, but more importantly, they reflect the feelings of betrayal and weakened obligation to the father that divorce and remarriage create. He said:

> The way I looked at it, it was my father betraying my mother . . . I thought that marriage was supposed to be for a lifetime . . . and when I found out my father had been cheating on my mother, I saw no excuse for that whatsoever. . . . I didn't speak to my dad for a period of 9 to 10 months because I didn't believe that he should have the satisfaction of having the love that a child should have for his parent.

Although this comment may not be representative of the reactions of most adults to parental divorce and remarriage, I think it reflects the psychology underlying some of the negative reactions we observe in stepfamilies involving older offspring.

REFERENCES

Bumpass, L. L. (1984). Children and marital disruption: A replication and update. *Demography*, *21*, 71–82.

Cooney, T. M. (1994). Young adults' relations with parents: The influence of recent parental divorce. *Journal of Marriage and the Family*, *56*, 45–56.

Gennep, A. van (1960). *The rites of passage*. Chicago: University of Chicago Press.

Riley, M. W., & Waring, J. (1976). Age and aging. In R. Merton & R. Nisbet (Eds.), *Contemporary social problems* (4th ed., pp. 355–410). New York: Harcourt Brace.

Uhlenberg, P., & Chew, K. S. Y. (1986). The changing place of remarriage in the life course. *Current Perspectives on Aging and the Life Cycle*, *2*, 23–52.

11 Stepfamilies: Selectivity of High-Risk Persons or Risk State?

Dennis P. Hogan
Pennsylvania State University

In chapter 9, White ably fulfills her assigned task of going beyond stereotypes about stepfamilies to determine who gains and who loses intergenerational social support in stepfamilies. Besides providing an excellent summary of the diverse interdisciplinary literature in this area, White provides an informative description of social support in stepfamilies of various configurations. The conceptual and empirical work in her chapter thus provides the groundwork for future, more focused and theory-driven studies of intergenerational social support in stepfamilies.

WHAT IS PARENTHOOD?

During 1993, there were a number of prominent child custody cases. These ranged from a case of adoptive parents who raised a child from birth, forfeiting their adopted daughter to the biological mother who had changed her mind about adoption, to the case of a child switched at birth and raised by others. While the legal system still relies most heavily on the biological definition of parenthood, recent advances in reproductive biology call this standard into question. What the chapters in this volume suggest is that the United States is moving toward the recognition that a parent is the person who works at being a parent day in and day out, providing an adequate home, caring for the child, and offering a secure, nurturant environment. White shows that the parent–child affective bond strengthens cumulatively over time and with experience, becoming an integral part of the identity of the parent and child. It is in this context that the perceived access to social support is more important to mental health than the actual provision of support.

White suggests that stepfamily roles that are of shorter duration can be more easily terminated, and because they are only vaguely defined by social norms and institutions, are inherently weaker than biological parent ties. But where the nonbiological parent behaves more like a parent than the biological one, definitions of parenthood can depart markedly from the legal standard. Furthermore, the effects of gender, duration of stepparenthood, and stability of the stepfamily are all consistent with the idea that stepparents who work at being parents are more often perceived as some form of such. This is especially true if there are no other biological children of the stepparent competing for resources. This behavioral difference, which we now measure only poorly in our studies, is probably a critical source of variation in who benefits and who does not in stepparent families.

IS A STEPFATHER MORE THAN AN INCOME GENERATOR?

Research on the consequences of divorce suggests that the major impact of father absence after a divorce is the economic loss suffered by the mother and the household she now heads (Angel & Angel, 1993; Cherlin et al., 1991; Garfinkel & McLanahan, 1986). Other social and mental outcomes follow on the income loss. These negative outcomes diminish over several years if the mother gains an independent financial footing, the family adjusts to its lower income, or the mother remarries.

White shows that the role of stepfather is much more common than the role of stepmother, and that such homes are generally more functional than other configurations. This is especially the case for stepfathers who lack biological children. Yet these stepfathers are the ones who, on average, are able to provide the stepfamily household with the greatest income. A stepfather with noncustodial biological children elsewhere must divide his earnings between his new family and alimony and child support for his prior family.

How are decisions about income allocation made? To find out, we need to collect detailed information on time allocation, income and expenses, and distribution of consumption in biological parent(s) and stepfamily households. It is possible that the lowered income of the stepfamily household (because of the need to support non-coresidential family) creates a fall in the standard of living that creates family stress. Elder's (1974) work on the Great Depression suggests that the level of stress in response to income loss will vary by class and by perceptions of appropriate gender roles. Decisions about the allocation of funds to custodial stepchildren and noncustodial children may be the source of tension in the household, tension that White identifies as critical to understanding some of the parent–child tension in stepfamilies.

This raises the possibility that the differences in kin ties and support White observes for different types of stepfamily configurations are a function of variations in economic contributions. The alternative explanation is that the differences are due to the limited extent to which some kind of stepfathers work at being fathers. White seems to emphasize the economic argument. She suggests that fathers do relatively little in families except earn an income and stay out of the way: "Although one can be a decent father by being a good provider and a nice guy. . . . " On the other hand, she also hints that the reason that stepmother families may appear to be more problematic than stepfather families lies with the gender of the biological parent, fathers being unable to form the necessary affective links. Future research must address these alternatives.

THE FATHER–CHILD LINK

Although most studies have focused on the mother–child link, it is critical that we better understand the father–child link, with particular attention to whether or not it, in fact, matters. We need to conduct studies (perhaps using the methods popularized by Rossi & Rossi, 1990) to determine what people expect fathers to do. We also need to get this information for people in particular roles—what fathers expect, what mothers expect, and what children (sons and daughters, both young and grown) expect.

Following studies of the normative expectations of fatherhood, we need to get measures of the economic contributions of fathers and stepfathers—financial contributions from all sources, and all expenses (including alimony and child support). We also need to better measure what responsibilities fathers and stepfathers take for child care: Do they help bathe the child, dress the child, play sports with the child, serve as a ball team coach? How often do stepfathers, compared to biological fathers, teach hunting, fishing, or car repair skills to their adolescent sons and stepsons? How do stepfathers with noncustodial children allocate their time to these activities? Rather than speculate on father–stepdaughter sexual tension and conflict, we need to study the sources of the conflict, its frequency and intensity, and its implications for the mother–stepfather relationship.

Some comparative information would be helpful in this regard. Are those same socioeconomic status and age groups in which fathers are involved in raising their child, also involved in the care of stepchildren? Are older men with young wives more involved in the child care of children and stepchildren than they were when they were younger? Do population groups in which marriage is regarded as a serious, lifetime commitment do better in a second marriage (having failed once), or do they fare more poorly at stepparenting? Finally, an important but largely neglected topic is the way in which the parent and stepparent met each other and became romantically involved. Did it occur after the first marriage, or was it a factor in that marriage ending? The impact of this factor may depend on the gender of the child and biological parent, and the age of the child.

STEPFAMILIES AND STEPFAMILY HOUSEHOLDS

Besides getting much more information on life in the stepfamily household, it is essential that we learn to pay much greater attention to non-coresidential parents and family. What is the consequence of having one instead of two sets of stepfamilies, or of being in a single-parent home? Are any measured results due to financial loss associated with divorce, parental stress from an unexpectedly large number of children to raise, or to less frequent contact and weaker affective bonds? This conference is on stepfamilies rather than stepfamily households. But, as in much of family research, this distinction is too often muddled. If fathers matter in ways other than as income generator, attention to noncustodial parents and stepparents is essential.

THE SELECTIVITY ISSUE

Even though they are becoming increasingly common, stepfamilies result from a series of very selective processes. Most commonly, stepfamily households will consist of a parent and stepparent who were previously married, and went on to have children. They are then selective of the divorced (with the stepparent as well as the parent subject to this risk). Then the parent and stepparent have married. Recent research by Cherlin et al. (1991) provides strong evidence that many of the supposed sequelae of divorce are due to the kind of marriage—and family experiences in that marriage—that lead to a divorce. In the case of stepfamilies, those formed as a result of an adulterous relationship may be permanently scarred by lack of trust between the parents, the parent and stepparent, the parent and child, or the child and the stepparent. Sexual conflict between a stepfather and stepdaughter might be accentuated in this situation.

The most common form of stepfamily is one that is formed by the marriage of a single or divorced woman with children and a man. The unmarried woman with children is in a very unfavorable marriage market position. Demographic theory would lead us to expect that she would form a poorer match (one that departs from the ideal) in order to marry again. The new husband might differ more in age, have an inferior education or occupational level, or be a relatively poor income generator. On average, then, it is likely that the stepfather is more poorly positioned for the breadwinner role, and may not be trusted for an affective role. This would seriously undermine the remarriage, and create conflict in the household that exacerbates the difficulty stepfathers face. In this way, economic stress in a family arising from the greater economic burdens of both a coresidential and a non-coresidential family, and from the relatively poor earning power of the stepfather, could predispose stepfamilies to conflict and disruption.

On the other hand, our research in this area does not seem to capture the advantages that attract remarriage and produce stepfamilies. White suggests that the earlier marriage of children from stepfamily households may be a way to escape. This is possible. But it is also possible that the child of a parent who has been married more than once considers marriage a normal and desirable state. Unless we learn why couples remarry, and the extent to which they will sacrifice marriage market preferences to remarry, our assumptions are not at all well-grounded.

Clearly, we have only begun to explore stepfamilies. But White gives us a sound beginning, from which we can proceed for more carefully conceptualized and designed studies of stepfamilies.

REFERENCES

Angel, R., & Angel, J. L. (1993). *Painful inheritance: Health and the new generation of fatherless families*. Madison: University of Wisconsin Press.

Cherlin, A. J., Furstenberg, F. F., Jr., Chase-Lansdale, P. L., Kiernan, K. E., Robins, P. K., Morrison, D. R., & Teitler, J. O. (1991). Longitudinal studies of effects of divorce on children in Great Britain and the United States. *Science*, 252, 1386–1389.

Elder, G. H., Jr. (1974). *Children of the Great Depression*. Chicago: University of Chicago Press.

Garfinkel, I., & McLanahan, S. S. (1986). *Single mothers and their children*. Washington, DC: Urban Institute Press.

Rossi, A. S., & Rossi, P. H. (1990). *Of human bonding: Parent–child relations across the life course*. New York: Aldine de Gruyter.

12 Intergenerational Ties in Adulthood and Childhood Experience

Judith A. Seltzer
University of Wisconsin—Madison

White's research and the work of the other authors and their colleagues (Cooney & Uhlenberg, 1990, 1992; Eggebeen & Hogan, 1990; Hogan, Eggebeen, & Clogg, 1993) provided a great deal of food for thought about parent–child relationships and the effects of stepfamily membership on exchanges between generations. Motivated by their work, I consider three questions: Is there a difference between step- and original families in the support that parents and adult children exchange? If so, what is the source of the difference? Finally, what questions should researchers address to elaborate an understanding of stepfamily relationships? To preview my conclusions, I see White's findings as suggestive, but incomplete. I propose ways to elaborate the analysis of intergenerational ties using existing survey data. Findings that stepfamilies exchange less support than original families, and that stepmother relationships are more troubled than those with stepfathers, are consistent with evidence from studies of parents and minor children. I argue that intergenerational exchanges in adulthood depend on behaviors rooted in younger families' experiences with divorce and remarriage.

IS THE DIFFERENCE BETWEEN STEP- AND ORIGINAL FAMILIES REAL?

White finds a small, but statistically significant difference between the contact and social support exchanged in stepfamilies and that exchanged between parents and children in original (biological) families. This finding has been replicated in several other studies, most of them also using data from the National Survey of Families and Households (NSFH). Despite the consistency of this finding, authors differ in their interpretation of the difference. White acknowledges that it is a small difference, but treats it as important in her speculations about what the pattern means for intergenerational relations, suggesting that this diminishes family support across our society. Aquilino (1993) reported a very similar finding, that remarried mothers have less contact with children and a lower quality relationship with children than do mothers in intact first marriages. Yet Aquilino essentially dismissed the finding, instead emphasizing the similarity between families with a stepparent and those with two biological parents. Whether to treat the small difference between step- and original families as a meaningful difference depends on whether we think that the finding is real, that is, whether it persists when we take account of other differences between step- and original families that might otherwise explain why the two differ on social support.

Alternative Explanations

There are two steps to evaluating the finding. The first is to ask whether the disadvantage of stepfamilies goes away when statistical controls are introduced to take account of other differences between step- and original families that might explain lower support in stepfamilies. Characteristics that might explain differences in social and economic support are dissimilarities between the two family types in the resources and needs of parents and of children. Resources and needs include such factors as number of children, ages of parents and children, marital status and whether the adult children have become parents, whether the older parents have another child still living with them, and the financial resources that stepparents and children control compared to those controlled by parents and children in original families. White does not consider many of these characteristics in the analysis for her chapter, but does take more of them into account in some of her other work with the NSFH (e.g., White, 1992). She documents that remarried parents provide less social support to adult children than do first-married parents, and that this difference persists even when differences in assets and numbers of children are taken into account. Other studies, for example, those by Aquilino (1993) and by Furstenberg, Hoffman, and Shrestha (1993), also found that, even after taking account of a wider array of family resources and needs, the lower levels of social and economic support exchanged between stepparents and children persisted. None of these analyses provides a full consideration of the relative resources and needs of parents and adult children in step- and original families, due in part, to limitations of existing data.

The availability of more complete information about parents and children in the 1992–1993 follow-up to the NSFH, as well as ongoing analyses of the detailed data in the 1988 wave of the Panel Study of Income Dynamics (e.g., Hill, Morgan, & Herzog, 1993), and of matched parents and children across cohorts of the National Longitudinal Surveys (e.g., Rosenzweig & Wolpin, 1993) provide an opportunity to elaborate investigations of alternative explanations for the lower level of support in stepfamilies. Improved measurement of differences in the resources and needs of stepfamilies compared to original families is likely to reduce the disadvantages of stepfamilies observed in studies to date.

Possible Bias in Sample Composition

The second step in evaluating the validity of White's finding of lower support in stepfamilies is to consider whether or not the sample she uses is biased in a way that would either deflate or inflate observed differences in the exchanges between stepparents and adult children, and those between biological parents and children. Serial monogamy, such as in the patterns of short-term marriage, divorce, and then remarriage in the United States, creates the potential for vast complexity in kin relationships (e.g., see Bartlema's, 1988, simulation). The question is whether the NSFH does a good job of identifying all of the stepparents and stepchildren of respondents. The NSFH data require a reasonably restricted definition of stepparents, and use a vague definition of stepchildren. Definitional problems work toward including step relationships that are more important to respondents and excluding those that are less important. As a result, analyses such as White's probably underestimate the differences between step- and original families.

Information about adult children's early experience of stepfamily living comes from the family history sequence, that asked respondents about periods during childhood when they lived with a stepparent for more than 4 months. Stepparents who marry a custodial parent live with their stepchildren, while stepparents who marry a noncustodial parent may see their stepchildren, but not live with them. Thus, the NSFH data underestimate the number of stepparents with whom adult children might be involved in exchanges. Studies of younger families show that minor children have little contact with noncustodial parents after separation, and that parents' remarriage reduced this contact (Furstenberg, Nord, Peterson, & Zill, 1983; Seltzer, 1991; Seltzer & Bianchi, 1988). This pattern suggests that stepparents with whom children do not share a period of co-residence are even less likely to give support to or receive support from adult children.

Parent respondents in the NSFH identify adult stepchildren by providing lists of all of their children by name. This strategy is reliable for determining the stepchildren who are salient to the respondent, but it runs the risk of omitting stepchildren who are not salient. The latter are considerably less likely to be in contact with the stepparent, let alone to be involved in exchanges with the stepparent. Identifying someone as a member of one's kin group reflects, in part, the degree of emotional attachment and involvement between the parties (e.g., Johnson, 1988). From both the perspective of the parent respondent and of the adult child respondent, then, the NSFH probably underrepresents stepfamilies in which the ties between parents and adult children are weak or do not exist at all. Thus, on balance, White's findings probably underestimate the relative lack of support in stepfamilies compared to original families.

VARIATION AMONG STEPFAMILIES

Intergenerational relationships vary among stepfamilies. The exclusion of less salient stepkin relationships and of stepparents and children who never lived together may also limit the observed variability of stepfamily relationships. This is because the data omit families or parent–child dyads at the extreme, low end of the distribution of involvement. Stepparents and children who are omitted are likely to have the worst relationships and to have little or no contact with each other. In contrast, the observed stepfamily respondents include both those with good and those with bad (but probably not the worst) relationships. Even with this qualification of limited sample coverage, White's findings suggest great variation among stepfamilies in the level of involvement and quality of relationships between parents and children. For instance, White reports that mean frequencies of contact between adult children and stepparents mask wide variation among stepfamilies, including large percentages of children who have no contact with stepparents, and others who have very frequent contact. That there is great variability in the quality and content of stepparent–child relationships is consistent with Rossi and Rossi's (1990) finding that individuals differ more in their beliefs about what obligations stepchildren and parents have to each other than about obligations between biological children and parents. Rossi and Rossi also showed that there is greater variation in people's understanding of obligations to stepchildren than to biological children.

Dimensions of Variation

Gender. Compared to men, women are more kin-oriented in their behavior, and they devote considerably more time and attention to rearing young children. Gender differences in stepparent–child relationships reflect these differences in women's and men's roles. Although most gender differences show greater obligations to female than male kin (Rossi & Rossi, 1990), and greater involvement of women in kin networks (Fischer, 1982; Hagestad, 1986; Roan, 1993), custody arrangements after divorce have a perverse effect on stepmothers' ties to stepchildren. Children usually live with their biological mother after a separation or divorce, and when their mother remarries, the children live with a stepfather. It is still unusual for children to live with biological fathers or biological fathers and stepmothers (see Seltzer, in press, for a review of residence patterns after divorce). Co-residence provides opportunities for intimacy and attachment that favor children's attachment to stepfathers, and hamper the development of bonds with stepmothers. Even in those rare families in which children do live with their father after separation, noncustodial mothers are more likely than noncustodial fathers to stay involved in their children's lives (Furstenberg et al., 1983; Seltzer & Bianchi, 1988). Similarly, divorced noncustodial mothers are more involved than noncustodial fathers in monitoring children's behavior and looking after the routine tasks of childrearing (Maccoby & Mnookin, 1992).

These patterns are at the root of adult children's lower quality of relationships with stepmothers (Aquilino, 1993). White found that adult children have higher quality relationships with their noncustodial biological mother and have more frequent contact with her than that which occurs in the relationship between an adult child and noncustodial biological father. She also showed that children who grew up in a stepmother household have very similar relationships with their stepmother and with their biological mother. However, children who grew up with a stepfather view their relationship with the stepfather as more positive than their relationship with their noncustodial biological father. That adult children are more likely to be involved with two mothers (their biological mother and their stepmother) than they are to be involved with two fathers, suggests that stepmother families may have to manage more conflict over role obligations than stepfather families (Ihinger-Tallman, 1988); this conflict may account for the lower levels of support received by children in stepmother families compared to stepfather families. Studies of younger families show that the custodial biological parent plays an important role in mediating a minor child's relationship to a stepparent (e.g., Marsiglio, 1992). Mothers may be more adept at this than fathers, and this gender difference in the way that the stepparent is introduced to the child, may also explain why stepfather relationships appear to be of higher quality than stepmother relationships in adulthood. White could begin to examine this by testing whether closeness to the biological parent has a bigger effect on a child's relationship with a stepfather than on a child's relationship with a stepmother.

Age at Entering a Stepfamily and Duration of Co-Residence.   How old children are when they acquire stepparents affects children's understanding of the events and the quality of their relationships to parents. Children's understanding of who is in their family affects their attachment to stepparents. For instance, in-depth interviews with young children show that they consider whether a person lives with them as a central determinant of who is in their family, and they treat co-residence as more important than biological ties. As children age, they begin to consider other factors, such as the quality of the emotional bond—family members are people who love each other—and whether the person fulfills important obligations (Beshers, 1991; Isaacs, Leon, & Kline, 1987).

Evidence is mixed about the effects on parent–child relationships of children's age and duration of co-residence in various household types (single-parent, parent–stepparent) during childhood. On one hand, Hetherington and Jodl showed earlier that children who are younger when their parents remarry appear to adjust to remarriage better than those who are adolescents when their parents remarry. Similarly, Furstenberg and his colleagues (1993) showed that when remarriages occur earlier in a child's life, mothers and adult children are more likely to transfer resources to each other than when divorce and remarriage occur after the child has grown up. Parents who have been remarried longer are also more likely to give support to stepchildren (Eggebeen, 1992). These patterns suggest that extended periods of co-residence enable stepfathers to develop bonds and a history of shared resources which facilitate exchanges in later life.

On the other hand, some studies of parents and minor children have shown that the amount of time stepfathers and children lived together had no effect on whether children considered the stepfather to be part of their family (Furstenberg, 1987) or on stepfathers' involvement in activities with minor children (Thomson, McLanahan, & Curtin, 1992). White's finding that a child's age at the parent's remarriage did not affect the quality of the stepparent–child relationship during adulthood is consistent with these studies.

Differences in the effects of age at entry and in effects of duration of stepfamily experience across studies may be due to sample differences (in the degree to which children lived with stepparents informally, in nonmarital cohabitation before remarriage), and differences across studies in the use of control variables. Finally, the differences across studies in treating the outcome as an affective or instrumental dimension of parent–child relationships may also account for the inconsistencies in findings. The question of how the timing of events in childhood affects adult stepfamily relationships deserves additional, systematic attention because of its theoretical importance and because of the rapid demographic change in the number and pace of children's stepfamily experiences (e.g., Bumpass & Raley, 1993).

ANOTHER LOOK AT VARIATION: VARIATION WITHIN STEPFAMILIES

The emphasis throughout White's chapter and in this volume has been on differences between original families and stepfamilies of various types. Understanding stepfamily relationships also requires knowledge of how parents treat biological and stepchildren in the same family. That is, to address concerns about equity and the extent to which parents treat stepchildren differently from biological children requires that we examine within-family variation in the quality of relationships and exchanges between parents and children. Do parents with both biological and stepchildren give more to their biological children, all else being equal? The structure of the NSFH data allows one to examine this by using the parent–child dyads that White identified for the second stage of her analysis. Parents report about exchanges with all of their adult children living apart from them. Because most older parents have more than one adult child, White had multiple observations for most parents. It is possible to use this information to determine whether a parent distinguishes between his step- and biological children in providing social and economic support. A simple first step would be to determine whether there is greater variation within stepfamilies than within original families in the way that parents share resources with their adult children. A within-family analysis of the type that I propose can also evaluate White's suggestion that parents in stepfamilies exchange less support with both biological and stepchildren because of the tensions and lack of emotional closeness in the family environment (see also White & Booth, 1985). A competing hypothesis suggested by Hetherington and Jodl earlier in this volume, is that, in stepfamilies with minor children, parents favor their biological children over their stepchildren.

The NSFH data on parent–child dyads within families may also be used to identify characteristics of stepfamilies in which stepchildren are treated differently from biological children. One hypothesis is that parents in stepfamilies in which the step- and biological children spent most of their childhood in the same household treat the children more similarly than if the stepchildren spent fewer years in the household. Within-family analyses can also address the question of how children's ages at the time they enter a stepfamily affect their attachment to stepparents in later life. Because siblings enter a stepfamily at different ages, a comparison of siblings within the same family identifies age effects, while at the same time holding constant other aspects of the family environment which affect all of the children in the family. (For an example of this strategy, see Kuo & Hauser, 1993.)

Whether or not adult stepchildren receive the same amount and type of support from their parents may also depend on how their parents make decisions about spending money, who controls the financial resources of the marriage, whether the husband and wife make joint decisions about how to spend a common pot of money, or whether they manage their money separately (e.g., Treas, 1991). Remarried parents who pool their financial resources may make equal transfers to both step- and biological children. Separate accounts, on the other hand, may facilitate distinctions between investments in step- and biological children. We know very little about how first-married parents with biological children manage their money (but see Blumstein & Schwartz, 1983; Pahl, 1989; Wilson, 1987), and even less about how parents in stepfamilies make financial decisions. Small, highly selective samples are useful for learning about how couples think about their money and individual versus joint control over resources (e.g., Coleman & Ganong, 1989). However, we must also have information from representative samples to understand differences between original and stepfamilies in the control and allocation of resources and to learn which patterns of financial control are more common in stepfamilies.

STEPFAMILIES AND PUBLIC POLICIES

Finally, White suggests that laws and social policies ignore or deny the rights and responsibilities of stepparents compared to biological parents. Recent reforms to the child support system, custody and access rulings, and paternity adjudication reinforce the priority of biological over step relationships between parents and minor children. This is in contrast to the trend in England, where stepparents who live with minor children acquire financial responsibilities to those children, even if the stepparent and biological parent divorce. Stepparents' responsibilities are in addition to those held by both custodial and noncustodial biological parents. In the United States, stepparents rarely supersede biological parents, except when the stepparent legally adopts the child. States vary widely in the laws and practices governing stepparent adoption (Chambers, 1990). Evidence from the 1987–1988 National Survey of Families and Households shows that a stepfather very rarely adopts his wife's biological children when the children's noncustodial biological father is still alive (fewer than 25 stepfathers with children under 18, out of about 500 unweighted cases).[1] Despite stepparents' absence of legal claims to children, welfare programs, such as Aid to Families with Dependent Children, assume that stepparents share their incomes with stepchildren in their household (e.g., Chambers, 1990). This is certainly a reasonable assumption. Children benefit from stepparents' income in a variety of ways, including the quality of their housing and the stepparents' contributions to daily expenses. However, as I have noted, we know very little about the extent to which stepparents contribute to minor children's other material needs, or how their contributions to stepchildren may differ from those to biological children.

---

[1] These figures ignore that the NSFH may undercount stepfamilies in which minor children live with a biological parent and stepparent. Questions at the beginning of the Wave 1 interview asked respondents which, if any, of their biological children were also the biological children of the respondent's spouse. Preliminary work by Bumpass and his colleagues suggests that these questions do not correctly classify all of the children in stepfamily (biological mother–stepfather) households (Bumpass, Raley, & Sweet, 1993). The underenumeration of stepfamilies may also affect how many children are identified as having been adopted by a stepparent, because questions about stepparent adoption followed the identification of stepchildren in the interview. Compared to other stepfamilies, those in which the stepparent had adopted the respondent's biological children may be underrepresented in the data if respondents in stepfamilies with adopted children think of the children as having equally close kin ties to both parents, regardless of their biological relationships. These respondents might have understood the NSFH question about their spouse's relationship to the children as asking who the children's "real" parents were, instead of asking about biological and legal relationships. Even taking account of these ambiguities, the NSFH data suggest that only a small percentage of stepfathers have adopted their stepchildren.

Fortunately, we do not live in a society in which there are likely to be differences within households in children's access to basic needs such as food, as in some developing countries (e.g., Haddad & Kanbur, 1990), but stepchildren may differ from biological children in the extent of parents' investments in presents, clothing, and educational expenses, including college. Only by going back to early family experiences and the relationships and exchanges between stepparents and minor children can we better understand why later-life relationships between stepparents and adult children are less supportive than those between biological parents and children.

SUMMARY AND CONCLUSION

On balance, I think that the evidence from White's research and other studies of social and economic support in adulthood shows that parents and children in stepfamilies are less involved with each other than those in original families. Unlike the gender differential favoring women in most kin relationships, stepmothers are disadvantaged compared to stepfathers in the quality of their relationships with stepchildren. Living arrangements during childhood and differences in biological mothers' and fathers' attachment to children explain, in part, lower quality relationships with stepmothers. We know little about the effects of timing and duration of residence with stepparents on the quality of intergenerational relationships in adulthood, because of inconsistent findings in both studies of minor and adult children. Existing data provide opportunities to examine whether, and to what extent, parents distinguish step- and biological children within the same family in the allocation of resources. Within-family analyses may shed light on the effects of children's ages at divorce and remarriage on exchanges with stepparents. Finally, new data on the horizon offer greater potential for examining the role that differences between the needs and resources of stepfamilies, and those of original families, play in explaining the lower support exchanged between stepparents and children.

ACKNOWLEDGMENTS

Preparation of this chapter was supported by a faculty development retraining grant from the University of Wisconsin and by a grant from the National Institute of Child Health and Human Development (HD-24571). I am grateful to Yvonne Brandreth for research assistance.

REFERENCES

Aquilino, W. S. (1993). *Impact of childhood family disruption on young adults' relationships with parents.* Unpublished manuscript, University of Wisconsin, Department of Child and Family Studies, Madison.

Bartlema, J. (1988). Modelling step-families: Exploratory findings. *European Journal of Population, 4,* 197–221.

Beshers, J. G. (1991). Strategies children use for the cognitive construction of kinship. *Sociological Studies of Child Development, 4,* 137–151.

Blumstein, P., & Schwartz, P. (1983). *American couples: Money, work, sex.* New York: Morrow.

Bumpass, L. L., & Raley, R. K. (1993). *Trends in the duration of single–parent families* (National Survey of Families and Households, Working Paper No. 58). Madison: University of Wisconsin, Center for Demography and Ecology.

Bumpass, L. L., Raley, R. K., & Sweet, J. A. (1993). *The changing character of stepfamilies: Implications of cohabitation and nonmarital childbearing.* Paper prepared for the Rand Conference, "Reshaping the Family: Social and Economic Changes and Public Policy," Santa Monica, CA.

Chambers, D. L. (1990). Stepparents, biologic parents, and the law's perceptions of "family" after divorce. In D. Sugarman & H. H. Kay (Eds.), *Divorce reform at the crossroads* (pp. 102–129). New Haven: Yale University Press.

Cooney, T. M., & Uhlenberg, P. (1990). The role of divorce in men's relations with their adult children after mid-life. *Journal of Marriage and the Family, 52,* 677–688.

Cooney, T. M., & Uhlenberg, P. (1992). Support from parents over the life course: The adult child's perspective. *Social Forces, 71,* 63–84.

Coleman, M., & Ganong, L. H. (1989). Financial management in stepfamilies. *Lifestyles: Family and Economic Issues, 10,* 217–232.

Eggebeen, D. J. (1992). Family structure and intergenerational exchanges. *Research on Aging, 14,* 427–447.

Eggebeen, D. J., & Hogan, D. P. (1990). Giving between generations in American families. *Human Nature, 1,* 211–232.

Fischer, C. S. (1982). *To dwell among friends: Personal networks in town and country.* Chicago: University of Chicago Press.

Furstenberg, F. F., Jr. (1987). The new extended family: The experience of parents and children after remarriage. In K. Pasley & M. Ihinger-Tallman (Eds.), *Remarriage and stepparenting: Current research and theory* (pp. 42–61). New York: Guilford.

Furstenberg, F. F., Jr., Hoffman, S., & Shrestha, L. (1993). *The effects of divorce and remarriage on intergenerational transfers: A preliminary analysis of the PSID.* Paper presented at the annual meeting of the Population Association of America, Cincinnati, OH.

Furstenberg, F. F., Jr., Nord, C. W., Peterson, J. L., & Zill, N. (1983). The life course of children of divorce. *American Sociological Review, 8,* 656–668.

Haddad, L., & Kanbur, R. (1990). How serious is the neglect of intra-household inequality? *The Economic Journal, 100,* 866–881.

Hagestad, G. O. (1986). The aging society as a context for family life. *Daedalus, 115,* 119–139.

Hill, M. S., Morgan, J. N., & Herzog, R. (1993). *Intergenerational aspects of family help patterns.* Paper presented at the annual meeting of the Population Association of America, Cincinnati, OH.

Hogan, D. P., Eggebeen, D. J., & Clogg, C. C. (1993). The structure of intergenerational exchanges in American families. *American Journal of Sociology, 98,* 1428–1458.

Ihinger-Tallman, M. (1988). Research on stepfamilies. *Annual Review of Sociology, 14,* 25–48.

Isaacs, M. B., Leon, G. H., & Kline, M. (1987). When is a parent out of the picture? Different custody, different perceptions. *Family Process, 26,* 101–110.

Johnson, C. L. (1988). *Ex familia: Grandparents, parents and children adjust to divorce.* New Brunswick, NJ: Rutgers University Press.

Kuo, H. D., & Hauser, R. M. (1993). *Gender, family configuration, and the effect of family background on educational attainment* (National Survey of Families and Households, Working Paper No. 93-19). Madison: University of Wisconsin, Center for Demography and Ecology.

Maccoby, E. E., & Mnookin, R. H. (1992). *Dividing the child: Social and legal dilemmas of custody.* Cambridge, MA: Harvard University Press.

Marsiglio, W. (1992). Stepfathers with minor children living at home. *Journal of Family Issues, 13*, 195–214.

Pahl, J. (1989). *Money and marriage*. New York: St. Martin's Press.

Roan, C. L. (1993). *Looking within families: Does parent's contact with an adult child depend on characteristics of other children in the family?* (National Survey of Families and Households, Working Paper No. 62). Madison: University of Wisconsin, Center for Demography and Ecology.

Rosenzweig, M. R., & Wolpin, K. I. (1993). Intergenerational support and the life-cycle incomes of young men and their parents: Human capital investments, coresidence, and intergenerational financial transfers. *Journal of Labor Economics, 11*, 84–112.

Rossi, A. S., & Rossi, P. H. (1990). *Of human bonding: Parent–child relations across the life course*. New York: Aldine de Gruyter.

Seltzer, J. A. (in press). Consequences of marital dissolution for children. *Annual Review of Sociology, 20*, 235–266.

Seltzer, J. A. (1991). Relationships between fathers and children who live apart: The father's role after separation. *Journal of Marriage and the Family, 53*, 79–101.

Seltzer, J. A., & Bianchi, S. M. (1988). Children's contact with absent parents. *Journal of Marriage and the Family, 50*, 663–677.

Thomson, E., McLanahan, S. S., & Curtin, R. B. (1992). Family structure, gender, and parental socialization. *Journal of Marriage and the Family , 54*, 368–378.

Treas, J. (1991). The common pot or separate purses? A transaction cost interpretation. In R. L. Blumberg (Ed.), *Gender, family and economy: The triple overlap* (pp. 211–224). Newbury Park, CA: Sage.

White, L. (1992). The effect of parental divorce and remarriage on parental support for adult children. *Journal of Family Issues, 13*, 234–250.

White, L. K., & Booth, A. (1985). The quality and stability of remarriages: The role of stepchildren. *American Sociological Review, 50*, 689–698.

Wilson, G. (1987). *Money in the family*. Brookfield, VT: Gower.

IV BUILDING RESEARCH AND POLICY AGENDAS—WHAT IS NEEDED?

13

Research on Stepparenting Families: Integrating Disciplinary Approaches and Informing Policy

Jeanne Brooks-Gunn
Columbia University

The goal of this volume is to take a critical look at what is known about marital transitions, in particular remarriage and stepparenting, as they influence children, parents, and stepparents. Of secondary interest is how children and their parents negotiate marital transitions in families, specifically moves of parents and stepparents, in and out of the child's household. This chapter highlights several research and policy issues related to marital and parental transitions, with an eye toward integrating findings from different disciplines and informing policy, using interdisciplinary approaches.

Six issues are addressed in this chapter. The first considers the distinction between household composition and parental and marital transitions. The second looks at what families might be included as stepparent families. The third focuses on the variety of methods and models used in the study of stepparenting.

The fourth takes the most consistent finding in the literature—namely the fact that children in stepparent families resemble those in single-parent families more than their counterparts in original-parent families, at least for some outcomes (Amato & Keith, 1991; Chase-Lansdale & Hetherington, 1990; Emery, 1988; McLanahan & Booth, 1989). Economic, psychological and family system explanations are explored. Various disciplines put more emphasis on certain mechanisms than others. Little comparative research exists that includes explanations from different disciplines. This section registers a plea for such comparative approaches. Variations in outcomes within family types are not the focus of this section; Hetherington and Jodl (this volume) present a cogent discussion of individual differences in children's outcome.

The fifth issue addresses possible variations in parenting behavior and child outcome as a function of the number of persons in the household and their gender. Almost all the research to date focuses on three family structures— single-mother, original parent and mother–stepfather families. Effects of living in single-father and father–stepmother families are less often studied, even though the gender of the parent may influence parenting. Additionally, the fact that single parents often live with other adults has not been addressed by many studies. Recent work on these family types is reviewed (McLanahan, Seltzer, Hanson & Thomson, in press; Thomson & McLanahan, 1993; Thomson, McLanahan, & Curtin, 1992)

The sixth issue broadens the perspective beyond the family within the household to examine effects of noncustodial parents upon children. Child support, contact and conflict have been the main variables studied. Regrettably, the literature focused almost exclusively on the effects of child support upon children's well-being in cases where the custodial parent was not remarried. Child support and changes in the child support system are likely to influence children in stepparent households. Federal policies, such as the Family Support Act (1988), are dedicated to increasing the number of noncustodial fathers paying child support, providing this support consistently, and paying custodial parents the full amount of the award. These policies should influence the behavior of noncustodial fathers (both present and absent) whose former wives are single, as well as those who have remarried (Garfinkel & McLanahan, 1990, in press; Garfinkel, McLanahan, & Robins, in press).

STUDYING HOUSEHOLD ARRANGEMENTS
AND PARENTAL TRANSITIONS

Much of the stepfamily research to date focuses on marital or parental states, rather than on changes in these states, as *transition* implies. Consequently, most studies focus on residence in various family forms. Much of the work is descriptive and comparative in nature, rather than process-oriented. The three family forms most often compared are: original-parent or traditional families (defined as a family with the biological mother and father residing with their children), ever-married single-parent families (in most cases, comprised of the mother and her children), and stepparent families (a biological mother who has been married previously, and a stepfather who reside with the children).

The benefits or costs of any particular household or parenting arrangement are not only studied by comparing different family forms, but also investigated by looking at changes in these arrangements. Marital transitions have become the object of longitudinal study, which allows for an understanding of how changes in parental marital status and household residence influence changes in children's adjustment (Amato & Keith, 1991; Baydar, 1988; Block, Block, & Gjerde, 1986; Chase-Lansdale & Hetherington, 1990; Cherlin et al., 1991; Hetherington & Arasteh, 1988; Kiernan, 1992; Maccoby & Mnookin, 1992; McLanahan &

Booth, 1989). A transition-oriented perspective allows for an examination of the characteristics of parents and families (and, to a lesser extent, children) that undergo transformations versus those who do not (Block et al., 1986; Cherlin et al., 1991; Hetherington & Clingempeel, 1992). Most of the research in this tradition focuses on the two primary transitions that result in the three most studied family configurations. These are the transitions of divorce and remarriage.

DEFINING STEPPARENTS

The most frequent stepparent family form studied is the custodial mother, her children, and her spouse. Other family forms are not typically studied, even though several include stepparents. These include at least five types of families.

1. Stepparent families may have the father as the custodial parent and the new wife as the stepparent. Recent research (Hetherington, 1993; Maccoby & Mnookin, 1992; Teachman, 1991; Thomson & McLanahan, 1993; Thomson et al., 1992; White, this volume) does address this stepfamily type, which is briefly discussed in this chapter.

2. Stepfamilies may also be formed when the custodial mother has not been married prior to her marriage to the stepfather. Although there is a voluminous literature on the life circumstances of the never-married single mother and the consequences for her children—especially those who give birth in their teenage years or in their early 20s (Chase-Lansdale, Brooks-Gunn, & Paikoff, 1991; Furstenberg, Brooks-Gunn, & Morgan, 1987; Hayes, 1987), little work follows these mothers and their children into stepparent situations. These stepparent families are also not included in most comparative analyses of the effects of residing in different family types, although recent work is separating out never-married and ever-married single mothers into two groups when comparisons among single, original-parent and remarried families are made (Knox & Bane, in press; McLanahan et al., in press; Thomson et al., 1992).

3. Never-married single fathers also may marry and become stepparents. This group received no research attention.

4. Custodial parents who marry a third or fourth time bring new stepparents into the household. The same is true for noncustodial parents who remarry several times. Little research has focused on multiple remarriages, or on transitions from one stepparent family to another. Additionally, almost nothing is known about the continued relationships of previous stepfathers (or stepmothers) and children. However, children will sometimes list a previous stepfather as someone "who is like a father to me." Research is needed on these more complex family relationships, and these larger but perhaps, more diffuse social networks.

5. The final stepparent family form to be mentioned involves cohabitating adults with children from a previous marriage. Although not a stepparent family in the legal sense, these families present similar challenges to remarried families in that the mother, her partner, and her children must forge new relationships, renegotiate old ones, and develop a new family system. While little research addresses this family form, a small but significant number of families consist of cohabitating adults with children from either the man or the woman (Thomson et al., 1993). This family form may evolve into a more traditional stepparent family. Its existence may confound some of the research findings for remarried families. Family systems seem to go through a period of disequilibrium in the several years following a remarriage (increased conflict, decline in parental responsibility, difficulties in acceptance of the stepparent/stepchild, decreased monitoring and supervision, and altered individual alliances), after which the family system seems to stabilize (Hetherington, 1993). The advent of cohabitation needs to be studied, since disequilibrium may occur when the adult partner enters the household and not when a remarriage occurs. Research on remarried family forms may be confounding length of time in the new family form with the actual remarriage, such that periods of disequilibrium might actually be periods of stabilization. Alternatively, it is possible that a remarriage after a period of cohabitation signals a second reorganization of family relationships (e.g., the stepparent takes on a more active parenting role, the stepchild accepts the inevitability of the stepparent staying in the household, the mother actively promotes a more active parenting role for her spouse, and so on). Neither the condition of cohabitation prior to remarriage nor the condition of cohabitation without eventual remarriage has been addressed. Cohabitation without remarriage probably confers different roles and responsibilities upon stepparents than does remarriage. Cohabitating partners may be less involved in family life than are stepparents, although one recent study did not support this premise (Thomson et al., 1992).

Cohabitation also may occur in families where the single mother has never married. Little information is available on this family form.

What is clear from this brief description of various stepparent forms is that remarriage and stepparenthood are not equivalent. Unfortunately, almost all of the research on stepparenting focuses on a first remarriage rather than a first marriage, cohabitation, or multiple marriages.

SPECIFYING METHODOLOGIES AND MODELS

Methodologies in the Study of Stepparenting

Several research traditions consider the effects of stepparenting upon family members. These include economic, demographic, sociological, developmental, and clinical disciplines. Disciplinary boundaries have led to somewhat separate methodologies and models being developed to study family processes (Brooks-Gunn, Phelps, & Elder, 1991). For example, the national data sets preferred by sociologists and economists provide rich and detailed descriptions of income, employment, fertility, marital status and change, but often characterize family functioning in terms of single items or short scales (e.g., conflict, contact, involvement in child's schooling). Even when home environment scales were used, given trade-offs in cost and staff training, short-forms relying on interview questions, rather than actual observations in the home are used (see Children of the National Longitudinal Study of Youth [NLSY]; Chase-Lansdale, Mott, Brooks-Gunn, & Phillips, 1991). At the same time, small, local samples provide rich family process data, but often include relatively few questions on income sources, employment, and the like (Duncan, Brooks-Gunn, & Klebanov, in press).

Sample composition also varies by research tradition. The most obvious example is whether or not a sample is representative of the children (or families) in the nation, a region, a city, or even a hospital birth cohort. Perhaps the biggest problem with the small, process-oriented samples is that they almost never include minority children. The ways in which families cope with marital transitions may be linked to cultural values, family poverty, recency of immigration, neighborhood residence, and religious beliefs (Brooks-Gunn, Duncan, Klebanov, & Sealand, 1993; Garcia-Coll, 1990; McLoyd, 1990; Rossi & Rossi, 1990). Our knowledge about stepparenting in African-American and, to a lesser extent, Hispanic-American families comes almost exclusively from analyses of the Panel Study of Income Dynamics (PSID), High School and Beyond (HSB), NLSY cohorts, National Survey of Families and Households (NSFH), and the Current Population Survey (CPS).

Investigators analyzed data either controlling for race/ethnicity or for separate groups. Given that the proportion of single-parent and stepparent families varies by ethnicity and that income differentials among ethnic groups are great, comparative analyses are necessary. The mechanisms underlying child and parent outcomes in different family forms may differ by ethnicity (McLanahan, Astone, & Marks, 1991).

Small, process-oriented studies do not include families across the entire income range. We have a great deal of information about the effects of divorce upon income loss and poverty and the effects of remarriage upon income gains (Duncan, 1991; Hernandez, 1993). The importance of family income, and sources of income, upon differential aspects of residing in various families constitute the central questions being asked by economists and demographers (Thomson et al., 1992). Process-oriented studies did not focus on income loss or volatility as potential causes of high family conflict and low social control and parental warmth, even though income, and income loss, are associated with these family processes (Conger et al., 1992; Elder, 1974; Elder, Conger, Foster, & Ardelt, 1993; Lempers, Clark-Lempers, & Simons, 1989; McLoyd, 1990). Income is often not included in analyses or, if used, is conceptualized as a control variable. Given its potential as a moderator or mediator of links between child and parent outcomes on the one hand and family processes on the other, income measures must be constructed carefully. For example, family processes such as conflict might be more tightly linked with negative child outcomes in single-parent or stepparent families who are poor than in those who are not poor. Poor families are more likely to experience the poverty co-factors of low quality schools, multiple moves to new neighborhoods or schools, impoverished or high crime neighborhoods, inadequate access to social services, and small and unreliable social support networks (Huston, 1991; Liaw & Brooks-Gunn, in press; McCormick & Brooks-Gunn, 1989; Parker, Greer, & Zuckerman, 1988). All of these characteristics can theoretically interact with poverty and with family configuration to influence child outcomes. Alternatively, family processes may make less of a contribution to the negative effects of marital disruptions upon poor children, because of the overwhelming negative effects of poverty itself upon children (Duncan, Brooks-Gunn, & Klebanov, in press). Research has not addressed issues surrounding poverty and marital disruptions adequately (Cherlin, 1992). More culturally sensitive research is suggested by ecological models such as those described by Bronfenbrenner (1986; Bronfenbrenner & Crouter, 1983).

Cross-national data exist, but have not been used extensively to look at stepparenting and remarriage (see, as notable exceptions, Cherlin et al., 1991; Kiernan, 1992). Cross-national residence may be particularly valuable for the examination of stepparent effects in countries where relatively more and relatively fewer divorces and remarriages occur. The example often given is the research of Cherlin, Kiernan and their colleagues using British longitudinal data sets. Divorce and remarriage are less common in Britain (the increase occurred much later there than in the United States). Whether effects are associated with how normative divorce and remarriage are, is a seldom studied but important topic.

Another example of the importance of family income upon outcomes involves higher income families. Research suggests that fewer youth living in stepparent families go to college (Kiernan, 1992). These effects might be more pronounced in children from higher income families, who have enough discretionary income for their offspring's college costs. If stepparent families invest less in the children than do original-parent families, then presumably less money would be allocated to college costs. Thus, the effects of stepparent family structure upon college attendance may be underestimated, in that all family income levels are included in analyses, rather than those income levels that are likely to yield discretionary income.

Different research disciplines tend to ask different questions. For example, almost none of the more psychologically oriented studies of family systems in stepparent families discuss the effect of noncustodial parents upon child outcome or upon the functioning of the family (Chase-Lansdale & Hetherington, 1990; Hetherington & Arasteh, 1988). The analysis by one of Hetherington's students, Gunnoe (1993), is a notable exception and, I hope, a harbinger of work to come.

Integrating findings across research traditions needs to be done. For example, the family-process studies in the tradition of Hetherington elegantly demonstrated the increased conflict following remarriage (Chase-Lansdale & Hetherington, 1990; Hetherington, 1993). And, as Hetherington & Jodl noted, intrafamily conflict is associated with negative child outcomes. Analyses of the national data sets also suggest that conflict is higher in single-parent and stepparent families (McLanahan et al., 1991). However, in these studies, increased conflict does not add much power to regression equations predicting child and youth outcomes, after family income and social demographic characteristics are taken into account. Variations in research findings need to be reconciled, or at least explored, vis-à-vis differences in measures, samples, and analytic procedures. The illustration just given is a case in point. Not only are the measures used by Hetherington and McLanahan vastly different, but so are the samples. Family income accounts for a large portion of the variance in youth outcomes across family types. Whether conflict would play a larger role for not-poor families (which would be more similar to the Hetherington samples) than for the poor families in the national data sets is not fully explored.

Another example focuses on parental resources. Money and time are resources that parents control. Income loss or gain that occurs in divorce or remarriage influences where families live and whether parents (or others) work or alter their work hours. Time available influences monitoring, supervision, and provision of learning experiences that, in turn, affect child outcomes (Coleman, 1988). Single mothers have less time available because of increased work hours (and no spouse substitute), and remarried mothers may have less time because of time spent with the new spouse. Little work addresses time and income trade-offs.

Models Used in the Study of Stepparenting

Many different models are used to frame the discourse on stepparents. It is beyond the scope of this chapter to summarize these models regarding their use and influence in studying stepparent families. Economic models consider the decisions on income distribution within the family, the provision of income to children living outside one's household, compliance with child support awards, and changes in economic behavior as a function of marital status changes (e.g., the remarriage of the noncustodial parent). Effects of income upon children's outcomes are also examined as a function of family type.

A series of family systems or parental behavior models focus on how individual family members, as well as the family as a whole, respond to changes in the family. Much of this research takes a transition-oriented approach, postulating that moves of parents and stepparents in and out of the child's household trigger a reorganization and renegotiation of relationships, roles, and responsibilities. Hetherington (1993; Hetherington & Clingempeel, 1992) has made the important distinction between the phase immediately following a parental transition and subsequent phases. The early phase is marked by disequilibrium in the family system; the system stabilizes after a period of several years.

Another conceptual approach is based in risk and resilience models, as championed by Rutter and Garmezy (1983). This approach takes as its starting point the fact that reactions to parental disruptions are quite variable. Individual differences in adaptation to events such as parental changes are the focus. Factors that promote positive adaptation to such an event are explored (protective factors) as well as those that impede adaptations (risk factors). The individual difference approach considers a wide range of characteristics within the child, the parent(s), and the stepparent, as well as the relationships among them. Risk and resilience models are often used in conjunction with family systems models. While comparisons among family types are not the focus, comparative questions arise regarding the pattern of associations among variables within each family type: for example, whether mother–child conflict operates similarly with regard to child outcomes in original-parent, single-mother or stepfather families, or whether certain children, by virtue of characteristics such as temperament or reactivity, respond differentially to such conflict across family types.

More contextual models attempt to place the child of a stepparent family in a broader context. Bronfenbrenner's ecological model is the prime exemplar of this approach (Bronfenbrenner, 1986; Bronfenbrenner & Crouter, 1983). How the peer, neighborhood, school, and kin networks are altered by a parental transition is the object of study. Whether these contextual changes influence the family and the child is explored, as well as whether the characteristics of contexts interact to influence children (see, as an example, Hetherington's work on the intersection of school and parenting style and its influence on children in stepparent families in this volume).

Social network and role theories are also useful in studying stepparent families. As White (this volume) beautifully demonstrated, contact and support between stepparents and stepchildren are relatively infrequent after the stepchildren become adults and no longer live with the stepparent. The demonstration of such loose step-ties leads us to question the stepparents' role in the family (Rossi & Rossi, 1990; Thoits, 1992). Loose step-ties also raise questions about the primacy of biological sameness in the commitment of parents to offspring.

Prevention models focus on approaches to altering behavior in families. Little prevention work has focused on stepparent families. However, programs have targeted high conflict families or families in which the spouses have just become, or are about to become, parents (Cowan & Cowan, 1990; Cowan, Cowan, Heming, & Miller, 1991; Markman, Floyd, Stanley, & Storaasli, 1988). Via social skills and conflict resolution training, and identification of common stressors on families, goals of such programs are to reduce conflict and potential marital disruption. Such approaches could easily be applied to stepparent families.

All of these models provide useful frames for the study of stepfamilies. They

often overlap in interesting ways. For example, all models speak to the investment and commitment of stepparents (or lack thereof). However, different measures and theory are garnered to support the premise that stepparents are, on
average, less committed to their stepchildren than are original parents. Much
more integrative research across models is needed.

PROCESSES UNDERLYING NEGATIVE OUTCOMES
OF CHILDREN IN STEPPARENT FAMILIÈS

The outcomes of children in two-parent families differ as a function of the
identity of the second parent in the household. Children in stepparent families
often have lower school-related achievement scores and more adjustment problems than children in original-parent families. They are similar to children in
ever-married single-parent households, although achievement decrements are
somewhat less likely to be seen in children of stepparent families than in single-
parent families (Thomson et al., 1992; Zill, Morrison, & Coiro, 1993). However, variations are seen with respect to timing of parental disruptions in the
child's and parents' life, duration of different family structures, and intensity of
initial responses to such disruptions. These critical topics are not discussed here.

Single parenthood is known to confer risk for children, in part due to low
income, drops in income (compared to family incomes prior to divorce), moves
to new neighborhoods and schools, and possibly, reduced amount of time in
parent–child interaction (due in part to the availability of one parent rather than
two parents in the household, and to employment patterns in single-parent families). Stepparent households have several advantages over single-parent households, which might be expected to translate into better adjustment for the
children residing in them, compared to single-parent households. Stepparent
households are not as poor, on average, as ever-married single-parent households. Additionally, two parents reside in the household, rather than one parent,
making adult time for child care and interaction more available.

Given these possible advantages, why do children in stepparent families look
so similar to children in single-parent families? Economic, psychological, and
family system perspectives all speak to these findings. Data from each of these
perspectives are discussed briefly, in order to elucidate the mechanisms underlying the poorer adjustment of children in stepparent than in original-parent households. Economic perspectives focus on income, moves to new neighborhoods or
schools, and adult time available for children in the household (see McLanahan
et al., 1991). The psychological perspectives considered here focus on parental
commitment to children in stepparent families. Family systems perspectives
address relationships among family members. Comparisons are typically made
among original-parent, ever-married single-parent, and stepparent families. Outcomes are school achievement (grades, high school drop-out, postsecondary

schooling) or emotional problems (behavior problems, leaving home early). The most comprehensive comparative work has been conducted by McLanahan and her colleagues (Garfinkel & McLanahan, 1986; McLanahan et al., 1991; McLanahan et al., in press; Thomson et al., 1992; 1993) on the first two perspectives and Hetherington (1993, Hetherington & Jodl, this volume) on the third perspective. Research across perspectives, however, still does not adequately address whether or not the negative effects of stepparent families are really due to the first description—the divorce of the original parents.

Economic Perspectives

Income Differences in Original-Parent, Single-Parent, and Stepparent Families. A marital dissolution results in many children living below the poverty threshold. This is because mothers are usually the custodial parents and because fathers earn more income and are more likely to be employed than children. As incomes for the custodial parent declines, it increases for the noncustodial parent. The incomes in households a year following a marital dissolution tell the story—single mothers have 67% of the pre-divorce family income and fathers have 90% of the pre-divorce income (based on data from the PSID; Duncan & Hoffman, 1985). Duncan (1991) provided estimates of the number of children who are poor in various family configurations.

Family incomes rise with remarriage, but not always to levels comparable with those of original marriages. McLanahan et al. (1991) documented that stepfamilies have higher incomes than single-parent families, but not always as high as those reported by original-parent families (race/ethnic and sample differences are found for these comparisons).

Even if the national studies uniformly documented that stepparent families have incomes comparable to those of original-parent families, children in stepparent families are more likely to spend time in low-income, single-parent families. Persistence of poverty conditions is associated with child outcomes: longer bouts of poverty are associated with decrements in well-being, compared to more transient spells of poverty (Duncan et al., in press; Haveman, Wolfe, & Spaulding, 1991). Consequently, stepparent families may have higher incomes than single-parent families, but children in both families are more likely to have spent some childhood years in poverty than children in original-parent families. Effects of living in stepparent families need to be modeled, taking into account income levels and changes in income levels over time, including the years preceding the formation of a stepparent family (see Knox & Bane, in press).

Income volatility is also more likely in single-parent households than in two-parent households. Women experience a sharp drop in income following a divorce or separation. Some gains are made for those who may respond to the loss of income by entering the work force or increasing the number of hours of work. Changes in labor force participation, or difficulty in securing a stable job, can precipitate further drops and possible rises. Remarriage results in a rise in income for many families and perhaps short-term income volatility. No studies accounted for income volatility in the study of stepparent effects upon children.

Income Differentials and Outcomes in Stepparent Families. Research has addressed whether income or family configuration explains more variance in child and youth outcomes. In an analysis of the outcomes of adolescent girls from the PSID, my research group found that income was a more potent predictor of high school drop-out and nonmarital teenage childbearing than was family configuration (Brooks-Gunn et al., 1993). However, income did not account for all of the negative effects of single parenthood following divorce or separation. The question may be framed: How much do income differentials among original-parent, single-parent and stepparent families account for the between-group variance in youth outcomes? PSID analyses by McLanahan et al. (1991) suggest that between two fifths to four fifths of the single-parent family effect on school-related outcomes is accounted for by family income. In contrast to the findings for single-parents, where income differences accounted for most of the between-group variance (original-parent vs. single-parent families) for youth outcomes, income accounted for very few of the differences between original-parent and stepparent families. (These analyses did not take into account the income differentials occurring during the years of single motherhood prior to a remarriage.) However, the risk of poor adolescent outcomes was high in step-parents, often as high as in single-parent families (McLanahan et al., 1991; Thomson & McLanahan, 1993).

Family Income and Neighborhood. While the line of research just reviewed suggests that family income explains many of the effects of residing in a single-parent family, it still does not provide any explanation of how poverty actually operates, nor why poverty does not explain differences between children in original-parent and stepparent families. One obvious possibility is that single parenthood and stepparenthood, operating through income, influences the stability of the family in several ways, including moves to a new neighborhood. Youth in single-parent households are more likely to live in poor neighborhoods than youth in original-parent households. This is not true of youth in stepparent families (McLanahan et al., 1991).

McLanahan and colleagues (1991) also examined the current school climate of youth in single-parent, stepparent and original-parent families. Using the HSB, they reported that White youth are more likely to attend a school with a high drop-out rate if they are in a stepparent household than if they are in an original-parent family. This effect was not significant for African Americans, but in the same direction (McLanahan et al., 1991). The same was true for youth in single-parent families. Youth in stepparent families also reported that their peers had lower academic aspirations than did the youth from original-parent families.

Is this because stepparent families are less likely to invest in the children than are original-parent families, the result being residence in neighborhoods with lower quality schools? The schools were rated as having more problems by the offspring in stepparent compared to original-parent households. Single-parent households were similar to original-parent households. Why are neighborhood or school characteristics more negative for youth in stepfamilies, as compared to original-parent families, than for youth in single-parent families?

Psychological Perspectives

A number of research lines suggest that parents who are remarried may invest less psychologically (and economically) in their children than do parents in first marriages. Investment is inferred from time spent with the child, supervision and monitoring of the child's activities, and participating in adolescent decision-making.

Stepparent households differ from single-parent households in that the former have more adults in the household. Higher adult-to-child ratios were associated with better child outcomes. However, it is not clear that children in stepparent households spend more time with parents than children in single-parent households. Newly married couples may spend more time together, rather than time with the child. And stepfathers may not spend much time with their stepchildren, as Hetherington's results on the high rates of stepparent disengagement suggest (1993; Hetherington & Clingempeel, 1992; see also Thomson & McLanahan, 1993). More time-use data in different family configurations, and possible links between time and child outcome, would be welcome additions to the field (Lazear & Michael, 1988).

Remarried, single-parent mothers seemed to exhibit lower degrees of social control in comparison to mothers in original-parent families. This was expressed by less routinized household schedules, less supervision of homework, and less assistance in academic plans (Dornbush et al., 1985; Hetherington, Cox, & Cox, 1978; McLanahan et al., 1991; Thomson et al., 1992). These findings were more pronounced for single-parent families. Disagreements about parental plans for their adolescents' further schooling were equally likely in stepparent and single-parent households, as compared to original-family households, at least for the White HSB sample (McLanahan et al., 1991).

How do such indicators of supervision relate to outcomes? In comparisons using the HSB data set, McLanahan and colleagues (1991) reported lower levels of involvement in homework and in planning of the high school program in stepparent families than in original-parent families, with this effect consistent across ethnic groups (stepparent families being one half as likely to be involved, similar to the findings for single-parent families). However, supervision, involvement, and aspirations did not alter differences in youth outcomes between stepparent and original-parent families, controlling for social and economic status. The question remains as to whether supervision is really an explanatory mechanism, or whether or not the measures used in national data sets are reliable (youth report vs. multiple respondents; single items vs. scales). Other types of analyses might be helpful, especially those that examine the effects of supervision as a function of poverty, maternal employment, time spent with child, and so on.

Investment also has been studied regarding the salience of the stepparent role. Thoits (1992) examined the importance of 17 roles to adults, rated using a 4-point scale. Parenthood was rated as the most important of all roles to individuals; stepparenthood (for those individuals who were stepparents) was rated as one of the least important roles. These findings suggest that the role of stepparent may not be seen as particularly salient to most stepparents, which would partially explain the findings on disengagement and low monitoring.

Family Systems Perspectives

Family systems perspectives chart the changes in relationships within the family as a function of parental transitions. The research clearly describes a number of disruptions or disequilibrium in families when a stepparent enters the system. Children are often very resistant to the entrance of another adult into the household. Consequently, when stepparents do try to establish a relationship, many children do not respond. In such cases, as Hetherington (1993) showed, stepparents become disengaged—exhibiting little warmth, control, or monitoring. Stepparents are not necessarily negative, they are just distant. Relationships with the custodial parent often change as well, with conflict increasing.

Distant parenting is not solely the result of children's feelings and responses to the intrusion of another adult—a person who also has ties to the parent. Stepparents are simply less involved with stepchildren, regardless of the children's reactions. They are less likely to exhibit authoritative parenting, for example. And the custodial parent in remarriages may respond with less monitoring, supervision, and less general support (Thomson et al., 1992).[1]

Clearly, the entire family system is altered by a remarriage. Hetherington (1993; Chase-Lansdale & Hetherington, 1990) pinpointed the developmental stages at which remarriage may have the most negative consequences for relationships and for children's outcomes—early adolescence. More developmentally oriented work on the interaction of child's life phase and parental transitions is needed.

---

[1]Family processes and relationships may be quite different in the equilibrium and stabilization (or restabilization) phases of a remarriage. Whether family processes operate in a similar fashion, vis-à-vis effects on child outcome during the stabilization and disequilibrium phases of a remarriage or divorce, are not well studied.

Hetherington and others charted the initial child (and, to a lesser extent, the family) characteristics that might moderate the effects of single parenthood and remarriage on families and children. This work is in the tradition of risk and resilience models. One finding is illustrative: Children of parents who divorced or separated were often quite different than children of parents who did not divorce prior to the actual marital disruption (Baydar, 1988; Block et al., 1986; Cherlin et al., 1991). It is believed that these differences arise because families that divorce actually experience more conflict and less cohesion prior to the transition than those who do not divorce. Some of the negative effects of marital disruptions upon children are accounted for by these pre-existing differences, and such findings lead to a re-examination of the ways in which marital disruptions are conceptualized. Children are not just influenced by the actual disruption, but by the entire process leading up to the disruption. Family system perspectives, in the tradition of Hetherington, could offer a way to study family reorganization and stability prior to a disruption, if samples existed where families who do and do not divorce are studied intensively.

Longer-term effects also need to be studied. Kiernan's (1992) recent analysis of the National Child Development Study in Britain suggests that children in stepparent families leave home earlier than do children in other family configurations (single-parent and original-parent families). Youth from stepparent families were more likely to say that conflict was the reason for their leaving home early. Thus, conflict in stepparent families may have significant effects on life course trajectories.

OTHER FAMILY STRUCTURES

Thus far, discussion has centered upon the three most studied family structures— original-parent, ever-married single-parent, and the stepfather families. The effects of divorce and remarriage upon children tend to be confounded with the gender of the custodial parent, as most research focuses upon the mother. A few studies explored both parenting behavior and child outcomes in single-parent and stepparent families including the original father rather than the mother. Using the NSFH, Thomson et al. (1992) looked at parental activities for several family structures, including original-parent families, single-mother, single-father, step-mother, and stepfather families to see whether gender of the parent was associated with parenting behavior within family structure types. Generally, step-mother and stepfather families were similar to one another and differed from original-parent families, being less positive towards the children and engaging in less frequent activities. Single-parent families, whether headed by a mother or father, were also similar to one another. They differed from all of the two-parent families in terms of control and supervision, suggesting that parental monitoring is facilitated by having more than one adult in the household.

While the gender of the parent did not explain differences between original-parent families on the one hand and single-parent and stepparent families on the other, the gender of the parent was associated with parental behavior. Across family structure types, mothers were more involved with their children's lives than were fathers. This is true for custodial and noncustodial mothers alike (see also, Hetherington, 1993).

Thomson and her colleagues examined parental behavior in households where the mother is cohabitating but is not married. In general, parents in this family structure reported behavior that was quite similar to that reported by parents in stepparent families.

These lines of research need to be extended. Additionally, more work on children's responses to these various family structure forms is recommended. Although custodial mothers and fathers are quite similar, the within-family processes, or reactions to the stepparent, may differ by gender of the parent as well as by gender of the child.

NON-CUSTODIAL PARENTS IN SINGLE-PARENT AND STEPPARENT FAMILIES

Thus far, the focus has been on intra-household economic, psychological, and family system perspectives. The noncustodial parent, typically the father, is also important in the child's life and in the family system. Issues to be discussed include child support payments, effects of child support upon contact and conflict, and potential effects of changes in the child support system (e.g., mandates) upon actual payment and upon noncustodial fathers' relationships with their children.

Almost all policy-relevant activity has focused on child support. Presumably, the economic well-being of children is not only perceived as a parental responsibility, but one of the few parental obligations that we as a society are willing to require of parents; that is, we provide legislative and judicial solutions to nonsupport, including sanctions such as wage withholding and prison. Contact, emotional commitment, monitoring and supervision—all ingredients of parenting— are not as likely to be the province of policy.

Child Support Payments

The average child support payment is about $2,500, for those parents who actually pay. About 60% of all women eligible for a child support award have an agreement. About one half of all children receive child support payments at the agreed to level, and one quarter receive nothing. The current child support levels are lower than what fathers would contribute if living in the household and, perhaps, lower than the best standard would award (Corbett, 1992; Garfinkel, McLanahan, & Robins, in press).

Little work has considered child support payment in cases of remarriage. It is believed that the remarriage of the noncustodial parent (father) results in a decrease in child support payments and in compliance. Somewhat surprisingly, then, the few studies performed did not support this premise. Teachman (1991), using the NLS 1972 cohort, found no effect of remarriage upon child support. Sonenstein and Calhoun (1990), using data from two states, reported that compliance increased when the noncustodial parents remarried.

The remarriage of the custodial parent is also believed to result in the noncustodial parent reducing support. Teachman (1991) found no support for this premise. However, two studies, one using CPS data and one using data from two states, did report that compliance dropped with remarriage of the custodial parent (Beller & Graham, 1991; Sonenstein & Calhoun, 1990). The CPS data included alimony as well as child support payments, so that the decrease could have been due to the change in alimony payments. Clearly, more research is needed on child support and remarriage.

Fathers who do and do not pay child support are quite different. Higher income, contact with child, age of child, voluntary rather than mandated payments, and time since divorce are all associated with compliance and higher child support payments (Beller & Graham, 1991; Maccoby & Mnookin, 1992; Sonenstein & Calhoun, 1990; Teachman, 1991). An example is taken from my work with Baydar (Baydar & Brooks-Gunn, in press). Children who were 5 years of age or younger in 1986 and who were living with their biological parents in 1986 (children of the NLSY) were divided into two groups—those who were still living with their father and mother in 1988, and those who were living with their mother in 1988. We then divided those children whose parents separated into two groups—those whose fathers reportedly paid child support, and those whose fathers did not. Family characteristics were less strongly linked to child support payment among children with separated parents than they were to whether or not parents had separated. Child support was more likely if fathers had higher education, if families had higher income, and if mothers worked prior to the separation. Mothers who received child support did not reduce their work hours, compared to mothers who did not receive child support. And the quality of the home environment was the same in the two groups. No comparable analysis exists for stepparent families and child support payments.

Effects of Child Support

Effects on Child Well-Being.   What effect does the receipt of child support payments have on children? Research has looked at sources of income and child well-being (Garfinkel & McLanahan, in press). Three papers at a 1992 symposium on child support presented relevant analyses, focusing on marital disruptions. Effects of income, and income derived from child support, were examined using the children of the NLSY (Baydar & Brooks-Gunn, in press), the PSID (Knox & Bane, in press), and the NSFH (McLanahan, Seltzer, Hanson, &

Thomson, in press). All had longitudinal data, and one (PSID) used family income data for 8 years (see also Furstenberg, Morgan, & Allison, 1987).

Using the children of the NLSY (Baydar & Brooks-Gunn, in press), we compared the outcomes of children in separated/divorced families where noncustodial fathers pay child support and where fathers do not. The premise is that receipt of child support income will have beneficial effects on children. Reading achievement scores (PIAT) of children who received child support or did not receive child support, were compared to those whose father did not leave the household. Regression analyses were conducted for those 437 children in 1986 who had Peabody Picture Vocabulary Test Scores (those children aged 3–5 in 1986 and, consequently, aged 5–7 in 1988). Effects of child support were found for girls, but not for boys. Girls whose fathers paid child support had similar achievement scores to girls whose fathers still lived in their homes, after controlling for initial child and family characteristics, but girls whose fathers did not provide child support had lower scores. These effects were not due to maternal working hours being different or quality of home environment being different for the two groups. Although including family income reduced the differences between the two groups, receipt of child support was still a significant factor in girls' outcomes.

Knox and Bane (in press) studied children who were 2–8 years of age in 1968 (PSID). The outcome of interest was school completion in 1987 (age 21). They examined the average child support payment received during all single-parent years, from 8 to 18. Child support was positively related to more years of schooling, even after controlling for income level and receipt of welfare.

McLanahan et al. (in press) looked at school grade point average (GPA) and behavior problems in the NSFH. Like the other two studies, child support receipt was associated with higher levels of child well-being.

It is unclear what accounts for these effects. Perhaps the receipt of child support provides mothers with more control over finances or allows them to work fewer hours or to stay off welfare (Knox & Bane, in press), or the provision of money reduces overall stress in the home. Regardless of how the father and mother perceive the payments, the child might see the child support as an affirmation of the father's commitment. This could be true even in the absence of increased contact. The perception of commitment might influence children's behavior without actual parental behavior being substantially different between those who do and do not provide child support. More research is needed on how this effect operates. Also, we do not know if the child support effect would be found in stepparent families where a remarriage had occurred.

Effects on Contact and Conflict.   Child support might influence contact with the child and conflict with the mother or family more generally. Child support is associated with contact, although it is unclear as to the direction of the relationship (McLanahan et al., in press; Seltzer, Schaeffer, & Charng, 1989). It is believed that contact with the noncustodial father has positive effects on children, although little research found such links (Baydar & Brooks-Gunn, in press; Furstenberg et al., 1987). It is important to note the low levels of contact between noncustodial parents and their children. Low levels of contact in many families bespeaks a lack of parental commitment, and may be perceived as such by the children. As Furstenberg (in press) noted, a parental divorce, in many cases, is a child divorce as well. How this might translate into child outcomes is not well understood.

Payment of child support is thought to increase conflict about how money is spent, or about visitation, the premise being that noncustodial parents might feel more entitled to a say in the spending of money and childrearing if they were providing for the child. In an analysis of NSFH children under the age of 18, McLanahan et al. (in press) reported that child support was associated with higher conflict in divorced families. In these analyses, conflict was negatively associated with child outcomes, while contact was not associated with child outcomes (GPA and school problems).

Changes in the Child Support System

Findings from the few studies of child support receipt may not speak directly to current child support policies. Mandated child support was not as widely implemented in the late 1980s, when the children and youth were assessed. Fathers who choose to pay child support may differ from those who pay support only after legal proceedings. How mandated child support will influence such factors as contact, commitment, supervision, and conflict is a policy research topic of utmost importance. For example, mandated child support may increase contact, since fathers who are paying child support might have stronger ties to the children as a function of their legitimacy in the family, given their contribution. On the other hand, mandates may cause resentment, decreasing ties or increasing conflict. Parents who had high levels of conflict might continue to experience conflict, if contact is assured via child support or if resentment over payments is high (Garfinkel & McLanahan, in press).

One study provided a model of what might happen to the links between child support and child contact as well as family conflict. Using the CPS Child Support Supplement data, McLanahan et al. (in press) provided estimates of predicted child support for each state in order to model differences in child support enforcement policy. Using coefficients derived from the CPS, they re-ran their analysis of the NSFH, finding that predicted child support was no longer associated with conflict, and that predicted child support was still associated with higher GPAs and lower school problem scores. The authors speculated that conflict and child support payments might not be associated in a system where more noncustodial parents paid, because the system would be seen as more equitable. However, research has not focused on stepparent families, nor on how child support mandates would influence children in remarriage situations.

CONCLUSION

This chapter focused on several research and policy agendas. Research needs to focus on how remarriage operates in families for whom the remarriage has positive income effects, versus those for whom it does not. How stepparenting and remarriage operate in different cultural or ethnic groups (using economic, psychological, and family systems perspectives) also needs to be considered.

The connection of the noncustodial father is still an understudied topic in remarried and stepparent families. Different custody and child support mandates might influence the process of adapting to the new stepparent family form. Much more research is recommended on these topics, particularly work integrating economic and family system perspectives. In addition, almost nothing has been done regarding policies related to family processes. All policy initiatives address family economics, although policy scholars are considering the potential impact of economic policies on parent–child contact and family conflict.

Programs could focus on helping stepparent families adapt to this sometimes difficult family setting. Programs focus on new parents, and some ventures have universal home visiting during the neonatal period. The programs probably meet with widespread acceptance because health and safety are considered paramount (rather than family conflict or adaptation to the new family form), and because parenthood is a transition experienced by 90% of all adults. The formation of a stepparent family is not normative. Research such as that by Hetherington suggests potential directions for prevention research programs.

Another vexing issue involves the low commitment of many stepparents to their stepchildren. We have not yet begun to grapple with the question of whether or not it is desirable to increase stepparents' commitment (i.e., would the commitment of noncustodial parents decrease with stepparents' commitment?). Even if the answer is yes, it is not clear how to alter parental commitment and concern.

Stepparenting is a family form for many children in the United States. If stepparenting is defined to include never-married parents after they marry a first time, multiple remarriages, and perhaps even cohabiting parents with children from previous unions, even more children would be living with stepparents than the statistics suggest. At the same time, it is important to remember that stepparent families are not the most frequent living arrangements for children who are not in original-parent family situations. Children living in nonoriginal-parent families are most likely to be residing in parent-only families, not stepparent families. The study of stepparent families might be embedded in a larger contextual framework that considers the effects of all types of parental transitions upon children and the family system.

Such a framework would also allow for a more precise explanation of the effects of stepparents upon children. Currently, it is not clear whether the untoward effects are due to the residual effects of the original marital disruption and move to a single-parent household, or to the entrance of a new and unrelated adult into the household, or to a second disruption (independent of the identity of the new parental figure). Looking at various parental transitions would help untangle these possibilities. What happens to children and families when the father moves back into the household after a separation—and many separations do not end in divorce (Baydar & Brooks-Gunn, in press). In what ways are the disequilibrium and restabilization processes similar and different to those in families where a stepfather enters the family? Another example may come from the work on cohabitation. Does remarriage to a cohabitating adult alter the family systems already in place?

A final example involves grandmothers, since so many never married single mothers co-reside and co-parent with their mothers or other female kin (Brooks-Gunn & Chase-Lansdale, 1991; Chase-Lansdale, Brooks-Gunn, & Zamsky, 1994). The move out of the grandmother's house is a common occurrence for many children in the preschool years. These children are losing a co-parent; how do the effects on the family system compare to those in a divorce situation? And how do these children and their mothers respond to a marriage or cohabitation situation? Although answers to these questions do not yet exist, they point to research agendas for the next decade.

ACKNOWLEDGMENTS

The writing of this chapter was supported by research grants from NIH and by the NICHD on Child and Family Well-Being Network. I wish to thank Elizabeth Peters and Sara McLanahan for their comments, Nazli Baydar for her collaboration, and Pia Rebello for her help in manuscript preparation.

REFERENCES

Amato, P. R., & Keith, B. (1991). Parental divorce and the well-being of children: A meta-analysis. *Psychological Bulletin, 110*, 26–46.

Baydar, N. (1988). Effects of parental separation and re-entry into union on the emotional well-being of children. *Journal of Marriage and the Family, 50*, 967–981.

Baydar, N., & Brooks-Gunn, J. (in press). The dynamics of child support and its consequences for children. In I. Garfinkel, S. McLanahan, & P. Robins (Eds.), *Child support reform and child well-being*. Washington, DC: Urban Institute Press.

Beller, A. H., & Graham, J. W. (1991). The effect of child support enforcement on child support payments. *Policy Research and Policy Review, 10*(2), 91–116.

Block, J. H., Block, J., & Gjerde, P. F. (1986). The personality of children prior to divorce: A prospective study. *Child Development, 57,* 827–840.

Bronfenbrenner, U. (1986). Ecology of the family as a context for human development: Research perspectives. *Developmental Psychology, 22*(6), 723–742.

Bronfenbrenner, U., & Crouter, A. C. (1983). The evolution of environmental models in developmental research. In P. Mussen (Ed.), *Handbook of child psychology* (Vol. 4, pp. 357–414). New York: Wiley.

Brooks-Gunn, J., & Chase-Lansdale, P. L. (1991). Children having children: Effects on the family system. *Pediatric Annals, 20*(9), 467–481.

Brooks-Gunn, J., Duncan, G. J., Klebanov, P. K., & Sealand, N. (1993). Do neighborhoods influence child and adolescent behavior? *American Journal of Sociology, 99*(2), 353–395.

Brooks-Gunn, J., Phelps, E., & Elder, G. H. (1991). Studying lives through time: Secondary data analyses in developmental psychology. *Developmental Psychology, 27*(6), 899–910.

Chase-Lansdale, P. L., Brooks-Gunn, J., & Paikoff, R. L. (1991). Research and programs for adolescent mothers: Missing links and future promises. *Family Relations, 40*(4), 396–404.

Chase-Lansdale, P. L., Brooks-Gunn, J., & Zamsky, E. S. (1994). Young multigenerational families in poverty: Quality of mothering and grandmothering. *Child Development, 65*(2), 373–393.

Chase-Lansdale, P. L., & Hetherington, E. M. (1990). The impact of divorce on life-span development: Short and long term effects. In P. B. Baltes, D. L. Featherman, & R. M. Lerner (Eds.), *Life-span development and behavior* (pp. 105–150). Hillsdale, NJ: Lawrence Erlbaum Associates.

Chase-Lansdale, P. L., Mott, F. L., Brooks-Gunn, J., & Phillips, D. (1991). Children of the NLSY: A unique research opportunity. *Developmental Psychology, 27*(6), 932–945.

Cherlin, A. J. (1992). *Marriage, divorce, remarriage.* Cambridge, MA: Harvard University Press.

Cherlin, A. J., Furstenberg, F. F., Jr., Chase-Lansdale, P. L., Kiernan, K. E., Robins, P. K., & Morrison, D. R. (1991). Longitudinal studies of effects of divorce on children in Great Britain and the United States. *Science, 252,* 1386–1389.

Coleman, J. S. (1988). Social capital in the creation of human capital. *American Journal of Sociology, 94,* S95–S120.

Conger, R. D., Conger, K. J., Elder, G. H., Jr., Lorenz, F. O., Simons, R. L., & Whitbeck, L. B. (1992). A family process model of economic hardship and adjustment of early adolescent boys. *Child Development, 63,* 526–541.

Corbett, T. (1992). The Wisconsin child support assurance system: From plausible proposals to improbably prospects. In I. Garfinkel, S. McLanahan, & P. Robins (Eds.), *Child support assurance* (pp. 27–54). Washington, DC: Urban University Press.

Cowan, P. A., & Cowan, C. P. (1990). Becoming a family: Research and intervention. In I. Sigel & A. Brody (Eds.), *Family research* (pp. 1–51). Hillsdale, NJ: Lawrence Erlbaum Associates.

Cowan, C. P., & Cowan, P. A., Heming, G., & Miller, N. B. (1991). Becoming a family: Marriage, parenting and child development. In P. A. Cowan & M. Hetherington (Eds.), *Family transitions* (pp. 79–110). Hillsdale, NJ: Lawrence Erlbaum Associates.

Dornbusch, S. M., Carlsmith, J. M., Bushwall, S. J., Ritter, P. L., Leiderman, N., Hastorf, A. H., & Gross, R. T. (1985). Single parents, extended households and the control of adolescents. *Child Development, 56,* 326–341.

Duncan, G. J. (1991). The economic environment of childhood. In A. C. Huston (Ed.), *Children in poverty* (pp. 23–51). New York: Cambridge University Press.

Duncan, G. J., Klebanov, P. K., & Brooks-Gunn, J. (in press). Economic deprivation and early-childhood development. *Child Development, 65*(2), 296–318.

Duncan, G. J., & Hoffman, S. D. (1985). A reconsideration of the economic consequences of marital dissolution. *Demography, 22,* 485–498.

Elder, G. (1974). *Children of the great depression*. Chicago: University of Chicago Press.

Elder, G. H., Conger, R. D., Foster, E. M., & Ardelt, M. (1993). Families under economic pressure. *Journal of Family Issues, 13*, 5–37.

Emery, R. E. (1988). *Marriage, divorce, and children's adjustment*. Newbury Park, CA: Sage.

Furstenberg, F. F. (in press). Dealing with dads: Changing roles of fathers. In P. L. Chase-Lansdale, & J. Brooks-Gunn (Eds.), *Escape from poverty: What makes a difference for children*. New York: Cambridge University Press.

Furstenberg, F. F., Brooks-Gunn, J., & Morgan, S. P. (1987). Adolescent mothers and their children in later life. *Family Planning Perspectives*, (4), 142–151.

Furstenberg, F. F., Morgan, S. P., & Allison, P. D. (1987). Paternal participation and children's well-being after marital dissolution. *American Sociological Review, 52*, 695–701.

Garcia-Coll, C. T. (1990). Developmental outcome of minority infants: A process-oriented look into our beginnings. *Child Development, 61*(2), 270–289.

Garfinkel, I., & McLanahan, S. (1990). The effect of the child support provisions of the Family Support Act of 88 on child well being. *Population Research and Policy Review, 9*, 205–234.

Garfinkel, I., & McLanahan, S. (in press). The effects of child support reform on child well being. In P. L. Chase-Lansdale, & J. Brooks-Gunn (Eds.), *Escape from poverty: What makes a difference for children*. New York: Cambridge University Press.

Garfinkel, I., McLanahan, S., & Robins, P. (in press). *Child support reform and child well being*. Washington, DC: Urban Institute Press.

Gunnoe, M. L. (1993). *Noncustodial mothers' and fathers' contribution to the adjustment of adolescent stepchildren*. Unpublished doctoral dissertation, University of Virginia, Charlottesville.

Haveman, R., Wolfe, B., & Spaulding, J. (1991). Childhood events and circumstances influencing high school completion. *Demography, 28*(1), 133–157.

Hayes, C. D. (Ed.). (1987). *Risking the Future: Adolescent Sexuality, Pregnancy and Child Bearing*. Washington, DC:National Academy of Sciences Press.

Hetherington, E. M. (1993). An overview of the Virginia Longitudinal Study of Divorce and Remarriage: A focus on early adolescence. *Journal of Family Psychology, 7*, 39–56.

Hetherington, E. M., & Arasteh, J. D. (Eds.). (1988). *Impact of Divorce, Single Parenting, and Step-parenting on Children*. Hillsdale, NJ: Lawrence Erlbaum Associates.

Hetherington, E. M., & Clingempeel, W. G. (1992). Coping with marital transitions: A family systems perspective. *Monographs of the Society for Research in Child Development, 57* (2–3, Serial No. 227).

Hetherington, E. M., Cox, M., & Cox, R. (1978). The aftermath of divorce. In H. J. Stevens, Jr. & M. Mathews (Eds.), *Mother–child, father–child relations*. Washington, DC: National Association for the Education of Young Children.

Hernandez, D. J. (1993). *America's children: Resources from family, government, and the economy*. New York: Russell Sage Foundation.

Huston, A. (Ed.). (1991). *Children in poverty: Child development and public policy*. Cambridge, MA: Cambridge University Press

Kiernan, K. (1992). The impact of family disruption in childhood on transitions made in young adult life. *Population Studies, 46*, 218–234.

Knox, V. W., & Bane, M. J. (in press). The effects of child support payments on educational attainment. In I. Garfinkel, S. Mclanahan, & P. Robins (Eds.), *Child support reform and child well-being*. Washington, DC: Urban Institute Press.

Lazear, E. P., & Michael, R. T. (1988). *Allocation of income within the household*. Chicago, IL: University of Chicago Press.

Lempers, J. D., Clark-Lempers, D., & Simons, R. L. (1989). Economic hardship, parenting, and distress in adolescence. *Child Development, 60*, 25–39.

Liaw, F. R., & Brooks-Gunn, J. (in press). Cumulative risk and poverty. *Developmental Psychology*.

Maccoby, E. E. & Mnookin, R. H. (1990). Co-Parenting in the second year after divorce. *Journal of Marriage and Family, 52,* 141–155.

Maccoby, E. E., & Mnookin, R. H. (1992). *Dividing the child: Social and legal dilemmas of custody.* Cambridge, MA: Harvard University Press.

Markman, H. J., Floyd, F. J., Stanley, S. M., & Storaasli, R. D. (1988). Prevention of marital distress: A longitudinal investigation. *Journal of Consulting and Clinical Psychology, 56*(2), 210–217.

McCormick, M. C., & Brooks-Gunn, J. (1989). Health care for children and adolescents. In H. Freeman & S. Levine (Eds.), *Handbook of medical sociology.* (pp. 347–380). Englewood Cliffs, NJ: Prentice Hall.

McLanahan, S., Astone, N. M., & Marks, N. F. (1991). The role of mother-only families in reducing poverty. In A. C. Huston (Ed.), *Children in poverty: Child development and public policy* (pp. 51–78). Cambridge, MA: Cambridge University Press.

McLanahan, S., & Booth, K. (1989). Mother-only families: Problems, prospects, and politics. *Journal of Marriage and the Family, 51,* 557–580.

McLanahan, S., Seltzer, J. A., Hanson, T. L., Thomson, E. (in press). Child support enforcement and child well-being: Greater security or greater conflict? In I. Garfinkel, S. Mclanahan, & P. Robins (Eds.), *Child support reform and child well-being.* Washington, DC: Urban Institute Press.

McLoyd, V. C. (1990). The impact of economic hardship on Black families and children: Psychological Distress, parenting, and socioemotional development. *Child Development, 61,* 311–346.

Parker, L., Greer, S., & Zuckerman, B. (1988). Double "Jeopardy:" The impact of poverty on early child development. *The Pediatric Clinics of North America, 35,* 1227–1240.

Rossi, A. S., & Rossi, P. H. (1990). *Of human bonding: Parent-child relations across the life course.* Hawthorne, NY: Aldine de Gruyter.

Rutter, M., & Garmezy, N. (1983). Developmental Psychopathology. In P. Mussen & M. Hetherington, (Eds.), *Handbook of child psychology: Socialization, personality and social development.* (pp. 775–911). New York: John Wiley and Sons.

Seltzer, J., Schaeffer, N. C., & Charng, H. (1989). Family ties after divorce: The relationship between visiting and paying child support. *Journal of Marriage and Family, 51,* 1013–1031.

Sonenstein, F. L., & Calhoun, C. A. (1990). Determinants of child support: A pilot survey of absent parents. *Contemporary Policy Issues, 8*(1), 75–94.

Teachman, J. D. (1991). Who pays? Receipt of child support in the United States. *Journal of Marriage and the Family, 53*(3), 759–772.

Thoits, P. (1992). Identity structures and psychological well-being: Gender and marital status comparisons. *Social Psychology Quarterly, 55,* 236–256.

Thomson, E., & McLanahan, S. (1993, August). *Family structure and child well-being: Economic resource versus parental behavior.* Paper presented at the annual meeting of the American Sociological Association, Washington, DC.

Thomson, E., McLanahan, S., & Curtin, R. B. (1992). Family structure, gender, and parental socialization. *Journal of Marriage and Family, 54,* 368–378.

White, L. (1993, October). *Stepfamilies over the Life Course: Social Support.* Paper presented at the National Symposium on Step-Parent Families with Children: Who Benefits? Who Does Not?, University Park, PA.

Zill, N., Morrison, D. R., Coiro, M. J. (1993). Long-term effects of parental divorce on parent-child relationships, adjustment, and achievement in young adulthood. *Journal of Family Psychology, 7*(6), 1–13.

14 Reformulating the Legal Definition of the Stepparent–Child Relationship

Margaret M. Mahoney
The University of Pittsburgh

Traditionally, the legal system has recognized and defined family status relationships exclusively for married couples and for parents and their biological or adopted children. These relationships entail many legal rights and responsibilities within the family unit, and vis-à-vis others who interact with children, parents, wives, and husbands. The general purposes of family related laws are to safeguard the interests of individual family members, protect the family unit, and vindicate particular interests of the larger society. For example, the law of support protects dependent family members, relieves the public from economic responsibility for them, and enhances the solidarity of the family unit. The growing number of adults and children in our society who reside in nontraditional family settings, including stepfamilies, has caused family scholars to question whether the legal recognition, benefits, and burdens associated with legal family status should now be extended beyond the traditional nuclear family (Bartlett, 1984; Fine, 1989; Jaff, 1988; Kargman, 1991; Mahoney, 1984; 1989; Melton, 1991; Polikoff, 1990).

In *Stepfamilies and the Law* (Mahoney, in press), I surveyed the various contexts in which lawmakers have been asked to extend some aspect of the legal parent–child status to stepfamily relationships. The book highlights the wide variety of situations in which family status matters. In addition to the obvious issues of child support and custody, questions have been raised about the proper treatment of stepfamilies under the laws governing inheritance, the construction of wills, family tort immunity, parent–child consortium claims, the vicarious liability of parents for the torts of their children, workers' compensation survivors' claims, the rights of parents to choose their children's surnames, the authority of parents to discipline children, the civil child protection system, special crimes of abuse in the family, and incest. This catalog of state law issues reveals the complexity of the legal parent–child status, which has provided the backdrop for reconsidering the legal definition of the stepparent–child relationship.

To date, most state legislatures and courts have failed to attach any significance to the stepparent–child relationship for most of these purposes. Frequently, this result was reached by reference to the policies behind particular legal doctrines, and without any reference to the nature of relationships within the stepfamily. For example, the Massachusetts Supreme Court relied upon general policies relating to the tort law system of compensation for personal injuries, when it refused to include stepchildren in the cause of action for loss of parental consortium. The consortium doctrine enables children in that state to recover for their own relational losses against the person who severely injures or kills a parent. The court denied a similar right to stepchildren, with the observation that "[l]imiting loss of consortium claims to members of legally cognizable relationships provides a clear, principled, easily ascertainable standard which adequately distinguishes those entitled to recover from those involved in the 'myriad of relationships' which exist in society" (*Mendoza v. B.L.H. Electronics*, 1988). The generally accepted, tort-related policies expressed in this statement justify doctrines that are easy to administer and that do not impose too great a financial burden on the person whose conduct harmed a family member. Missing here is any reference to the nature of the losses suffered by stepchildren when their stepparent is wrongfully disabled or killed. Those losses might (or might not) support the court's conclusion that drawing a line between biological children and stepchildren is a "principled" method of achieving these goals for the compensation system.

The current "law of stepfamilies" consists of a series of limited exceptions to the premise, expressed in the *Mendoza* opinion, that stepparents and their stepchildren are legal strangers to one another. Furthermore, the exceptions that validate stepparent–child relationships for a particular limited purpose are not consistent from one state to another. For example, there is no uniform position among the 50 states on the question of the capacity of a stepparent and an adult stepchild to marry each other after the stepparent's marriage to the stepchild's biological parent has been terminated by death or divorce. Currently, the civil marriage statutes in 12 states refuse to recognize the validity of such a marriage. Furthermore, in 9 states (including 2 states that impose the civil marriage prohibition), the attempt to marry is a crime. In the remaining states, there is no civil or criminal marriage restriction. A similar lack of uniformity exists as to many other important issues. Clearly, a comprehensive definition of the stepfamily in U.S. law has yet to be formulated.

The absence of a clear and comprehensive legal definition becomes more troubling as a growing number of U.S. citizens come to reside in stepfamilies. However, the task of formulating a definition of the stepparent–child relationship that is fair and workable for stepparents, stepchildren, other family members, and the larger society is a daunting one. In defining the stepparent–child status in the future, two important questions must be answered. First, what relationships between children and the spouses of their custodial parents should be legally significant? And second, what rights and responsibilities should be associated with stepfamily membership? The empirical research about stepfamilies discussed in this volume and the research agenda being prepared for the future are relevant in answering these questions.

As to the first issue, the threshold question is whether the marriage between a custodial parent and another adult should automatically give rise to a legally significant stepparent–child relationship, or whether something more should be required before any legal status is attached. Existing legal doctrines have not answered this question in a consistent fashion. Some state laws, such as the criminal and civil marriage regulations described earlier, apply to every stepparent and child in the state. By way of contrast, certain statutory and judicial doctrines, which recognize stepfamilies for other legal purposes, inquire into the nature of the stepparent–child relationship in each case. For example, the common law in loco parentis doctrine asks whether or not the stepparent has voluntarily assumed a parental role toward the stepchild. In some states, the courts have recognized certain stepparent rights—including the authority to discipline stepchildren, and visitation rights following a divorce—when the stepparent stands in loco parentis (in the place of a parent) toward the child. A more restrictive test appears in the California inheritance statute, which allows stepchildren to inherit as children from their stepparents only when "(1)the relationship began during the [stepchild's] minority and continued throughout the parties' joint lifetimes and (2)it is established by clear and convincing evidence that the . . . stepparent would have adopted the [stepchild] but for a legal barrier."

Both the California inheritance statute and the common law in loco parentis doctrine attempt to identify situations where certain meaningful ties exist between a stepparent and child, beyond their residence together with the custodial parent, as the basis for imposing legal rights and duties. The empirical studies relating to the many variations in relationships established within stepfamilies tend to support this more refined approach. That is, given the wide variety in actual relationships, it would be inappropriate to impose a full array of legal entitlements, benefits, and responsibilities in every stepfamily formed by the marriage of a custodial parent.

In the future, policymakers must establish clear legal standards for distinguishing between stepfamilies where relationships are so tenuous that legal status is inappropriate, and those where recognition is a fair result. Furthermore, the standards should be relatively clear and easy to administer, so that family members know where they stand in the eyes of the law. As highlighted by many of the authors in this volume, information is available regarding the variable factors that appear to affect the nature and quality of relationships established within stepfamilies. This information, along with the results of future empirical studies, may be helpful in establishing standards for identifying legally significant stepparent–child relationships.

Once these standards are developed, the legal analysis must turn to the second question posited earlier. That is, what rights and responsibilities are properly associated with stepfamily membership? For each family related doctrine, in areas of law including custody, support, property, torts, and criminal law, the inquiry must be made as to whether or not the policies that justify regulation in the biological family also extend to the stepfamily. If so, then a decision must be made about the appropriate form of regulation in the nontraditional family. For example, if stepparent support duties are determined to be wise policy, should the stepparents' duty be the same as that of biological parents, or different, in terms of quantity or duration? Similarly, if stepparent visitation rights following divorce are recognized, should the rights be coextensive with those of noncustodial biological parents? The task of analyzing these issues, as part of the process of formulating a legal definition of the stepparent–child relationship, is complex and challenging. Here, too, many of the research agendas highlighted in this volume can provide assistance to the policymakers who undertake this task.

Empirical information about stepfamilies may have a direct application in analyzing certain aspects of the legal status of stepparents and stepchildren. For example, inheritance statutes in all states list the relatives who are entitled to property when the owner dies without a will. The legislative purpose is to pass the property to those persons who most likely would have been the beneficiaries if the owner had made a will. The statutes assume that the average person would desire to benefit his or her closest relatives, usually the surviving spouse and children. With the exception of the California statute quoted above, state inheritance laws exclude stepchildren from the definition of close relatives entitled to inherit. In reassessing this doctrine, it would be useful to know how often stepparents who die with a will include their stepchildren as beneficiaries. It would also be useful to know whether living stepparents would desire their stepchildren to inherit in the event the stepparent died without a will.

Since the average stepparent's preference is the key to determining general standards for intestate distribution of stepparents' estates, empirical data about actual stepparent preferences would be relevant here. Indeed, the results of a 1965 study of 453 wills probated in Cuyahoga County, Ohio suggests that donative interests do arise in many nontraditional family relationships. In this study, which did not focus exclusively on stepfamilies, 63% of the wills included gifts to "nonrelated inheritors." More than one half of these nontraditional gifts were made to stepchildren or to other relatives-by-marriage (such as in-laws), all of whom would have been excluded from inheritance if the owner had died without a will (Sussman, Cates, & Smith, 1970). This study provides some support for the proposition that many stepfamily members desire to benefit each other at death, and that the inheritance laws, which are designed to reflect average testamentary intent, should recognize stepfamily relationships. Of course, more refined studies, focusing exclusively on testamentary goals in stepfamilies, would be more informative.

For other legal issues, the relevance of empirical information about families to the process of legal policymaking is more tenuous. For example, in formulating rules regarding child custody and visitation, the primary concern of the legal system is the future welfare of family members, especially (or exclusively) the children. The process of creating and applying legal rules in this field has been a complex and uneasy one for legislatures and judges. Defining the best interests of children is even more difficult in the stepfamily setting, where complicated fact patterns and multiple adult–child relationships are likely to exist. No single factor, nor any set of factors, will ever serve as a certain predictor of a child's future welfare. Still, as policymakers work to achieve the most just definition of custody and visitation rights in the stepfamily, they may productively look to objective data about the well-being of children in a variety of circumstances. This is a policy agenda that admittedly requires greater definition in the future.

Finally, the law in general, and family law in particular, serves a normative function. In the words of legal scholar Mary Ann Glendon (1987):

> Much of family law is no more—and no less—than the symbolic expression of certain cultural ideals. . . . Probably no other area of law is so replete with legal norms that communicate ideas about proper behavior but that have no direct sanctions. (p. 10)

I believe that proposals to enhance the recognition of stepparent–child relationships must be considered in light of this important function of the law.

The proponents of change in the legal definition of the family believe that, for many members of society, the family law system is failing to accomplish its basic purposes by denying recognition to nontraditional family styles, and that this is wrong. The call for reform raises an additional question about the likelihood that legal validation of the stepfamily would be consistent with both public expectations and the private expectations of stepfamily members. An affirmative answer to this question, which can be tested in a scientific fashion (as noted in White's chapter), would support the case for legal reform.

In a law review article entitled "To Have and Have Not: Assessing the Value of Social Science to the Law As Science and Policy," Faigman (1989) described the role of the social sciences in this situation:

> Virtually every legal judgment is composed of both factual premises and normative principles. . . . [S]cience cannot contribute to the normative debate. . . . [S]ubjective belief (or disbelief) . . . does not implicate a fact question that is susceptible to testing. Subjective beliefs may be examined in the sense that their prevalence can be assessed. (pp. 1015–1016)

This type of objective information about social acceptance of the stepfamily status, like the other types of information highlighted in this chapter, would be relevant in reassessing the legal definition of the stepparent–child relationship.

REFERENCES

Bartlett, K. T. (1984). Rethinking parenthood as an exclusive status: The need for legal alternatives when the premise of the nuclear family has failed. *Virginia Law Review, 70*, 879–963.

Faigman, D. L. (1989). To have and have not: Assessing the value of social science to the law as science and policy. *Emory Law Journal, 38*, 1005–1096.

Fine, M. A. (1989). A social science perspective on stepfamily law: Suggestions for legal reform. *Family Relations, 38*, 53–58.

Glendon, M. A. (1987). *Abortion and divorce in Western law.* Cambridge, MA: Harvard University Press.

Jaff, J. (1988). Wedding bell blues: The position of unmarried people in American law. *Arizona Law Review, 30*, 207–242.

Kargman, M. W. (1983). Stepchild support obligations of stepparents. *Family Relations, 32*, 231–238.

Mahoney, M. M. (1984). Support and custody aspects of the stepparent–child relationship. *Cornell Law Review, 70*, 38–79.

Mahoney, M. M. (1989). Stepfamilies in the law of intestate succession and wills. *University of California at Davis Law Review, 22*, 917–250.

Mahoney, M. M. (in press). *Stepfamilies and the law.* Ann Arbor: University of Michigan Press.

Mendoza J. B.L.H. Electronics, 530 N.E.2d 349, 350–51 (Mass. 1988) (concurring opinion).

Melton, R. L. (1991). Legal rights of unmarried heterosexual and homosexual couples and evolving definitions of "family." *Journal of Family Law, 29*, 497–517.

Polikoff, N. D. (1990). This child does have two mothers: Redefining parenthood to meet the needs of children in lesbian-mother and other nontraditional families. *Georgetown Law Journal, 78*, 459–575.

Sussman, M., Cates, J., & Smith, D. (1970). *The family and inheritance* (8th ed.). New York: Sage.

Social Policy Pertaining to Stepfamilies: Should Stepparents and Stepchildren Have the Option of Establishing a Legal Relationship?

15

Mark A. Fine
University of Dayton

Family scholars have often claimed that the United States does not have a clear, integrative, and coherent policy to support families (Aldous & Dumon, 1990). This statement is even more applicable to stepfamilies than it is to families in general. Not only are there few programs designed specifically to assist members of stepfamilies, but the rights and obligations of stepfamily members are not clearly specified in most existing laws. Although the rights of stepparents and stepchildren and the responsibilities of stepparents have become clearer in the last decade, there is still considerable variability among states in their laws affecting stepfamilies. Unlike most other Western nations, family law in the United States is primarily governed at the state level. Courts and legislatures have been slow to recognize the possibly enduring nature of stepparent–stepchild relationships (M. Fine & Fine, 1992).

It is noteworthy that the most commonly addressed legal and policy issues pertaining to stepfamilies are concerned with what occurs after a residential stepfamily is disrupted following parental divorce or death. These issues address whether or not, following termination of the remarriage, stepparents have an obligation to financially support stepchildren, have visitation rights after the end of the remarriage, and have a right to contest custody of stepchildren. Policy issues pertaining to intact stepfamilies have rarely been addressed.

In this chapter, I propose some principles that I believe should underlie any policy initiative. After these principles are presented, I discuss one specific policy initiative relevant to both adults and children in intact stepfamilies: whether or not stepparents should have the option of legalizing the relationship with their stepchildren. After describing the proposed policy initiative, I review its potential advantages and disadvantages and identify research questions that need to be answered.

Before proceeding to stepfamily policy, I wish to explicitly state two beliefs that underlie my position. First, I believe it is inappropriate to attempt to reduce the prevalence of stepfamilies, as suggested by Popenoe in his chapter. Because marital conflict and divorce will, in my opinion, inevitably occur in many families, stepfamilies will continue to be a common family form in our society. Therefore, my agenda is to conduct research and to propose policy that improves the lives of stepfamily members, rather than reduces the number of stepfamilies. Second, although I believe that empirical research needs to inform the process of policy planning, it is naive and erroneous to assume that empirical research will answer all important policy questions.

PRINCIPLES THAT SHOULD UNDERLIE
POLICY INITIATIVES

Two principles should underlie any policy initiatives that directly affect stepfamilies. First, policies need to take into account that stepfamilies, perhaps more so than other types of families, are a diverse group. Because policies that are helpful for some stepfamilies may not be helpful for others, laws need to be flexible and judges need to take into account the unique aspects of specific cases.

The second principle is that policy reform needs to recognize that steprelationships, particularly the stepparent–stepchild relationship, can be satisfying and meaningful to both parties (Coleman & Ganong, 1990). Should the remarriage terminate, the relationships may continue to be important. Of course, steprelationships are not always mutually satisfying and of enduring importance. However, unlike the assumption of many current laws that these relationships are not important and of ongoing meaningfulness, laws should be established that take into account the possibility that these relationships are of enduring importance.

A POLICY PROPOSAL: STEPPARENTS
AND STEPCHILDREN SHOULD HAVE
THE OPPORTUNITY TO ESTABLISH LEGAL
RELATIONSHIPS WITH EACH OTHER

Currently, unless stepparents adopt their stepchildren—which affords the stepparents the same rights as biological parents—stepparents and stepchildren in this country have no legal ties. In this section, I discuss the policy proposal that stepparents and stepchildren should be allowed to develop legally sanctioned relationships with each other.

A residential stepparent should be allowed to petition the court to establish a legal relationship to his or her stepchild. This relationship would not affect the parental rights and responsibilities of the noncustodial parent. Consequently, for those who seek such a relationship, there would be three adults—the biological parents and the stepparent—who would have parental rights and responsibilities. Therefore, the proposed policy differs from adoption, which terminates the rights of the noncustodial parent.

Because the cooperation of the child's custodial biological parent(s) would be critical to the success of a legal stepparent–stepchild relationship, the petition would require the approval of the child's custodial parent (or both biological parents in cases of joint custody). In addition, recognizing children's rights to have their needs considered in legal decisions that affect them (Koocher & Keith-Spiegel, 1990), the stepparent and biological parent(s) would have to claim that the petition was in the child's best interests and that the child's input was sought in a manner consistent with his or her level of cognitive development. If custody resides solely with one parent, the noncustodial parent could not prevent the petition from being granted. Once granted, the legal relationship would last until the child reached the age of 18, unless the stepparent petitioned the court to end the legal tie.

Stepparents with legal relationships to their stepchildren would be granted the same basic rights (e.g., to participate in the child's education, to consent to medical treatment for the child), and would have the same responsibilities as custodial parents (e.g., to financially support the child). For some decisions that are potentially very impactful to the child (e.g., moving the child out of the country, adopting the child), the stepparent with such a relationship would not be able to make the decision without the consent of the custodial parent(s). Depending on the circumstances in a particular case, the court would be allowed the flexibility to modify the responsibilities and obligations of the stepparent with a legal relationship with the stepchild.

The English Policy

England's Children Act 1989 (see also Cretney & Masson, 1990), which took effect in 1991, established a new concept in English law—"parental responsibility"—maintaining as its theme the notion that parenthood involves continuing and enduring responsibility. The Act regards children no longer as their parents' property, but rather as their parents' responsibility. Because most parental responsibility can be exercised only while a parent is caring for a child, the Act dictates that the court's powers should be directed to allocating the time the child spends with his or her parents, and not with dividing responsibilities and obligations between the parents (Cretney & Masson, 1990). Thus, both parents retain parental authority following divorce and, consequently, the courts are concerned primarily with determining the residence of the children and not with custody (Duquette, 1992).

Consistent with its emphasis on allowing adults who care for children to exercise parental responsibility, the Act provides an opportunity for stepparents to have a legal relationship with their stepchildren that is similar to, and a model for, the policy proposed in this chapter. The Act allows a residential stepparent who has been married for at least 2 years to the child's biological parent to petitition for a residence order. These petitions are typically granted and ex-spouses do not have the right to deny them. A stepparent with a residence order has parental responsibility for the child for the duration of the order, which typically lasts until the child is age 16 (Cretney & Masson, 1990). In this system, the child can have legal relationships with at least three adults (i.e., both biological parents and the stepparent), unlike the present situation in the United States, that allows for only two adults to have parental rights and responsibilities.

Stepparents who have residence orders have similar rights to biological parents. For example, changing the child's name or removing the child from the United Kingdom for more than 4 weeks requires the approval of all persons with parental responsibility, including stepparents with residence orders (Cretney & Masson, 1990). However, there are instances when stepparents with residence orders do not have the same rights as biological parents. For example, adoption only requires the agreement of all parents and does not require the approval of stepparents with residence orders.

The simplest version of the residence order merely stipulates with whom the child will live. However, the court is granted considerable discretion to establish detailed provisions which provide more control than that granted in the statute, if it considers these to be in the best interests of the child (Cretney & Masson, 1990). In particular cases, for example, the court may impose a condition on the residence order that stipulates that the child will receive certain medical treatments in an emergency, regardless of the objections of the stepparent.

Potential Advantages and Disadvantages of the Proposed Policy

There are several potential advantages for stepfamilies that may result from allowing a stepparent to petition for a legal relationship with the stepchild. Because granting this legal relationship requires the approval of the custodial biological parent(s) and requires a consideration of the interests of the stepchild, stepfamilies who seek to have such a legal relationship must initiate discussions between the biological parent(s), and the stepparent, and these might include the stepchild. These deliberations could lead to enhanced stepfamily cohesion and greater consensus about the parenting role of the stepparent. In addition, for those who wish it, the stepparent–stepchild relationship may be legitimized, and less conflict may result as the stepparent exercises his or her parental responsibility. Thus, for those stepfamilies with such a legal relationship, the policy might enhance the commitment that stepparents and stepchildren feel toward each other, reduce the ambiguity inherent in the stepparent role, and add to the stability of the remarriage.

Creating such a status might also affect the way that stepfamilies interface with societal institutions. For example, creating a sanctioned relationship might allow parents in stepfamilies (with the approval of the biological parent(s) and with input from the child in a manner consistent with his or her level of cognitive development) a mechanism to allow the stepparent to be involved in the stepchild's education and medical treatment. Allowing a stepparent to have a legal relationship with the stepchild might also affect whether or not stepchildren can be covered by health insurance policies and can inherit in the event of the stepparent's death—issues that can be ambiguous (D. Fine & Fine, 1992).

I argue that the proposed policy might have several advantages for those stepfamilies in which stepparents and stepchildren establish a legal tie. Clearly, those stepfamilies that choose to establish such a relationship are likely to be those that already have positive stepparent–stepchild relations. An important question is whether or not the proposed policy initiative would increase the quality of family relations for stepfamilies that have distant or conflictual stepparent–stepchild relations. For these stepfamilies, the availability of such a legal option could lead to improved relations. Whether or not the proposed policy would have this effect awaits future research, particularly from studies that address the association between stepfamily members' awareness of their legal circumstances and the quality of family relations (discussed later). The proposed policy could have positive effects on family relations only for those stepfamilies whose adults are aware of their legal options.

Possible disadvantages of the proposed policy are that it might: (a) add another level of bureaucracy to public institutions concerned with child welfare, without evidence that the policy initiative would lead to enhanced child well-being; (b) be perceived as interfering with noncustodial parents' attempts to remain actively involved with their children, which could have the effect of reducing contact between noncustodial parents and their children; (c) encourage stepparents to become excessively involved in the discipline of their stepchildren, which can be problematic, because some studies have found that the adjustment of stepchildren is facilitated when stepparents initially do not actively discipline their stepchildren, but support the discipline of the biological parent (Hetherington, 1993); and (d) be perceived by potential stepparents as an obligation, rather than a choice they must pursue, which may make them reluctant to marry biological parents with children.

Research Questions That Need to be Addressed

To determine the viability of the proposed policy, a number of research questions need to be investigated. Several of these are described here.

What Effects Will the English System Have?   To my knowledge, there have been no studies that have empirically investigated the utility of the English system. Clearly, careful evaluation of the English experience is warranted. How many stepparents petition and are granted residence orders? For those who do, how often is stepchildren's input sought and considered? How do stepchildren react to the legal nature of their relationship with the stepparent? To what extent are stepchildren aware of residence orders?

How are family relations affected? Are stepparent–stepchild relations enhanced following the granting of residence orders? Is the stability of remarriages enhanced with a spouse who has been granted residence orders? Is the ambiguity of the stepparent's role lessened following the granting of residence orders? Will a clear role emerge for stepparents who have sought and been granted residence orders?

The financial sequelae of obtaining residence orders also need to be investigated. What happens to the financial well-being of children in stepfamilies with residence orders? How is financial support from nonresidential parents to their children affected when stepparents seek and obtain residence orders?

There are also research questions that involve extrafamilial institutions. What happens to children's relations with their nonresidential parents after residence orders are granted to the stepparent? Is it easier for stepparents with residence orders to be involved in the education of their stepchildren? Do such institutions as health-care agencies and insurance companies treat stepparents as more legitimately responsible and involved in the lives of their stepchildren following the granting of residence orders?

To study these and other important questions, longitudinal designs are necessary. Simple comparisons between stepfamilies with stepparents that have and do not have residence orders are not likely to be informative. This is because those stepfamilies with stepparents that have residence orders are likely to have more harmonious stepparent–stepchild relations before the acquisition of residence orders than those stepfamilies with stepparents who do not have these orders. Family relations within stepfamilies that have these orders must be studied repeatedly over time.

Issues Needing Investigation in the United States.   Within the United States, there are several issues that need to be investigated to begin to determine the viability of this policy. Elsewhere, I proposed that the uncertain legal status of stepparents and stepfamilies may exacerbate adjustment difficulties in stepfamilies (M. Fine, 1989). However, to my knowledge, there are no empirical data to support this claim. To test the proposition, several lines of inquiry need to be pursued. At the most basic level, investigators need to determine how aware parents and stepparents are of their legal circumstances. How many parents and stepparents are aware of their rights and responsibilities in their particular state? Of those who have some awareness, how thorough is their level of understanding? How aware are stepchildren of the legal nature of their relationship with their stepparents?

In addition to examining the level of legal awareness of stepfamily members, it would be useful to know the effects of this awareness on stepfamily experiences and adjustment. Do stepparents who have a high level of legal awareness have a clear sense of their roles in the family? Is legal awareness associated with positive adjustment to the potentially stressful circumstances facing stepfamilies?

Researchers could also fruitfully examine how attractive a legally sanctioned stepparent–stepchild relationship is for stepparents and custodial biological parents. After being informed of what such a status might consist of, stepparents and their spouses could be asked if they would avail themselves of this opportunity if it became available. Members of stepfamilies, including noncustodial parents, could be asked how they think this might affect family relations. While these perceptions would not directly assess the effects of the proposed policy on family relations, they would give some preliminary insights into the expectations of stepfamily members.

Finally, piloting the policy initiative on a demonstration basis may provide useful information. If a local jurisdiction or state is willing to serve as a test site for the proposed policy, investigators could evaluate the utility of the policy by examining the same types of research questions presented earlier with reference to the English system.

CONCLUSION

This policy initiative was proposed to stimulate discussion about whether or not such a system would be viable in the United States. Because family law in the United States is governed at the state level, it is unlikely that issues pertaining to stepfamily policy will be given the national coverage in this country that they might receive in others (Glendon, 1987). Nevertheless, it would be useful for policy specialists to engage in deliberations concerning the viability of the proposed policy, and for family scientists to conduct the evaluations to inform these deliberations.

REFERENCES

Aldous, J., & Dumon, W. (1990). Family policy in the 1980s: Controversy and consensus. *Journal of Marriage and the Family*, *52*, 1136–1151.

Children Act 1989. (1989). England and Wales.

Coleman, M., & Ganong, L. G. (1990). Remarriage and stepfamily research in the 1980s: Increased interest in an old family form. *Journal of Marriage and the Family*, *52*, 925–940.

Cretney, S., & Masson, J. M. (1990). *Principles of family law* (5th ed.). London: Sweet & Maxwell Ltd.

Duquette, D. N. (1992). Symposium, child protection legal process: Comparing the United States and Great Britain. *University of Pittsburgh Law Review, 54*, 239–294.

Fine, D. R., & Fine, M. A. (1992). Learning from social sciences: A model for reformation of the laws affecting stepfamilies. *Dickinson Law Review, 97*, 49–81.

Fine, M. A. (1989). A social science perspective on stepfamily law: Suggestions for legal reform. *Family Relations, 38*, 53–58.

Fine, M. A., & Fine, D. R. (1992). Recent changes in laws affecting stepfamilies: Suggestions for legal reform. *Family Relations, 41*, 334–340.

Glendon, M. A. (1987). *Abortion and divorce in Western law*. Cambridge, MA: Harvard University Press.

Hetherington, E. M. (1993). An overview of the Virginia Longitudinal Study of Divorce and Remarriage with a focus on early adolescence. *Journal of Family Psychology, 7*, 39–56.

Koocher, G. P., & Keith-Spiegel, P. C. (1990). *Children, ethics, and the law: Professional issues and cases*. Lincoln: University of Nebraska Press.

16

Policies for Stepfamilies: Crosswalking Private and Public Domains

P. Lindsay Chase-Lansdale
University of Chicago

OVERVIEW OF VOLUME GOAL

The purpose of this chapter is to consider the policy implications of the research findings embodied in the other chapters of this volume. In my opinion, the title of the book, *Stepfamilies: Who Benefits? Who Does Not?* is a strategic focus, and one I use to set the parameters for this chapter. First, I define the *who* in this issue, and second, the term, *benefit*.

Who

Here we have extensive complexity, as all of the chapters eloquently illustrate. Included in the who are:

1. Children: biological children, stepchildren, and half-stepchildren.
2. Mothers: custodial mothers, stepmothers, and noncustodial mothers.
3. Fathers: custodial fathers, stepfathers, and noncustodial fathers.
4. Dyads: given the emphasis on remarriage, the main focus is on marital dyads. However, other dyads are important to consider, as well: all combinations of parent–child dyads (including biological and stepparents with biological and stepchildren), and sibling dyads, again involving siblings who are biologically related because they are offspring of one parent, stepsiblings, and biologically related siblings, born in a newly created stepfamily.
5. The family as a whole: in this case, the remarried family, with concerns regarding who is defined as being part of the remarried family and who is not.

6. The extended family or families that become increasingly complex as marital transitions occur.

7. Society as whole: This, too, needs to be disaggregated into categories, such as the federal government, state and local governments, communities, neighborhoods, and schools.

Benefit

Multiple definitions of *benefit* have been introduced in this volume. Possible benefits include, for children: higher levels of socioemotional adjustment in young children, preadolescents, and adolescents, better performance in school, high school graduation, college attendance and graduation, adequate occupational attainment, and healthy family formation (specifically including the avoidance of teenage pregnancy and childbearing). For adults, potential benefits involve higher marital satisfaction, improved economic standing for some members of some families, lower levels of depression, and effective parenting. In addition, some benefits may be related to less strain (defined economically and socially) on social groups, such as communities, states, and our larger society or country.

Missing in this list of definitions is the notion of time, although a number of authors have addressed this point in useful ways: for example, lifetimes of children and adults, length of remarriage, age of children at remarriage, multiple marital transitions, and, of course, the future of our society.

Policy Implications

In topics related to families, and especially when focused on marriage, divorce, and remarriage, I clarify my policy approach by conceptually dividing issues into private versus public matters. Private matters concern those which occur within family boundaries and are not readily placed on the policy agenda, such as marital interaction. Public matters involve behaviors of individuals and families that affect others outside the family, or society as a whole. Such issues seem squarely within a policy agenda, for example, fathers' failure to pay child support.

The following policy analysis involves four parts: an enumeration of public issues related to stepfamilies that may have policy implications; a listing of private issues along the same lines; a brief discussion of these issues, the policies in place, future options, and related research questions; and the illustration of how, particularly for stepfamilies, there seems to be blurring or crosswalking between the public and private domains, more so than for either continuously married or divorced families.

Public issues
  1. *Adults*:
   • Economic implications for society.
   • Higher rates of second divorce.
   • Failure of stepfathers to pay child support.
  2. *Children*:
   • Lower levels of educational attainment.
   • Lower levels of occupational attainment.
   • Higher rates of nonmarital childbirth.
   • Possibly higher rates of divorce in adulthood.
  3. *Society*:
   • "Incomplete institutionalization" (Cherlin, 1978), namely unclear or absent societal norms and standards for how to define the remarried family, individual roles and relationships of its members, and connections with society.

Private issues
  1. *Within the family*:
   • Lower family functioning, higher conflict.
   • Difficulties in parenting by custodial mothers and stepfathers.
   • Higher levels of behavior problems in adolescence.
   • Disengagement by adolescents from the family.
   • Possibly improved levels of marital satisfaction.
   • Possibly higher marital discord.
   • Complexity within the family as to feelings about roles, relationships, commitments, views of the outside world, namely a complicated, personal definition of family.

Policy Implications of Public Issues.   Beginning with the economic implications for our society, women experience a precipitous drop in income after divorce (Duncan, 1991). Especially for those with weak attachment to the workforce, entering our nation's welfare system—Aid to Families with Dependent Children (AFDC)—tends to be a mode for managing this economic crisis. Indeed, longitudinal data from the Panel Study of Income Dynamics (PSID) showed that the majority of women on AFDC are divorced, and they exit the system within 2 years (Duncan, 1984). The exit is usually due to remarriage. As one British journalist recently noted, "Single parents cost the tax payer two billion pounds a year. Remarriage costs the taxpayer very little if anything" (Drummond, 1991).

  Thus, one policy proposal that could be put forth is that remarriage should be encouraged via various financial incentives. As Brooks-Gunn (this volume) and

McLanahan and Sandefur (in press) point out, so should the marriage of single mothers to someone who is not the father of their child. This is already occurring in a number of states, for example, New Jersey and Wisconsin, where AFDC checks increase in value if the mother remarries (or marries). The research in this volume suggests that this policy may be simplistic for several reasons. First, as noted earlier by Brooks-Gunn, many remarriages end in divorce, especially in the early years, so there may be multiple returns to poverty or low economic standing and a subsequent drain on state and federal AFDC budgets. Second, remarried families are not as likely to have the same economic standing as families with continuous first-time marriages. As Thomson's chapter showed, even when earnings are similar for first marriages and remarriages, home ownership and other indications of economic well-being are lower for remarriages. Economic strain may also be due to the financial obligations to children from prior marriages or unions and to increases in stepfamily size.

The third, a selection effect may be operating regarding multiple transitions. Research on patterns of self-selection into divorce and remarriage is beginning to take place, and is not possible without longitudinal data sets. But cross-sectional studies by Capaldi and Patterson (1991) and Lahey, Hartdagen, Frick, McBurnett, Connor, and Hynd (1988) suggest selection into multiple marital transitions by certain subgroups of individuals who have difficulties with relationships due to antisocial behavior. Selectivity may also occur because of economic difficulties. Duncan and Hoffman's research (1985) showed that economic difficulties also precede divorce, thus being a part of the dissolution process and a possible causal factor. If a subset of stepfamilies are also economically burdened, then redivorce is more likely. Of course, the opposite is possible for some proportion of remarriages, where the stepfather's earnings improve the economic situation of the mother, and less funding is required from government programs. Clearly, longitudinal work is needed on this topic, especially to differentiate subgroups.

The final economic issue presented here is child support. Mothers and children seem to be a package deal for fathers, whether biologically determined or demographically defined in society as stepfamilies (Furstenberg & Cherlin, 1991). The package deal aspect means that fathers support the women and children with whom they live. Serial marriage or serial monogamy is used to describe the changes in our society pertaining to marriage. Serial fathering also occurs. Those who remarry tend to form new economic units: the stepfamily household. Economic ties to biological children from prior marriages weaken substantially. Again, the field could use a much stronger database regarding the child support behavior of remarried fathers.

Beginning in 1994, new policy regulations have been implemented for all noncustodial fathers, not just those whose children are on AFDC. Due to the stringent provisions of the Family Support Act of 1988, the wages of all noncustodial with new court orders regarding child support fathers are automatically withheld by employers, as of January 1, 1994 (Chase-Lansdale & Vinovskis, in press; Garfinkel & McLanahan, in press). Thus, the economic link to children from first marriages will be strengthened. What this means for stepfamilies is not known. One might hypothesize that, given the higher likelihood of conflict and dissolution in the early years of remarriage, and well-established patterns of economic support by stepfathers to stepchildren over prior children in stabilized remarriages, this new policy may add to or promote conflict in stepfamilies, as well as diminish their level of economic standing. The impact of this new child support policy on stepfamilies is an important topic for study.

Turning to the issue of "incomplete institutionalization" of stepfamilies, as Cherlin pointed out in 1978, there were few studies on remarriage, but at least research progress was a considerable improvement over the previous decade. It is unfortunate that the United States did not have, as a national investment, a longitudinal study to examine the "incomplete institutionalization" of step-families hypothesis in detail, and more importantly, to follow possible changes over the past 15 years. White's chapter using the National Survey of Families and Households (NSFH), is an excellent example of the type of phenomenon that Cherlin described in 1978, namely that societal norms and rules for behavior of the stepfamily within its social context and within itself are weak. We do not have good data to examine whether or not there has been improvement along these lines since 1978, but with the second wave of the NSFH fielded in 1993, there is the potential for future longitudinal investigation.

Demographic data, amply presented in this volume, suggest that because divorce and remarriage have become dramatically more prevalent in the past few decades, the experience of adults and children in our society (as Hetherington and Jodl point out) is not to view stepfamilies as a small, pathological minority. Clinicians, school counselors, other practitioners, and support groups such as "Stepfamilies of America" worked to place divorce and remarriage on the map in schools and communities, so that individuals—adults or children—can pursue the meaning of this family state and adjust to it, if they so choose (e.g., Turner-Bielenberg, 1991). It is now a common experience in the workplace, community groups, religious institutions, and schools, for adults and children to learn who is married for the first time, who is divorced, and who is remarried. Years of dealing with complex extended families at holidays, graduations, and weddings have gone by. New terms have sprouted up, so that someone easily says, "We're a blended family," when first meeting a neighbor or someone at the PTA. Yet, despite the superb snapshot views of incomplete institutionalization as presented in White's chapter, we cannot, on the basis of data in this country, draw firm conclusions regarding changes in the institutionalization of remarriage over the past 15 years. Future investigations represent much more potential.

The other items on the list of public issues—lower levels of education, lower occupational attainment, higher frequencies of leaving home early and of non-marital childbearing—represent rather straightforward policy concerns. Our society holds participation in the labor force, or the creation of productive members of society, as a critical goal for our nation's well-being. The problematic outcomes cited above are all counter to this goal, portending individual life trajectories of low socioeconomic status or poverty for subsets of children from stepfamilies. In the case of leaving home early, one attendant, policy implication is the challenge of dealing with homeless youth.

The findings in this volume on child, youth, and young adult outcomes represent an example of how research has progressed considerably, and policy has yet to catch up. For the past several decades, remarriage has been regarded as a positive event by society. There has been a collective sigh of relief when remarriage occurs, because once again children will have a two-parent family. One major assumption has been that most of the problems associated with divorce are related to economic decline for mothers and children, so if a struggling divorced mother remarries, "things are whole again". At the very least, the divorced mother and children (so the argument holds) will escape poverty or the incessant daily struggle of making ends meet, which is positive for all concerned. There was also the belief—idealized and not well-researched—that a stepfather could come into the new family and fix family dynamics, restoring discipline, supporting beleaguered mothers who could not break coercive cycles of interaction with their sons, and essentially recreate the "idealized two-parent family". The net result would be to send a public problem, single motherhood, back into the private domain of marriage, a taboo topic of conversation in our society.

It was surprising for many researchers and policymakers to learn that remarriage brings its own set of challenges, and that difficulties within these families remain, even after improved economic levels are taken into account. Contributing to the state of shock for policymakers are the findings reported by Hetherington and her colleagues (this volume) and the new negative, long-term effects of remarriage on young adults. Given the U.S. emphasis on forging a productive adult society, policymakers are particularly affected by deleterious consequences of childhood experiences on adult functioning.

Kiernan's (1992) research is a dramatic example of the impact of negative, long-term research findings on public policy in Great Britain. Recall that her study, using the National Child Development Study, a nationally representative cohort of 17,000 children followed from birth to age 23, found even stronger negative impacts of remarriage than those of divorce during childhood, on educational and occupational attainment, and healthy family formation in young adulthood. Both remarried and divorced groups were significantly worse off than young adults from nondivorced families. One might view Great Britain as an interesting natural experiment in the interaction of research and policy regarding divorce and remarriage. The divorce rates in Great Britain have increased substantially in the past two decades, and along with Denmark and Sweden, are the highest in Western Europe, with two out of five first marriages ending in divorce (Kiernan & Chase-Lansdale, 1993). While these rates are not as high as those of the United States, their relative rise within Great Britain has recently placed divorce policy in the limelight (Kiernan & Wicks, 1990).

The idealized view of remarriage was particularly widespread in Great Britain when Kiernan's results were released by the Family Policy Studies Centre in London in 1991 (Family Policy Bulletin, December, 1991). No fewer than 12 major newspapers carried the findings as a major story; Kiernan was interviewed extensively; the results were discussed on national television; and visiting Senator Moynihan asked to meet Kiernan for lunch. The same British journalist wrote, "The wonder is [that] we have managed to ignore the problems of stepfamilies for so long" (Drummond, 1991).

The findings of the study were made public at a time of significant ongoing reform in divorce laws in Great Britain. At that point, divorce could be granted after 2 years of separation if both parties agreed, and after 5 years of separation if only one party agreed. The reform involved a variety of legal changes to make divorces easier to obtain. The media furor developed because Kiernan's article focused on young adult outcomes, controlling for economic standing. The Lord Chancellor, who had been reviewing proposals from the Law Commission to ease divorce laws, went on record as "having second thoughts" regarding the reform movement ("Consider the Children," 1991). Since this period of outspoken and prolonged discussions by policymakers, divorce reform has dropped to a low priority on the policy agenda. Although other events in Great Britain (e.g., economic policies) contributed to putting divorce reform on the backburner for now, there is no question that Kiernan's study affected the policy debates. In my opinion, this type of policy reaction to research that demonstrates that a subset of children from stepfamilies may have long-term difficulties—even after their economic situation has improved—brings the private issues, namely the quality of marriage, parenting, family conflict and cohesion, to the fore.

Policy Implications of Private Issues. What can be done regarding such private issues? I would like to address the concept of supporting marriage in our society without being placed in the same category as Popenoe, meaning that I do not agree with his thesis that the nondivorced two-parent family is the only family type that should be featured in U.S. society. I believe that single mothers and stepfamilies are and should be accepted and supported. At the same time, I believe our society could do more to support marriage without denigrating other family forms. The extent to which marriage is private and not within any public arena in the United States is staggering, with the exception of abusive and violent situations, where the state eventually intervenes; and even this has been slow to happen (Emery, 1989).

Marriage is not a topic of conversation in our society. The experiences about how to strengthen and create a marriage over time is not part of everyday discourse. A difficult time during marriage might be discussed among friends, but only after the issue has been resolved, or when the couple is irrevocably headed toward separation (Cowan & Cowan, 1992). Once a divorce occurs, the family is publicly labeled, whereas prior to that time, experiences within marriage—including development and growth, the transition to parenthood, conflict and heartache, communication and intimacy—are strictly private and generally not known by those outside the family. This is unfortunate and means that most young adults enter marriage uninformed about what it entails, with expectations that are either idealized, based upon difficult or happy family-of-origin experiences, and for the most part, barely developed and articulated.

Stepfamilies are a blend of the private and public domains. This is indeed a marriage, so it is private. Yet, stepfamilies are now more publicly labeled. The marital histories of the partners are either inferred or more openly discussed.

Should marriage (in this case, remarriage) be supported in our society without being coerced, and how? Can expectations and attendant skills be taught to stepfamilies and others in order to promote adjustment? One might hypothesize that stepfamilies would benefit if expectations were discussed regarding: (a) how to create a marital relationship in the presence of children of many ages; (b) how daughters of divorced mothers respond to stepfathers; (c) how stepfathers cannot be "Mr. Fixits," nor will they likely ever fill the role of father; (d) how to go about gaining the trust of stepchildren. Several interventions to prevent marital distress and dissolution have been undertaken and evaluated for first-time marriages (e.g., Cowan & Cowan, 1992; Markman, Renick, Floyd, Stanley, & Clements, in press), and a few interventions have been designed for children of divorce (e.g., Alpert-Gillis, Pedro-Carroll, & Cowen, 1989). Yet, similar interventions with strong evaluation components have not been targeted toward stepfamilies.

I do not intend to convey these ideas in an overly optimistic fashion, when such programs require innovative, multidisciplinary approaches and are highly costly. However, I raise these issues as examples of the crossing of the public and private domains. If there is a societal concern about stepfamilies, and if there are to be broader policies and programs aimed at the challenges facing children and adults in stepfamilies, then we definitely need research information about whether or not these intervention ideas are valid and worthy directions.

My final point in the private arena involves what psychologists would call the construction of a world view—a view of the self and family, defined internally and in interaction with the social world. Not enough attention is being paid to children's construction of the meaning of their experiences of parents' multiple marital transitions. A case in point is Hetherington's findings (this volume) that child characteristics drive how remarried adults parent effectively at subsequent points in time. A second example from the work of Hetherington and her colleagues is the phenomenon of disengagement of adolescents from their stepfamilies. This, too, is an important change, initiated by the child.

I would argue that we do not give enough credit to children's abilities to deal well with enormous complexity. Specifically, they cope with changes in family structure, changes in the behavior of parents, the entrance of stepparents and new extended families, reactions from peers, community members, teachers. While on the one hand we can bemoan the complex world of stepfamilies, we should also have a research agenda that asks how and why certain children (both biological and stepchildren) sort out the complexities of their worlds. This question applies to the majority of children in stepfamilies and would also better inform us regarding the subset who are most vulnerable, thus making targeted interventions more possible.

The clear policy issue related to this argument is tied to the disengagement of adolescents. There is broad meaning to the term disengagement, ranging from spending considerable time with another family in the neighborhood, to linking up with deviant peers, to becoming homeless. In the United States today is a large youth development movement, focused on offering adolescents experiences outside the family that promote positive development (Wynn & Pittman, 1993). The programs involved offer another system outside the family where the adolescent can benefit emotionally, socially, and cognitively. These programs do not have a deficit model, but rather, are patterned after authoritative parenting (Baumrind, 1989). Successful programs require a combination of firm limits (in this context "required helpfulness," Garmezy, 1991), such as being a companion to the elderly, or rehabilitating inner city housing, with emotional support and the development of a meaningful relationship with a program leader. The resiliency literature identified this combination as an important factor in healthy development, despite risky contexts (Garmezy, 1991). Thus, there is the possibility for adolescents who are having difficulties in stepfamilies to construct positive self-images and world views based on experiences outside of the family. Again, these programs are so consumed with obtaining funding and operating effectively that few have been evaluated, clearly a needed direction for new research.

In summary, to pursue a more delineated policy agenda for stepfamilies, I conclude that stepfamilies should be studied, and policies and interventions developed, with the combination of public and private perspectives in mind. Perhaps the most important conclusion related to the crossing of public and private domains, is that if we can learn about how the internal workings of stepfamilies are linked to external and bidirectional influences of families with larger social contexts (such as schools, intervention programs, communities, the work place), the result will be a more useful basis for developing effective social policies.

REFERENCES

Alpert-Gillis, L. J., Pedro-Carroll, J. L., & Cowen, E. (1989). The Children of Divorce Intervention Program: Development, implementation, and evaluation of a program for young urban children. *Journal of Consulting and Clinical Psychology, 57,* 583–589.

Baumrind, D. (1989). Rearing competent children. In W. Damon (Ed.), *Child development today and tomorrow* (pp. 349–378). San Francisco: Jossey-Bass.

Capaldi, D., & Patterson, G. R. (1991). Relation of parental transitions to boys' adjustment problems: I. A linear hypothesis. II. Mothers at risk for transitions and unskilled parenting. *Developmental Psychology, 27,* 489–504.

Chase-Lansdale, P. L., & Vinovskis, M. A. (in press). Whose responsibility? An historical analysis of the changing roles of mothers, fathers, and society in assuming responsibility for poor U.S. children. In P. L. Chase-Lansdale & J. Brooks-Gunn (Eds.), *Escape from poverty: What makes a difference for children?* New York: Cambridge University Press.

Cherlin, A. J. (1978). Remarriage as an incomplete institution. *American Journal of Sociology, 84,* 634–650.

Consider the children. (1991, March 12). *The Independent.*

Cowan, C. P., & Cowan, P. A. (1992). *When partners become parents: The big life change for couples.* New York: Basic Books.

Drummond, M. (1991, December 2). Step this way for the growing cause of family breakdown. *Daily Telegram.*

Duncan, G. J. (1984). *Years of poverty, years of plenty: The changing economic fortunes of American workers and families.* Ann Arbor: University of Michigan, Survey Research Center, Institute for Social Research.

Duncan, G. J. (1991). The economic environment of childhood. In A. C. Huston (Ed.), *Children in poverty: Child development and public policy* (pp. 23–50). New York: Cambridge University Press.

Duncan, G. J., & Hoffman, S. D. (1985). Economic consequences of marital instability. In M. David & T. Smeeding (Eds.), *Horizontal equity, uncertainty, and well-being* (pp. 427–470). Chicago: University of Chicago Press.

Emery, R. (1989). Family violence. *American Psychologist, 44,* 321–328.

Family Policy Bulletin. (1991, December). *Step-children at risk.* London, England: Family Policy Studies Centre.

Furstenberg, F. F., Jr., & Cherlin, A. J. (1991). *Divided families: What happens to children when parents part.* Cambridge, MA: Harvard University Press.

Garfinkel, I., & McLanahan, S. (in press). The effects of child support reform on child well-being and proposals for the future. In P. L. Chase-Lansdale & J. Brooks-Gunn (Eds.), *Escape from poverty? What makes a difference for children?* New York: Cambridge University Press.

Garmezy, N. (1991). Resilience in children's adaptation to negative life events and stressed environments. *Pediatric Annals, 20,* 459–466.

Hetherington, E. M., & Clingempeel, W. G. (1992). Coping with marital transitions: A family systems perspective. *Monographs of the Society for Research in Child Development, 57*(2–3, Serial No. 227).

Kiernan, K. E. (1992). The impact of family disruption in childhood on transitions made in young adult life. *Population Studies, 40,* 35–54.

Kiernan, K. E., & Chase-Lansdale, P. L. (1993). Children and marital breakdown: Short- and long-term consequences. In A. Blum & J. L. Rallu (Eds.), *European population. Vol. II. Demographic Dynamics* (pp. 295–308). London, England: John Libby & Company Ltd.

Kiernan, K. E., & Wicks, M. (1990). *Family change and future policy.* London: Family Policy Studies Centre.

Lahey, B., Hartdagen, S., Frick, P., McBurnett, K., Connor, R., & Hynd, G. (1988). Conduct disorder: Parsing the confounded relation to parental divorce and antisocial personality. *Journal of Abnormal Psychology, 97,* 334–337.

Markman, H. J., Renick, M. J., Floyd, F. J., Stanley, S. M., & Clements, M. (in press). Preventing marital distress through communication and conflict management training: A 4- and 5-year follow-up. *Journal of Consulting and Clinical Psychology.*

McLanahan, S., & Sandefur, G. (in press). *Uncertain childhood, uncertain future*. Cambridge, MA: Harvard University Press.

Turner-Bielenberg, L. (1991). A task-centered preventive group approach to create cohesion in the new stepfamily: A preliminary evaluation. *Research on Social Work Practice, 1*, 416–433.

Wynn, J., & Pittman, K. (1993). *Profiles of youth development programs in the United States*. Unpublished manuscript, University of Chicago, Chapin Hall Center for Children.

17 Stepfamilies: An Overview

Judy Dunn
Alan Booth
Pennsylvania State University

What is the nature and extent of the impact of living within stepfamilies on children and their parents? Two powerful lessons are evident from the research described in this volume. First, the variability in the relationships between stepparents and children, and in the effects of growing up in a stepfamily on children, is striking (Amato, Hetherington, Kurdek, White, Seltzer, this volume), as is the variability in the relations between the parents themselves (Popenoe, Thomson, Brooks-Gunn, this volume). Second, although large-scale studies consistently find that children in stepfamilies do have a higher probability of behavioral and health problems, poorer educational achievement (Hetherington & Jodl, Zill, this volume), and tend to leave home earlier and with less support (White, this volume; see also Cherlin et al., 1991; Kiernan, 1992), the effect size of many of such differences is small.

It is the questions of who benefits, who is particularly vulnerable, and what processes are implicated in these differences, that are of real significance. The change from a pathogenic model of the impact of divorce and remarriage to one that focuses on the diversity of changes and outcomes is, as Hetherington and Jodl note, recent, but of key importance. So is the idea that biological and cultural processes may be implicated in understanding the differential attachment of parents to birth and stepchildren. In this final chapter, we summarize some of the themes and lines of evidence identified earlier that begin to suggest some answers to these questions, and that also highlight the gaps and lessons for research design and policy that deserve attention.

WHO BENEFITS AND WHO SUFFERS?

The chapters highlight many important themes concerning the experiences of those in stepfamilies; we focus on just a few that bear on the issue of which children appear most vulnerable.

First, the extent and significance of the chain of changes for children that follow problems and breakdown of a marriage is increasingly evident. As Hetherington and Jodl noted, divorce and remarriage are not static events but part of a complex sequence of transitions and alterations in family relationships and household arrangements. The sequence begins as the marriage deteriorates, and the chain often involves more than one separation and remarriage. Research strategies have hardly begun to come to grips with the dynamics of household and family changes that follow parental separation, and with the significance of children's experiences as they move from one household to another. However, as Coleman noted, it appears that children in certain stepfamilies face a greater chance of a second or third breakup—namely those whose parents are of lower educational achievement and who married as teenagers. And the experience of multiple divorce and changes in family life is linked to a greater chance of problems for children (Kurdek, White, this volume; see also Ochiltree, 1990). Why this should be so is not yet clear. Have the children who have experienced several divorces also been exposed to more parental conflict and stress than the children who have experienced only one divorce? Are there systematic differences in the initial parent–child relationships in these families—or differences in the children even before the first divorce? The evidence that children who experienced divorce had more behavior problems and poorer academic achievement than children in intact families before divorce is of key importance (see the British national data set involving 11,000 families: Cherlin et al., 1991; Kiernan, 1992). A study on why remarriages are more unstable than first marriages suggested that both explanations should be explored (Booth & Edwards, 1992).

Second, as Hetherington and Jodl commented, the developmental stage of the child at the time of the remarriage, and his or her gender, appear to affect adjustment and outcome—at least in some of the studies (Hetherington & Jodl, this volume; see, however, Zill, 1988). Adolescents appear likely to react negatively to the constellation of events surrounding parental remarriage, although these effects may be linked to other factors of timing. As Brooks-Gunn and Thomson suggested, subsequent research needs to focus on disentangling the effects of the child's age at the time he or she joins the stepfamily (a cohort effect) from the youngster's current age (a period or developmental stage effect) and from the duration of the stepfamily experience (a family age effect).

Third, in many studies, different outcomes for children in stepmother and stepfather families are reported, and this too may be linked to children's gender (Brooks-Gunn, Kurdek, Hetherington & Jodl, Thomson, White, this volume). However, the pattern of findings is complex and not always consistent. Clearer patterns must await more extensive study of the rarer categories of stepfamilies (e.g., those with stepmothers, or with biological mothers cohabiting with a person who is not the child's father).

Fourth, there is the significance of the presence of stepsiblings and half siblings, and of differential parental treatment of own and stepchildren. Children with half siblings do less well in terms of adjustment, and those with stepsiblings continue to receive less support in later life than those without such siblings. To understand the processes that lead to such differences in outcome we need to look at variation in relationships within stepfamilies (White, Seltzer, Hetherington & Jodl, this volume). The adjustment of children in stepfamilies—as in nonstepfamilies (Dunn, Stocker, & Plomin, 1990)—is poorer if they perceive or receive less favored treatment than their siblings.

The lesson is that we need to look at within-family variation in relationships to understand children's outcome. This is of equal importance for non-stepfamilies (Dunn & Plomin, 1990). So, too, is another theme evident in the chapters: the importance of recognizing not just stepparent-to-child effects, but also the power of child-to-stepparent effects, documented by Hetherington and Jodl, and Seltzer (this volume). Images of stepfamilies dominated by the mythic importance of the wicked stepmother have to be adjusted to include the key role of the resentful or troubled stepchild in the dynamics of the stepfamily. These child effects may begin well before remarriage—when single parents begin to become involved with someone (for a particularly poignant account of the power of a child to destroy her mother's relationship with a potential stepfather, see Emile Zola's novel, *A Love Affair*).

UNEXPECTED FINDINGS

In the evidence for the power of child effects and of differential experiences within the family, there are important parallels between step- and non-stepfamilies. But there are also unexpected findings in the research on stepfamilies that challenge our usual assumptions about family functioning. First, Hetherington and Jodl reported that among the adolescent stepsiblings in the families they studied, there was less negative interaction than between the biological siblings of the control sample. And relations between adolescent children and their biological mothers were more conflicted than the more distant relations between adolescent stepchildren and their stepmothers. What may be the long-term consequences of such distant relations (as opposed to conflicted-but-involved parent–child relations in non-stepfamilies) is not yet clear.

Another unexpected finding was found in White's pioneering research with adult stepchildren. She showed that support for children is lower in stepfamilies than in nonstepfamilies. Although it is not surprising that stepparents are less supportive, what is surprising is that biological parents in stepfamilies are less supportive of their children than biological parents in nonstepfamilies. Another challenge to conventional views of family systems lies in the evidence that the quality of the marital relationship in stepparent households bears a very different relation to the quality of parent–child relationships and children's outcome than it does in non-stepfamilies. A happy remarriage is not a predictor of happy stepparent–stepchild relationships, it seems—especially from the perspective of the stepchild (White & Booth, 1985).

GAPS IN RESEARCH

It is of course likely that children's relationships with their noncustodial parents are of major significance in influencing their development and well-being. Relationships operate across households, as Cooney pointed out, yet we still have very little systematic information on the links between different strands in children's complex networks of relationships. What information on noncustodial parents that we do have suggests that noncustodial mothers have closer relationships with their children than do noncustodial fathers—a finding that adds to the growing evidence on the resilience of the maternal role and the commitment of mothers. This is just one of a number of major gaps in the research bases from which conclusions about stepfamilies are drawn.

Before we can answer the "who" questions adequately, it is clear that several gaps in our information base need to be addressed. First, we have little information on minority stepfamilies, yet it is likely that the ways in which stepfamilies function, and their impact on children and parents, will differ in different ethnic and cultural groups, as Brook-Gunn, Chase-Lansdale and White noted (for a study of minority stepfamilies, see Fine, McKenry, Donnelly, & Voydanoff, 1992).

Second, the complexity of the range of different types of stepfamilies is daunting; Burgoyne and Clark (1982) delineated 26 different types. We have hardly begun to grapple with the difficulties of studying the implications for children's and parents' outcomes in these different types of family. These many types also multiply the problems in conducting legal and policy research on legislation and programs that might influence stepfamilies.

Third, much of the research on stepfamilies has not included studies of families in which the adults are cohabiting, rather than remarried. As both Thomson and Cooney pointed out, this may have serious implications for the size of the effects we find and the kinds of conclusions that we draw.

Fourth, research has given little attention to selection effects. Many of the differences we observe between step- and non-step families may be due to unobserved characteristics of those who enter stepfamilies (Thomson, Hogan, this volume). Were systematic differences detected, the finding would have implications for the conclusions we draw about the effects of living in stepfamilies.

There are also many notable gaps in what we know about functioning within the family. Most studies are based on small and unrepresentative samples and very few focus on stepfamilies with adult children (White, Cooney, Seltzer, this volume). Moreover, we know little about marital and family functioning in stepfamilies with children from both parents, about the immediate or long-term impact of new children born within the stepfamily, about the significance of grandparent relationships (Brooks-Gunn, Chase-Lansdale, this volume), about what fathers and stepfathers actually do by way of family support (Hogan, this volume), about the relations between peer relationships and stepfamily relationships, or between noncustodial and stepfamily relationships (Brooks-Gunn, this volume)—which the divorce literature suggest are of central importance.

Perhaps most important of all, we are ignorant of the feelings and perceptions of children, themselves, about their experiences within their stepfamilies. These do not always mesh with the perceptions of others in the family. For instance, Brand and colleagues showed that whereas the perceived quality of the stepparents' marital relationship was positively associated with the stepparents' view of the stepchild, from the child's viewpoint, a good marital relationship was either negatively or not associated with their perceptions of the stepparent (Brand, Clingempeel, & Bowen-Woodward, 1988). It is interesting that the 1989 Children Act in Britain, discussed by Fine, potentially provides children with a more powerful voice in the arrangements that affect them following parental separation (they must be given an opportunity to express their wishes and feelings). At present, we know little about those views.

METHODOLOGICAL CONSIDERATIONS

There are two research traditions in stepfamily research: small sample, in-depth research such as that of Hetherington and Jodl, and large sample surveys, such as those utilized by Thompson, White, and Zill. The small studies of homogenous populations contribute a richness not captured by surveys, and the large-scale surveys are essential to discern the effects of variability in income, prior history, and rare stepfamily forms. Research using both methods can illuminate the issues better than either alone. Small sample homogeneous studies can provide detailed information on family processes at work, and large sample surveys can give us information on the prevalence of behavior that may put children at risk. Involving investigators in each tradition in the design of the other's research will enrich both types of studies. And ethnographic, descriptive studies of stepfamilies— which are at present lacking—could usefully contribute to developing theoretical ideas on stepfamilies. Research on stepfamilies is still notably atheoretical.

It is clear from past research that multiple informants on each stepfamily are needed. The perspective of the custodial and noncustodial parent and children would help us to fill many of the gaps in our knowledge, as suggested above.

Evaluation research should also be a priority. As states change the laws to make provisions for stepfamilies, the consequences of these changes should be monitored. In addition, as indicated in our discussion of policy issues to follow, research will be needed to assess the effect of the Family Support Act of 1988 and other legislation. Special attention should be given to assessing possible unanticipated consequences.

POLICY ISSUES

The evidence for stress and difficulties that stepfamilies experience makes it all the more important that we should reflect on how support can be provided, both to individuals in intact marriages which are in difficulty, and to lone parents and stepparents. The real difficulties faced by both stepparents and stepchildren suggest that we should devise and support policies that will make family life less stressful through increasing the availability of good childcare, education and counselling in family issues. With all the evidence for the serious consequences of parental conflict on children's adjustment and outcome, policies aimed at making divorce more difficult appear both inhumane and unlikely to help children.

Regarding the legal issues addressed by Fine and Mahoney, a brief comment on the working of the Children Act 1989 in England discussed by Fine is in order. A detailed discussion of the changes in the Act which apply to stepfamilies has recently been published by the National Stepfamily Association in Britain (Dimmock, 1992). This considers the Act from the perspective of stepparents, and highlights the point that the Act gives greater rights than before to non-resident parents, who share continuing parental responsibility for their children, even if they no longer care for them. It is argued that this may, in fact, be disruptive to existing stepfamilies, since it enables non-resident parents to take a greater part in decisions relating to their biological children. Stepparents can acquire parental responsibility by means of a residence order, but this does not mean that the nonresident parent relinquishes parental responsibility. Masson (1992) commented that:

> the Children Act 1989 has not made it any easier to be a stepparent . . . parental responsibility does not..place the stepparent in the position of a parent because it does not give the right to make major decisions about adoption or guardianship nor does it impose the obligation to support the child. Stepchildren do not inherit on their stepparent's intestacy, so a will must still be made. Parental responsibility does give the stepparent independent decision-making power but in doing so may be seen to reduce the parents' authority. (p. 14)

Others consider this an unduly negative view of the Act: It is clear that evaluation of the Children Act 1989 should be continued for several years in order to assess its impact after it has been more thoroughly incorporated into family life, and the response to the legislation has stabilized.

New legislation in the United States that forces childcare payments by biological fathers is a sound policy, but we must be alert to possible negative effects. While the income from an ex-husband may improve family finances, it may also increase conflict in cases where the biological father who has remarried must allocate a larger portion of his family's income to another family. It may reduce the income of his new family enough to put the children at risk. Also, it may increase marital conflict, which we know has adverse effects on children and could lead to dissolution of the second marriage. As states implement the Family Support Act of 1988, funds should be allocated to assess the relative impact of the different ways that states implement the law.

It is possible that research on siblings may be of use in understanding stepfamilies. One cannot fail to be struck by the parallels between the experience of siblings and those of steprelatives. Like steprelatives, siblings do not choose each other, but are obliged to live together in conditions of daily unremitting intimacy and familiarity; they are inevitably jealous of the relationship of their most-significant-other with this new person, and (for firstborn individuals) their relationship begins with a major life transition—one that has marked effects on their behavior and well-being. The limitations of drawing on such research is that the history of each relationship is much shorter in stepfamilies, and children in stepfamilies have other families (those of the noncustodial parent) of which they are a part. This more complex family structure may have both beneficial and deleterious effects. On the one hand, the home away from home may be a refuge from tension in the family of residence and an additional source of financial and other support; on the other, it may be a source of conflict and rejection that multiplies the sources of stress.

Finally, in assessing the developmental impact of stepfamily experiences on children and adults, it is important to take a long-term view. As children reach maturity, parental marital relationships may improve in quality, and parent–child relationships may weaken, but it is also possible that parent–child relations may strengthen later in life. To test whether or not this is true for steprelatives, we need to heed the cogent argument in White's chapter for more studies of stepfamilies with individuals 18–80 years of age.

REFERENCES

Booth, A., & Edwards, J. (1992). Starting over: Why remarriages are more unstable. *Journal of Families Issues, 13*, 179–194.

Brand, E., Clingempeel, W. G., & Bowen-Woodward, K. (1988). Family relationships and children's psychological adjustment in stepmother and stepfather families. In E. M. Hetherington & J. D. Arasteh (Eds.), *Impact of divorce, single parenting, and stepparenting on children* (pp. 299–324). Hillsdale, NJ: Lawrence Erlbaum Associates.

Burgoyne, J., & Clark, D. (1982). Parenting in stepfamilies. In R. Chester, P. Diggory, & M. B. Sutherland (Eds.), *Changing patterns of child-bearing and child-rearing* (pp. 133–147). London: Academic Press.

Cherlin, A. J., Furstenberg, F. F., Chase-Lansdale, P. L., Kiernan, K. E., Robins, P. K., Morrison, D. R., & Teitler, J. O. (1991). Longitudinal studies of effects of divorce on children in Great Britain and the United States. *Science, 252*, 1386–1389.

Dimmock, B. (Ed.). (1992). *A step in both directions: The impact of the Children Act on Stepfamilies.* London: National Stepfamily Association.

Dunn, J., & Plomin, R. (1990). *Separate lives: Why siblings are so different.* New York: Basic Books.

Dunn, J., Stocker, C., & Plomin, R. (1990). Nonshared experiences within the family: Correlates of behavioral problems in middle childhood. *Development and Psychopathology, 2*, 227–244.

Fine, M. A., McKenry, P. C., Donnelly, B. W., & Voydanoff, P. (1992). Perceived adjustments of parents and children: Variations by family structure, race, and gender. *Journal of Marriage and the Family, 54*, 118–127.

Kiernan, K. (1992). The impact of family disruption in childhood on transitions made in young adult life. *Population Studies, 46*, 218–234.

Masson, J. (1992). Stepping into the Nineties: A summary of the legal implications of the Children Act 1989 for stepfamilies. In B. Dimmock (Ed.), *A step in both directions* (pp. 4–14). London: National Stepfamily Association.

Ochiltree, G. (1990). *Children in stepfamilies.* Brookvale, Australia: Prentice-Hall.

White, L., & Booth, A. (1985). The quality and stability of remarriages: The role of step-children. *American Sociological Review, 50*, 689–698.

Zill, N. (1988). Behavior, achievement, and health problems among children in stepfamilies: Findings from a national survey of child health. In E. M. Hetherington & J. Arasteh (Eds.), *The impact of divorce, single parenting and stepparenting on children.* Hillsdale, NJ: Lawrence Erlbaum Associates.

Zola, E. (1957). *A love affair* (J. Stewart, Trans.). New York: Citadel Press.

Author Index

Subject Index